History of Computing

Founding Editor
Martin Campbell-Kelly

Series Editor
Gerard Alberts, Institute for Mathematics, University of Amsterdam,
Amsterdam, The Netherlands

Advisory Editors
Gerardo Con Diaz, University of California, Davis, CA, USA
Jack Copeland, University of Canterbury, Christchurch, New Zealand
Ulf Hashagen, Deutsches Museum, München, Germany
Valérie Schafer, ISCC, CNRS, Paris, France
John V. Tucker, Department of Computer Science, Swansea University,
Swansea, UK

The *History of Computing* series publishes high-quality books which address the history of computing, with an emphasis on the 'externalist' view of this history, more accessible to a wider audience. The series examines content and history from four main quadrants: the history of relevant technologies, the history of the core science, the history of relevant business and economic developments, and the history of computing as it pertains to social history and societal developments.

Titles can span a variety of product types, including but not exclusively, themed volumes, biographies, 'profile' books (with brief biographies of a number of key people), expansions of workshop proceedings, general readers, scholarly expositions, titles used as ancillary textbooks, revivals and new editions of previous worthy titles.

These books will appeal, varyingly, to academics and students in computer science, history, mathematics, business and technology studies. Some titles will also directly appeal to professionals and practitioners of different backgrounds.

Ashley Sweetman

Cyber and the City

Securing London's Banks
in the Computer Age

 Springer

Ashley Sweetman
King's College London
London, UK

ISSN 2190-6831   ISSN 2190-684X   (electronic)
History of Computing
ISBN 978-3-031-07935-1   ISBN 978-3-031-07933-7   (eBook)
https://doi.org/10.1007/978-3-031-07933-7

This Springer imprint is published by the registered company Springer Nature Switzerland AG
The registered company address is: Gewerbestrasse 11, 6330 Cham, Switzerland

Acknowledgements

This book is based upon my PhD research undertaken in the Department of War Studies at King's College London. For this comprehensive schoolboy from Neath, South Wales, writing those words still feels surreal.

There are so many to thank for their support along the way, including the official – who shall remain unnamed – who prompted this work by suggesting there was little understanding in government of what might happen should a bank collapse as a result of a cyberattack.

Thanks must go to Michael Goodman, Thomas Rid, Jon Agar, Richard Aldrich and John Ferris, all of whom provided support and input to this and related work as either supervisors, external examiners or interested reviewers. Thanks also to Peter Hennessy, whose writing of contemporary history provided the ultimate inspiration, and whose tea, cake and wisdom have always been gratefully received. The same must also be said for Mark, with whom many hours have been spent ruminating on cyber security, and the world, over hot chocolate.

Studying for a PhD was made far easier by being part of a cohort in the form of my Strand Group colleagues. Jack, Michelle, Martin, Eleanor and Jan all provided fun and friendship, and a commitment to teaching and writing contemporary history that was infectious. The Strand Group's visiting professors, including Iain Lobban and Simon Case, must also be thanked for sharing what they could of their knowledge and experience.

Conversations with experts have also provided vital background to this work. Among those to be thanked are Gordon Corera, Jeffrey Yost, Will Dixon, Paul Dorey, Mark Waghorne, Fred Piper and Maria Vello. I am grateful to all at Springer for their work in pushing this book through to publication.

It would be an understatement to say that meeting Jon Davis was a pivotal moment in my academic career. Thank you, Jon, for the patience to read multiple versions of this work along the way, for the opportunity to pursue postgraduate study at all, and for your friendship.

To all four of my parents, and to Amie and Lydia, I could not be more grateful for your love and support in all its forms.

And finally, Elle – for absolutely everything, including finding me a place at the Mile End Group event which set me on this path – thank you.

Contents

Chapter 1
Introduction

Banks have acted as secure stores of wealth for millennia. William Mitford, in his famous *History of Greece,* described how temples fulfilled such a role in that country's Ancient existence. 'In the general insecurity of property in the early ages … it was highly desirable to convert all that could be spared from immediate use into that which might more easily be removed from approaching danger', wrote Mitford. 'Gold then and silver having acquired their certain value as signs of wealth, a deposit secure against the dangers continually threatening not individuals only but every town and state in Greece would be a great object of the wealthy. Such security offered nowhere in equal amount as in those temples.'[1] And, with remarkable consistency, the broad parameters of banking have continued since.

Today's temples are the giant global banks whose vast buildings stand at the centre of major cities. They form a critical part of the global financial infrastructure responsible for storing and transferring trillions of pounds around the world on a weekly basis. Those institutions' understanding of security is different than that of their Ancient Greek predecessors, despite the continuity in their fundamental purpose.

Cyber security is universally recognised as crucial to the successful operation of the financial sector, with little questioning of the vast sums of money invested by organisations in capabilities required to protect them. But how did banks become so reliant upon computers and networks that their business operations – and very existence – came to depend so heavily upon "cyber"?

To answer this question, an historical approach is informative, though scarcely forthcoming. Understanding *how* banks have defined computer or information security (what is broadly referred to today as "cyber" by chief executives and world leaders), *what* they perceived to be the main threats they faced and *how* they defended themselves against them, allows us to trace the origins of cyber security in the financial sector and explore in detail how, in the second half of the twentieth

---

[1] William Mitford, *The History of Greece: Volume I* (London: T.Cadell, 1829), p. 193.

© Springer Nature Switzerland AG 2022
A. Sweetman, *Cyber and the City*, History of Computing,
https://doi.org/10.1007/978-3-031-07933-7_1

century and beyond, "cyber" has emerged as the pre-eminent concern for major public and private entities.

For the London clearing banks as they were then known – the largest, most prominent financial institutions, including Barclays Bank, Lloyds Bank, Midland Bank, National Westminster Bank, Coutts (part of National Westminster from 1969), and Williams & Glyn's (established in 1970) – this process began in the early 1960s, prompted by their first purchases of mainframe computers. Over the following decades, these institutions embedded computer and network technology into their operations at unrelenting speed. From the outset, they recognised the fundamental importance of protecting the data and wealth that they stored and transferred for their clients. It is to this era of rapid modernisation and technological advancement that the origins of cyber security in banking can be traced. And it is this era that is explored in detail for the first time herein.

Security and Trust

At the heart of this story is the relationship between security and trust. Customer trust *was* and *is* vital to these institutions' survival. A bank could not tolerate a reputation for insecurity. Without the ability for customers, be they individuals or organisations, to trust institutions to secure their wealth, the banking sector would likely exist in a very different form, if it existed in any formal way. The stark images of customers queuing outside branches of the British building society Northern Rock to withdraw their deposits in late 2007, following the announcement that it required Bank of England support in the early months of the global financial crisis, demonstrate how quickly consumers can react, albeit in an extreme case, when they lose trust in financial institutions. Certainty and security are therefore not just prized currency for banks but operational necessity, whether guarding precious metal in Ancient Greece or computer records of shareholdings and account balances in twenty-first century London.

So deeply embedded at the core of their function, maintaining the trust and confidence of customers drove' computer security thinking and action for banks in the second half of the twentieth century. This was visible both in their institutional decision-making and in the system-wide infrastructure they developed in collaboration with each other. It was the justification, often unspoken, for substantial investment in security features and the reason for detailed discussion and continual reassessment of their security approaches.

Explicit references to trust are found throughout the documentation of banks in this period. A 1972 booklet produced jointly by the clearing banks, for example, described what they felt was 'the most important of all the characteristic features of banking', namely: 'nobody will trust his wealth with an untrustworthy person.'[2]

---

[2] HSBC, File UK1793-0013, 'A History of Banking', *Bank Education Service*, March 1972, p. 6.

They described how historically the 'merchants who turned to banking had to be men who were trusted by the whole community.'[3] The banks maintained this view and extended it to encompass the new systems they created and the software and hardware they became reliant upon. 'Nobody can use the system if it can't be trusted,' was how Barclays summarised the importance of this quality to their development of a real-time dealing system in the mid-1980s.[4] This succinct statement epitomises the outlook of the banks throughout this period.

"Cyber" in Context

This book explores the clearing banks' comprehension and management of computer security as a means of garnering trust from their customers before the invention of the World Wide Web. In doing so, it injects rare historical context into contemporary debates around cyber security, particularly in the financial sector. As the historian of computing Paul Ceruzzi has said, 'We live in an age transformed by computing. This is also the reason why we need to understand its origins.'[5] This book attempts to add detail to our existing understanding of computer security, which as Jeffrey Yost has argued, has a much longer history than most of the literature on the issue implies.[6] Few attempts to understand the historical context of "cyber" in banking exist, despite how long it has been a concern for those institutions and therefore the potential that exists to learn lessons by revisiting past actions and events.

Held in the archives of the aforementioned banks are troves of evidence relating to computer security in this period. Little to none of this has been explored in academic work until now. It is difficult to know what, if any, material is yet to be released, but the documents which are available provide a solid basis for a first writing of history, offering a detailed insight into the thinking and decision-making of the major clearing banks in the late decades of the twentieth century. Researching these archives and piecing together the available evidence into a coherent narrative has therefore been both the primary opportunity and challenge of this project. Presented here is the first exploration of the origins of financial sector computer security in the United Kingdom.

---

[3] Ibid.

[4] Barclays File 0222-0049, 'Real-time Dealing System for BZW', 27 March 1985, p. 2.

[5] Paul Ceruzzi, *A History of Modern Computing: Second Edition* (Cambridge: MIT Press, 2003).

[6] Jeffrey Yost, 'A History of Computer Security Standards', *The History of Information Security: A Comprehensive Handbook* (London: Elsevier, 2007), p. 596.

Modernisation Drive

Technological developments, first the commercialisation of computers and later networking technology, revolutionised the operations of banks in the decades following World War II. In the City of London, the capital's oldest area and historically its business and commerce hub, the colossal clearing banks – whose function involved the settlement of debts between parties in the financial system, normally their peer banks – increasingly employed electronic computers whose processing power transformed the highly clerical clearing and settlement process. This book argues that the current day fundamentality of "cyber" to banks, including how computer security is defined and managed, can be traced to this particularly intense period of technological change which prompted British banks to re-evaluate their function and aptitude as trusted protectors of wealth.

Armed with the resources to do so, these banks – led by Barclays, Lloyds, Midland and National Westminster – invested prodigious resources from the early-1960s onwards in automating pre-existing manual, labour-intensive operations.[7] Each institution was individually motivated to invest in computer hardware and software by long-term cost savings, but their representative body, the Committee of London Clearing Bankers (CLCB), took a more strategic view, deeming such innovation crucial to the maintenance of the City's reputation as the leading global financial centre.

Unfolding over the following three decades was a relentless modernisation drive, revolutionising the way that banks and other financial institutions conducted business and interacted with each other and permanently altering the speed and scale at which the United Kingdom's financial sector functioned. The most historic area of the nation's capital became a hotbed of technological advancement.

There is broad consensus among historians that these decades of technological adoption were pivotal for banking, both in the UK and the United States. Davide Consoli labelled the period 1951–1980 the 'rise of the machines', while Bernardo Batiz-Lazo had described the periods 1965–1980 and 1980–1995 as 'emergence' and 'diffusion' respectively in reference to technology change in banking institutions.[8] This book adds nuance to these labels, particularly through its focus on the development of payments systems throughout the 1970s. In fact, this study adds vital context to the existing literature, which focuses heavily on parallel development in the United States, and extends James Cortada's argument in *The Digital*

---

[7] In 1962 the five biggest clearing banks, of the eleven in existence, were Barclays Bank, Lloyds Bank, Midland Bank, National Provincial Bank and Westminster Bank, see Bank of England Archive (hereafter BoE), File G1/13, 'Notes on Bank Amalgamations', 17 September 1962. The six banks listed here represent the primary London clearing banks as of January 1972. See HSBC Archive (HSBC hereafter), File UK1793-0013, 'The Clearing System', January 1972, p. 1.

[8] Davide Consoli, 'The dynamics of technological change in UK retail banking services: An evolutionary perspective', *Research Policy,* 34 (2005), pp. 461–480; Bernardo Batiz-Lazo and Douglas Wood, 'A Historical Appraisal of Information Technology in Commercial Banking', *Electronic Markets,* 12/3 (2002), pp. 192–205.

Hand that the 'history of the evolution of banking in America over the second half of the twentieth century cannot be written without discussing the use of computing technology' to the United Kingdom. Cortada's contention that computer adoption in the American banking sector was driven by business requirements is also mirrored in the findings of this research.[9]

Though other industry sectors experienced this period in a similar manner, led by military organisations in the UK and US and closely followed by manufacturers of all kinds, banking institutions were certainly pioneering in using technology to enhance reach and capability of their operations.

It is perhaps unsurprising that these institutions embraced this change so willingly: armed not only with the resources required for investment, but also underpinned by the City's longer history of adaption and agility. Iain Martin, in his account of the "Big Bang" liberalisation of the City in the mid-1980s, argued that 'invigorating innovation and openness to the outside world' were two key themes that emerged from the City's history over five centuries.[10] This outlook was also self-sustaining, allowing for the "demystification" of computers, and dispelling concerns from staff about being replaced by technology, that propelled forward their deployment to key banking functions. But the drive for banks was also utilitarian: saving significant amounts of time and money.

Information technology, and specifically the application of computers, transformed the UK financial sector in the second half of the twentieth century, starting in the 1950s and gathering pace in 1960s and 1970s. London's major banks started thinking strategically about automation in the 1950s. Though individual institutions did make their own earlier choices pushing them further towards automated processes, the CLCB, its representative body, created an electronics sub-committee which acted as the catalyst for this outlook. Two areas they investigated were clearing and book-keeping. For the banks, it was about *how*, not *if*, this would happen or not.[11] The political backdrop was, after all, one of optimism, with Labour leader Harold Wilson's speech on the 'white heat' of technology making headlines in 1963. And although much of the practical thinking was being done by large organisations both in the financial sector and elsewhere, a significant amount of published work in academic journals and conferences sought to understand the practical implications of new technology on banks and the commercial world more generally.[12]

---

[9] James Cortada, *The Digital Hand: How Computers Changed the Work of American Financial, Telecommunications, Media, and Entertainment Industries, Volume II* (Oxford: Oxford University Press, 2006).

[10] Iain Martin, *Crash, Bang, Wallop: Inside the Financial Revolution That Changed The World* (London: Sceptre, 2016), p. 6.

[11] See, for example, Philip Augar, *The Bank that Lived a Little: Barclays in the Age of the Very Free Market* (London: Allen Lane, 2018).

[12] See Dean Champion and Edward Dager, 'Automation man in the counting house', *Trans-action*, 3/3 (1966), pp. 34–36; Paul Armer, 'Computer Aspects of Technological Change, Automation, and Economic Progress', *The RAND Corporation*, February 1966; John Winthrop, 'Layman's View of Computer Power', *Financial Analysts Journal*, (1969), pp. 101–103; Gerald M Lowrie, 'ACM '70 Proceedings of the 1970 25th annual conference on Computer and crisis: how computers are shap-

Automation and Security

The 1960s was the decade of automation by computer. In the 1960s, core banking operations, particularly the clearing and settlement process for funds transferred between the London clearing banks, quickly became reliant upon the new computer hardware, software and telecommunication lines linking bank computer centres. Accompanying new opportunities, therefore, were new risks. Embracing technology into its critical operations brought with it new requirements: to secure this software and hardware and minimise the risk of its malfunction or manipulation. Such dependence came as a result of the clear and compelling benefits of computerisation, as argued by Donald MacKenzie, exemplified later on in the twentieth century by the contingency planning required for the Millennium Bug.

Banks immediately realised the importance of securing their computers and later their networks. They recognised that the security of their new operations – which they primarily understood to mean the *confidentiality* of information transmitted across their systems, the *integrity* of the communicated data and high levels of service *availability* – would be vital to their future success. For both their internal operations and the cross-sector apparatus they were involved in creating, the banks saw it as crucial that they fulfilled their side of the traditional banker-customer relationship in these contemporary developments, to both their individual and corporate clients: offering a trustworthy service for the protection and management of their money and information.

In this sense, the evidence provided in this book supports Donald MacKenzie's assertion that almost as soon as computers began to be used to control critical systems, the 'potential for disaster appeared'.[13] Though this is true, it is clear from archival records that banks understood from the very outset, even before computers were embedded in their operations, that they needed to think about how their existing process and procedures, and associated security requirements, would be altered by these new machines. This runs counter to arguments made by some historians that computers were not considered a security risk, not even in light of some of the more stark depictions of the time, such as Stanley Kubrick's 1964 film Dr Strangelove.[14]

The major banks certainly saw computers as a security risk and, perhaps due to their experience of accumulating and mitigating financial risk, acted swiftly to understand and manage this new issue. Though it is also true, as Stanley Winkler and Lee Danner have argued, that a combination of increasing numbers of

---

ing our future', *American Bankers Association,* (1970). For a legal viewpoint, see James Baxendale, 'Commercial Banking and the Checkless Society', *Rutgers Journal of Computers & Law,* 88 (1970), pp. 88–98.

[13] Donald Mackenzie, Mechanizing Proof: Computing, Risk and Trust (Massachusetts: MIT Press, 2004), p. 13.

[14] Hans Meijer, Jaap-Henk Hoepman, Bart Jacobs and Erik Poll, 'Computer security through correctness and transparency' in Karl de Leeuw and Jan Bergstra (eds), *The History of Information Security* (London: Elsevier, 2007), pp. 637–654.

individuals accessing greater amounts of software and hardware, increasing numbers of individuals being trained in computer science and the amount of data stored in computers increasing focused the minds of large organisations to protect the data in their computer systems, the banks were certainly an exception to this, recognising the importance of doing so from the very outset.[15]

Computer Security and History

While the history of 'computer security' in banking, and more broadly, can be more traced to this period, the longer history of information security dates back to the seventeenth century and beyond, as many, including Karl de Leeuw, have argued.[16]

More recently there have been attempts at substantive histories of key aspects of cyber security and technology more broadly. Thomas Rid's *Rise of the Machines,* a history of the concept of cybernetics throughout the twentieth and twenty-first century, explores the development of computers, computing power and its application by individuals and organisations, and Gordon Corera's *Intercept: The Secret History of Computers and Spies* tells the story of technology and espionage over the same period.[17] Both provide useful background, given the interrelation between histories of technology, security and computing which form the backdrop of the develops in this study.

Simon Singh's *The Code Book* and Steven Levy's *Crypto* both provide an historical perspective on the development of encryption and secure communications and demonstrate the continuity of thought in conceptualising security in relation to confidentiality, integrity and availability, as argued here.[18] Also of note is a 2012 article by Michael Warner entitled *Cybersecurity: A Pre-history.* Warner argued that the 'cyber' issue is not new at all but has taken half a century to develop and described four insights that have dawned on American policy-makers in particular decades, two of which concern the period covered in this book: computers can spill sensitive data and must be guarded (1960s); computers can be attacked and data stolen (1970s).[19] Though these insights now represent common understanding, these two

---

[15] Stanley Winkler and Lee Danner, 'Data security in the computer communication environment', *Computer,* 7/2 (1974), pp. 23–31.

[16] Karl de Leeuw, 'Introduction' in *The History of Information Security: A Comprehensive Handbook* (London: Elsevier, 2007), p. 1.

[17] Thomas Rid, *Rise of the Machines: A Cybernetic History* (London: W.W. Norton & Company, 2016); Gordon Corera, *Intercept: The Secret History of Computers and Spies* (London: Weidenfeld & Nicolson, 2015).

[18] Simon Singh, *The Code Book: The Secret History of Codes and Code-Breaking* (London: Fourth Estate, 2000); Steven Levy, *Crypto: How the Code Rebels Beat the Government – Saving Privacy in the Digital Age* (London: Penguin, 2001).

[19] Michael Warner, 'Cybersecurity: A Pre-history', *Intelligence and National Security,* 27/5 (2012), pp. 781–799.

pointers act as useful single-line explainers for how large organisations' thinking about computer security developed, and are supported by the evidence provided by the banking archives employed in this study.[20]

The fundamental requirements of banks to retain confidentiality in the messages passing between them and their counterparts of course has parallels with communication security that reaches even further back in time, given the inclusion of the Old Testament of what David Kahn described as "protocryptography".[21] Broader histories of banking also provide vital context here, and notably Davide Consoli's observation, in a study of the period 1840–1990 which posited that communication technologies 'have been and still are' at the core of a process of 'structural change' in retail banking, is certainly reflective of the period in focus for this book.[22] Similarly, Bernardo Batiz-Lazo's *Cash and Dash*, a monograph that explored from an historical perspective the impact of cash machines on banking and finance, provides a wider insight into the impact of technological change on banks and the banking process.[23]

Finally, the field of history of computing provides multiple historical accounts that supply useful background for understanding the significance of the events covered in this work. Prolific in this field is Martin Campbell-Kelly, his 1989 book *ICL: A Business and Technical History,* the official history of the information systems company ICL, charted their evolution within the wider context of the industry, with which, Campbell-Kelly argued, ICL's history is synonymous.[24] Starting in the early decades of the twentieth century and continuing through the dawn of the computer age in the 1950s and subsequent decades, the book focused on the growth of ICL from a business and technical viewpoint. Useful context is also provided by works that take a similarly focused approach to the study of individual companies, organisations or technologies.[25] Simon Lavington's *Early British Computers,* published

---

[20] Some of the protagonist banks in this work have been the subjects of larger authorised institutional histories which provide useful background to this work. See Margaret Ackrill and Leslie Hannah, *Barclays: The Business of Banking 1690–1996* (Cambridge: Cambridge University Press, 2001); Lloyds Banking Group, *250: 1765–2015* (London: Lloyds Banking Group, 2015); and Richard Roberts and David Kynaston, *The Lion Wakes: A Modern History of HSBC* (London: Profile Books, 2015).

[21] David Kahn, The Codebreakers: The Comprehensive History of Secret Writing (New York: Scribner, 1967), pp. 76–79.

[22] Davide Consoli, 'The dynamics of technological change in UK retail banking services: An evolutionary perspective', *Research Policy,* 34 (2005), pp. 461–480.

[23] Bernardo Batiz-Lazo, *Cash and Dash: How ATMs and Computers Changed Banking* (Oxford: Oxford University Press, 2018).

[24] Martin Campbell-Kelly, *ICL: A Business and Technical History* (Oxford: Clarendon Press, 1989).

[25] For example, see Simon Lavington, *History of Manchester Computers* (Manchester: NCC Publications, 1975); Peter Bird, *LEO: The First Business Computer* (Wokingham: Hasler Publishing, 1994); Peter Salus, *A Quarter Century of UNIX* (Reading: Addison-Wesley, 1994); Peter Salus, *Casting the Net: From ARPANET to INTERNET and Beyond…*(Reading: Addison-Wesley, 1995).

half a decade before *ICL*, assessed the evolution of computing in the United Kingdom specifically and provides a valuable account.[26]

Paul Ceruzzi's *A History of Modern Computing,* published in 2003 presented a broad historical assessment of computing, beginning with its commercialisation in the 1950s. It focused primarily on the United States of America, but is relevant to this work in its exploration of the emergence of computers, their adaption by business and how this history informs the current role and functions of computers in organisations and wider society. Earlier historical works examined wider themes related to the rise of computers, but Ceruzzi's work represents an all-encompassing account of the technologies and ideas most prevalent in the history of computing.[27]

Other recent work has focused on the business of computing. Such contributions again offer useful context to the subject matter of this study. Jeffrey Yost's 2005 book *The Computer Industry* took a wide historical scope and examined that industry as a whole, from its 'Prehistory' in the years 1880–1939 to the 'Computer Networking Revolution' between 1990 and 2004 and also provided a timeline of developments in the history of computing.[28] Its focus was primarily though not exclusively on the computer industry in the United States, particularly hardware companies, using as its evidence a base of secondary sources. Yost's contribution is therefore useful both as more contemporary assessment of the backdrop to adoption of computers by businesses and as an entry into the wider secondary literature around computing history, including valuable sections of recommended reading relevant to each chapter.[29] A decade on, Martin Campbell-Kelly and Daniel Garcia-Swartz published a similar though more ambitious contribution than Yost's. They took the history of the international computer industry as their subject and offered a chronological economic history covering the period from the 1950s which argued that a key theme of the industry's evolution has been its shifting core from hardware to software and services.[30] Campbell-Kelly and Garcia Swartz helpfully summarised the existing work on the history of the computing industry: on the one hand, lengthy

---

[26] Simon Lavington, *Early British Computers* (Bedford: Digital Press, 1980).

[27] See Herman Goldstine, *The Computer from Pascal to von Neumann* (Princeton: Princeton University Press, 1972); John Kemeny, *Man and the Computer* (New York: Charles Scribner's Sons, 1972); Brian Randell, *The Origins of Digital Computers: Selected Papers* (Berlin: Springer-Verlag, 1975); Nick Metropolis, J. Howlett and Gian-Carlo Rota (eds), *A History of Computing in the Twentieth Century* (New York: Academic Press, 1980); James Beniger, *The Control Revolution: Technological and Economic Origins of the Information Society* (Cambridge: Harvard University Press, 1986); Charles Eames and Ray Eames, *A Computer Perspective: Background to the Computer Age* (Cambridge: Harvard University Press, 1990).

[28] Jeffrey Yost, *The Computer Industry* (London: Greenwood Press, 2005).

[29] Other attempts to take an historical perspective on the industry include Kenneth Flamm's *Creating the Computer: Government, Industry and High Technology* (Washington, DC: Brookings Institution, 2007).

[30] Martin Campbell-Kelly and Daniel Garcia-Swartz, *From Mainframes to Smartphones: A History of the International Computer Industry* (Cambridge: Harvard University Press, 2015).

scholarly works dealing typically with a relatively narrow facet of the industry and on the other, the shorter, livelier and lightly documented.[31]

A seminal work in the history of computing literature, and therefore providing authoritative and thorough background for this research, is *Computer: A History of the Information Machine,* the third edition of which was published in 2014. Martin Campbell-Kelly, William Aspray, Nathan Ensmenger and Jeffrey Yost provided a thorough account, beginning in the early nineteenth century and tracing the rise of the computer over the course of the following centuries. It argued that new understandings of computer history, particularly as the field has burgeoned since the early 1990s, should not refute or supersede earlier histories but deepen knowledge, noting that the history of the computer has become inextricably intertwined with the history of communications and mass media.[32] *Computer* represents essential background reading which complements the comparatively narrow focus on security in this research, placing the developments traced here into a longer historical narrative.

Early Computer Security

If we take 'early' in this context to mean the period roughly covering the 1960s and the early 1970s, then it is difficult to counter Jeffrey Yost's argument that early computer security was relatively straightforward, posing few additional problems regarding the protection of confidential information. For example, a significant amount of early computer security focus was upon access control, often physical access to spaces and machinery, which had significant parallels to existing security practices. Security was also about understanding and classifying the sensitivity of information process by machines, which had been the case, as Yost has said, since the creation in the 1940s of the ENIAC, the first meaningful computer. Although Yost's argument that computer security was simply one element of the more general security of the installations where computers were housed, with protocols designed to focus upon and prevent or address theft, vandalism or sabotage, there was certainly concern from banks over technical security measures including the ability for messages to be eavesdropped or listened in on. Some academic work at this time also provided detailed practical guidance on the mechanics of protecting data stored in computers, with the express aim of bolstering the lack of expertise in industry and the management of this new risk.[33]

---

[31] Martin Campbell-Kelly and Daniel Garcia-Swartz, *From Mainframes to Smartphones: A History of the International Computer Industry* (Cambridge: Harvard University Press, 2015), p. 6. One such work is by Campbell-Kelly himself: Martin Campbell-Kelly, *From Airline Reservations to Sonic the Hedgehog: A History of the Software Industry* (London: MIT Press), 2003.

[32] Martin Campbell-Kelly, William Aspray, Nathan Esmenger and Jeffrey Yost, *Comptuer: A History of the Information Machine* (Boulder: Westview Press, 2014).

[33] See Jerome Saltzer and Michael Schroeder, 'The Protection of Information in Computer Systems', *Proceedings of the IEEE,* 63/9 (1975), pp. 1278–1308. On risks see Roy Freed,

However, as we move through the 1970s, security certainly became less straight-forward as the banks shifted focus from the institutional to the inter-bank payment systems. This involved protecting information not only when stored but also in transit. As Yost said, electronic radiation was an issue, and it became harder to simply shield computer machinery as minicomputers proliferated, and networks soon after, as exemplified by the Bank of England's concern over that particular issue from the late 1960s and into the early and mid-1970s. Physical security persisted but was complemented by increasingly technical measures, such as through the creation of BACS. Here we start to see security take into account issues of information transmission. Security was built into these payment systems from the outset as the banks had learnt the importance of that from their own internal systems, and so carried this combined experience into development of payment systems. Note, the cost of computer security investment did not temper their ambition, but was seen as a cost of doing business.

Yost argued that the complexity and specialised knowledge involved in operating early mainframes ensured and justified limited access and contributed a substantial degree of security, and this thinking was certainly indicative of the banks' approach. They saw security as a continuous endeavour, and in payment systems such as BACS, whose encryption keys would change, they recognised that a breach would require significant knowledge of the network as well as actually gaining hold of encryption keys. They recognised quickly that you couldn't achieve perfect security. This was about minimising risks and plans for recovery, being resilient, echoing the current approach and messaging provided by the Bank of England today, and the requirements for all banks to meet "operational resilience" requirements in the coming years.

Consolidation

By the late 1970s the major London clearing banks were in a period of consolidation. They had contributed to significant, co-ordinated progress in the implementation of new technology in the sector in major projects such as BACS and SWIFT, and were continuing to bolster their internal operations through investment in new hardware and software. These institutions' dependency on such technology was still growing deeper, and so efforts to develop contingency plans were maintained, alongside the consideration being given to the overall security of these operations. Banks had far bigger and more powerful technological installations to manage and protect against damage and fraud.

'Computer fraud – a management trap: Risks are legal, economic, professional', *Business Horizons,* 12/3 (1969), pp. 25–30; Rein Turn and H.E. Petersen, 'Security of Computerized Information Systems', *The RAND Corporation,* July 1970. On mitigation measures see Dennie van Tassel, 'Proceedings of the May 14–16, 1969, spring joint computer conference', *American Federation of Information Processing Societies,* (1969), pp. 367–372.

New computer networks enabled individuals to commit fraud on an unprecedented scale and at unprecedented speed. Mirroring Yost's observation that for
American companies, the replacement of physically isolating machines by digital
computer networking from the 1950s to 1970s altered the computer security landscape, meaning that confidentiality and integrity became even greater concerns for
organisations sending and receiving sensitive financial data and transactions. Meijer,
Hopman, Jacobs and Poll argue that three main aspects of computer security define
this period: "security", or protection against attackers; "accuracy", or the absence of
error; and "privacy", or protection against sniffers. This broadly holds true, but as
evidenced by the London clearing banks, the focus on confidentiality, integrity and
availability was not the only focus from the 1980s onwards, as those authors suggest. It is more helpful, perhaps, to consider information security in this age to
encompass both the deliberate and non-deliberate, and to focus on the potential
methods of breaking this security, to truly understand how major financial institutions conceptualised and managed the threat. Finally, though it is true, as those
authors argue, that the Internet has since emphasised the importance of authorisation and authenticity, it is in the development of these payment systems that its
importance was first given primacy.

This book argues that throughout the period 1960–1990 the major London clearing banks operated under a consistent and shared definition of computer security.
They took computer security to mean managing the use, access to and manipulation
of both software and hardware in their computer-dependent infrastructure, such as
electronic funds transfer and communication systems, to achieve certainty, predictability and control over operations. Confidentiality and integrity of information
alongside the availability of new systems were thought to be the values most at risk.
Achieving these qualities required the implementation of sufficient measures to
ensure that communication and financial transactions could be undertaken privately,
legitimately and at the time of the individual or institutions' choosing. Such measures were designed to minimise the risk involved in depending on computer and
telecommunications technology to acceptable levels for all involved parties.
Computer security manifested itself practically in physical and technical measures
including control of access to buildings and rooms and the scrambling of transmissions. Proportionality, more specifically the trade-off between cost and security,
played an influential role in banks' decision-making.

The consistency and stability of the London clearing banks' computer security
concerns over time is in large part due to the relative continuity in the role played by
those institutions, with the relationship between the banks and their customers at the
core of their business. As protectors of wealth for customers in the face of both
financial and operational risk remained unchanged, with computer security treated
as just that – another form of risk to manage. The historical importance which the
banks assigned to customer confidentiality – one of the key components of security
for the banks – underpinned this consistency. 'Bankers have a traditional duty to

keep secret their customers' affairs', read a guide published jointly by the clearing banks in the early 1970s.[34]

Connected to this rise in networking and computer security more broadly was the evolution of computer security experts, as Jerome Lobel has argued. The 'computer security and privacy expert seems to have evolved … sometime between 1968 and 1972', he said, noting that from a 'very slow start', interest in computer security and privacy blossomed in the early 1970s and then accelerated into a subject of acute national interest by the early 1980s.[35] It is certainly true, and argued here, that computer security expertise was both sought after and expensive, and only a very small number of individuals could provide banks with the required abilities – often at a significant cost, and often emanating from the United States rather than the UK. Lobel's argument that the acceleration and rapid application of computer technology caused unparalleled difficulty for system security and privacy also rings true.[36]

Furthermore, these banks often sought the advice of a limited number of private consultants, including Logica, so it is unsurprising that definitions of computer security persisted. Underpinning the deployment of practical security measures was a desire on the part of all the banks to employ computers for efficiency savings, to employ state of the art machinery and to do this in a way which made their customers trust in its necessity and benefit. A shared goal such as this ensured that computer security was not a competitive endeavour but one where collaboration and continuity were deliberate choices.

Networked Dependency

By the mid-1980s, banks depended upon the computer networks which linked the machines in their branches and computer centres. Meanwhile, the UK Government was for the first time taking an interest in how technology was impacting the sector. The development of the CHAPS payment system was focusing attention on all three elements of computer security – confidentiality, integrity and availability – given the vast sums of money due to be transferred across it. Much of the discussion in CHAPS' creation related to proportionality of security measures and the risks and benefits of methods of encryption.

It was in the development of CHAPS that a key theme of this period came to the fore: finding a balance between the level of investment in security measures and the level of risk that those measures eliminated. Susan Hubbell Nycum, writing in the mid-1970s, noted that the cost of ignoring security or providing poor security was

---

[34] HSBC, File UK1793-0013, 'Role of the Banks', *Bank Education Service*, March 1972, p. 12.

[35] Jerome Lobel, 'The State-of-the-Art in Computer Security', *Computers & Security,* 2/3 (1983), pp. 218–222.

[36] For a general overview of the banking sector in the UK across the period see John Grady and Martin Weale, *British Banking: 1960–85* (Basingstoke: Macmillan, 1986).

unimaginably greater than the cost of investment.[37] Although potentially true, the banks certainly grappled with this question and ultimately came to the view that perfect security was not achievable, but that setting the bar sufficiently high for criminals would provide sufficient protection. Agreeing on that level was not simple, but their belief that success on the part of criminals required both the opportunity and expert knowledge. Using these two assumptions, the banks played-out varying scenarios to ascertain the practical level of risk that they were willing to accept.

Hubbell Nycum, also in 1976, published an article on security in electronic funds transfer (EFT) systems such as CHAPS, in which she concluded that EFT could be 'one of banking's greatest boons and greatest threats', and outlined the areas of activity that she felt warranted particular consideration: personnel access; physical security; data security; systems security; and communication security and access controls.[38] Each of these were of particular concern to the London clearing banks at this time, the mix of both physical and technical security here reflecting the reality of the threat that banks faced throughout the period 1960–1990.

Until the mid-1980s, most contributions of relevance to this book concentrated upon computers and security in the United States rather than the United Kingdom. In 1986, however, Andrew Kinnon and Robert Davis wrote an article which specifically referred to BACS and CHAPS, two of the critical pieces of financial infrastructure developed by the major London clearing banks and case studies presented as chapters in this book.[39] Though Kinnon and Davis simply outlined the general features and functions of BACS and CHAPS, and the same for the SWIFT system,

---

[37] Susan Hubbell Nycum, 'Security for Electronic Funds Transfer System', *University of Pittsburgh Law Review,* 709 (1976), pp. 709–724. For a general overview of the development of electronic funds transfer systems by this point see Craig Ford, 'Electronic Funds Transfer: The State of the Art – Present and Project', *University of Pittsburgh Law Review,* 37/4 (1976), pp. 629–640. See also Donn Parker, *Crime By Computer: Startling New Kinds of Million-Dollar Fraud, Theft, Larceny and Embezzlement* (New York: Charles Scribner's Sons, 1976).

[38] Susan Hubbell Nycum, 'Security for Electronic Funds Transfer System', *University of Pittsburgh Law Review,* 709 (1976), pp. 709–724. For a general overview of the development of electronic funds transfer systems by this point see Craig Ford, 'Electronic Funds Transfer: The State of the Art – Present and Project', *University of Pittsburgh Law Review,* 37/4 (1976), pp. 629–640.

[39] Andrew Kinnon and Robert Davis, 'Audit and Security Implications of Electronic Funds Transfer', *Computers & Security,* 5/1 (1986), pp. 17–23. For a snapshot of EFT systems in the UK financial sector at this time, and the broader implications of technology on banking and finance, see Colin Lewis, 'Information management: the industrial need', *ASLIB Proceedings,* 37/3 (1985), pp. 137–145; John Langdale, 'Electronic funds transfer and the internationalisation of the banking and finance industry', *Geoforum,* 16/1 (1985), pp. 1–13; Glenis Moore, 'An end to the paper chase?', *Electronics and Power,* 33/9 (1987), pp. 554–556; Nick Cowan, 'The Technical Environment of Banks and Its Implications', *International Journal of Bank Marketing,* 5/4 (1987), pp. 15–31; Henry Holloway, 'Information Technology and Company Policy: 4. Banking', *Journal of Information Technology,* 3/4 (1988), pp. 265–271; Bruce Summers, 'Electronic Payments in Retrospect', *FRB Richmond Economic Review,* 74/2 (1988), pp. 16–19; and Harry Scarbrough and Ronnie Lannon, 'The Successful Exploitation of New Technology in Banking', *Journal of General Management,* 13/3 (1988), pp. 38–51. For a geographical perspective see Barney Wharf, 'Telecommunications and the Globalization of Financial Services', *Professional Geographer,* 41/3

which was created through global collaboration between banks and is also the subject of a case study in this research, they usefully explained internal audit functions within banks and the characteristics of shared networks developed by financial institutions alongside preferred characteristics of computer staff, providing relevant context. Kinnon and Davis described the aim of Electronic Funds Transfer security, in their assessment, as the development of measures 'sophisticated enough to prevent any invasion of a bank's financial and communication systems, no matter how ingenious the attacker or how well equipped he may be, while allowing swift, convenient, specifically limited access to those authorised and correctly equipped to do so.'[40] However, this study demonstrates that banks were actually more pragmatic about their computer security than Kinnon and Davis. Rather than preventing 'any invasion', they sought to minimise risk to a tolerable level, but accept that their defences would not be invincible. The authors shared a pessimistic conclusion for the future of computer security. They believed that it was 'likely that the criminal will stay a jump ahead [of bank security experts] indefinitely.'[41]

Direct reference was also made to the security of CHAPS by R.T. Clark in his 1984 article *Electronic funds transfer: The creeping revolution.* He discussed the 'extraordinary lengths to ensure reliability and security' its creators had gone to in order to safeguard the flows of billions of pounds that it facilitated each day, though the primary focus of Clark's article was the overall utilisation of technology in banking operations, rather than computer security specifically.[42]

Towards the end of this period, banks were certainly concerned more with the potential "technical" threats which could disrupt their network operations or render them inaccessible. Computer viruses and trojan horses were met with great apprehension. Bernard Zajac who, in 1990, wrote specifically on computer viruses and quoted first *The New York Times'* description of them as 'the letter bomb of the 1980s' but, going further, cited Dr Harold Highland, who said 'We ain't seen nothing yet!'[43] These quotations certainly reflected the apprehension held by banks towards the potential disruption which viruses and trojan horses had the potential to cause.

In 2012, Ian Martin made use of the Barclays archive in his article *Too Far Ahead of Its Time: Barclays, Burroughs, and Real-Time Banking* in the IEEE Annals of the

---

(1989), pp. 257–271. For an overview of electronic funds transfer in Canada see James Grant, 'Electronic banking and telecommunications', *Information & Management,* 11/1 (1986), pp. 3–7.

An historical perspective, with particular reference to BACS, is provided by J.B. Howcroft and John Lavis, 'Evolution of the Payment Systems of London Clearing Banks', *The Service Industries Journal,* 7/2 (2006), pp. 176–194.

[40] Kinnon and Davis, p. 22.

[41] Ibid., pp. 22–23.

[42] R.T. Clark, 'Electronic funds transfer: The creeping revolution', *Environment and Planning A: Economy and Space,* 16/4 (1984), pp. 437–450. For an overview of the banking sector in the UK at this time see John Cooper, *The Management and Regulation of Banks* (Basingstoke: Macmillan, 1984).

[43] Bernard Zajac, 'Computer viruses: Can they be prevented?', *Computers & Security,* 9/1 (1990), pp. 25–31.

History of Computing.[44] Martin argued that focusing on failures in the history of computing in banking studies can gain insight into the nonlinear nature of technological change, and this book supports this view though with a focus on computer security specifically. This, alongside Martin's earlier chapter 'Britain's First Computer Centre for Banking: What Did This Building Do?', represents a significant contribution to the field of computing history, particularly relevant to this book in their use of primary source evidence which was used to describe some of the early computerisation approaches taken by Barclays and the other London clearing banks.[45]

Demonstrated here is the complex web of interrelated work that, to varying extents, is relevant to this book.

Consistency

Consistency in the banks' understanding of computer security ultimately led to their successful management of the issue. The banks engendered enough trust and confidence from customers to use their systems, with the number of users, variety of services and amounts of money transferred growing over time. No evidence of a major security incident throughout this period exists in the archives, and although computer viruses by the end of the period caused some minor difficulties, discussion of security threats was often hypothetical. Continual focus on achieving the trio of aims – confidentiality, integrity and availability – gave the stakeholders involved the ability to evaluate potential security measures based on their ability to achieve one or more of those qualities. Such consensus, and the absence of any serious dissent, allowed the banks to progress towards their shared security goals in a productive manner, wasting little time debating what successful outcomes looked like and allowing them to spend more time understanding new technology and how they could offer themselves and their customers sufficient protection. Such consistency is also likely a factor in the longevity of the sector-wide infrastructure that they developed during this period.

Combined with this continuity of role was the strong relationships that existed between the major clearing banks. Formal mechanisms for collaboration, for example through the Committee of London Clearing Bankers (CLCB) meant that decisions were often made collectively. The creation of payment infrastructure like BACS, CHAPS and SWIFT, in which the banks took ownership, allowed for the entrenchment of views on computer security, as these dominant institutions combined their expertise and worked through the minutiae of security concerns in these

[44] Ian Martin, 'Too Far Ahead of Its Time: Barclays, Burroughs, and Real-Time Banking', *IEEE Annals of the History of Computing*, 34/2 (2012), pp. 5–19.

[45] Ian Martin, 'Britain's First Computer Centre for Banking: What Did This Building Do?' in Bernardo Batiz-Lazo, J. Carles Maixe-Altes and Paul Thomes (eds), 'Technological Innovation in Retail Finance: International Historical Perspectives (New York: Routledge, 2011).

vast new systems. A small number of banks, combined with a relatively limited amount of computer security expertise during this period, likely contributed to such stability and consensus.

City Security in Context

This books seeks to redress the balance of understanding by providing an objective, measured and rigorous historical assessment of how the City of London's major clearing banks first confronted, understood and managed computer security over the course of the 1960s, 1970s and 1980s.

Histories of security covering the second half of the twentieth century focus on national security, the Cold War backdrop and international relations framing their narrative. Security in this context was understood as a public policy aim, sought after by what David Omand has described as first the secret state and later the protective state.[46] While it is unlikely that a topic as specific computer London clearing banks would warrant inclusion in an attempt at an authoritative history of security akin to Christopher Andrew's history of intelligence, *The Secret World,* some of the themes that emanate from the subject of this book are of significance to contemporary understanding of security. Firstly, a substantial amount of what is designated by governments as "Critical National Infrastructure (CNI)", including financial services, essential services like electricity and water supply, are run by private companies. Cyber security for these crucial services is therefore the responsibility of private sector organisations, albeit with assistance from the intelligence services and law enforcement.

This work offers perhaps the origins of such a process and, while not concentrating in substantial detail on the relationship between the banks and central government, offers an insight into how the current relationships have come into being and what factors have impacted such relationships over time. Secondly, the clearing banks' understanding of security as resilience might also be seen to have wider historical significance. Such thinking begun during this period and is now the means through which the Bank of England encourages the sector to think of cyber security management.

The London clearing banks were persistent in their belief that security should be understood as resilience, and this belief resonates with contemporary thinking. Alongside these two points of significance, any wider history of cyber security would be incomplete without an understanding of how industry has managed computer security historically, and the account in this work offers an insight into how that was done, helping historians understand how cyber security thinking and management in industry has reached its current state.

---

[46]David Omand, *Securing the State:* (London: Hurst & Company, 2010), p. xviii. See also Christopher Andrew, *The Secret World: A History of Intelligence* (London: Allen Lane, 2018).

Chapter Outline

This book is comprised of 7 chapters: a combination of three overview chapters inter-spersed with three detailed case study chapters that closely examine collaboration between the major London clearing banks over the creation of major financial market infrastructure. Overview chapters introduce technological developments and govern-ment actions that impacted the sector alongside wider industry context and policy decisions on computer security taken by individual banks. Case study chapters further elucidate the viewpoint of those institutions by presenting the minutiae and nuances of company meetings, reports and reviews. Deploying this combination of chapters equips readers with the background knowledge to contextualise and understand the significance of specific detail in the case studies. As a result, this work offers readers an exploration of significant new information on computer security in the financial sector from a new perspective allowed by primary documents, that of the banks them-selves: their attempts to define and understand computer security and the threats to it, their practical implementation of security measures and their growing awareness of their increased reliance upon new technology.

Chapter 2 provides the reader with necessary overview of initial computerisation in the British financial sector in the 1960s and 1970s. It offers context on how infor-mation technology was adopted by the banks up to the 1960s, how this began to deepen over the course of the 1960s, and how this intensified further in the 1970s. For example, it details the types and number of computers utilised by Midland Bank in the early 1960s.[47] It then details the computer installations used by the Bank of England, with descriptions of the activities they were used for from the mid-1960s onwards.[48] Initial security measures are then explored, for example the methods used at Midland Bank's computer centres, such as contingency plans and physical security measures.[49] Also examined here is a 1975 memo directly from the Director of the Communications Electronic Security Group (CESG) within Government Communications Headquarters (GCHQ), the British signals intelligence agency, to the Bank of England regarding the security of Bank data.[50]

Chapter 3 presents the first case study. It outlines the development of Bankers' Automated Clearing Services (BACS) from its inception in 1968 until 1980. Providing the basis for this chapter are annual and bi-annual security reviews of this new infra-structure undertaken by the private sector banks who owned and developed the sys-tem. It explores the physical and increasingly technical security considerations of those banks over the course of the 1970s. For example, the 1973 security report notes the need for off-site back up facilities in case of catastrophe at the BACS computer

---

[47] HSBC Archives, Midland Bank, *Banking on Computers,* October 1981, p. 2.

[48] See Bank of England Archive, File 7A386/1, 'The Use of Computers at the Bank of England', 24 January 1969.

[49] HSBC Archives, Midland Bank, 'Computer Services Division News: South Yorkshire Computer Centre', December 1978.

[50] BoE, File 5A199/6, 'Computer Systems – Security of Bank Data', 10 June 1975.

centre as well as console logs to check for fraudulent data input to computers.[51] The 1978 report highlights concern that BACS' software was inadequately backed-up at the remote security store.[52] By 1980, the reports discuss the transmission of data between Scottish banks and BACS in London and how secure that process was.[53]

Chapter 4 introduces the second case study. Detailed here is the creation of the Society for Worldwide Interbank Financial Telecommunication (SWIFT). It traces the development of security in SWIFT from approximately 1972 until 1984, when the system experienced some software integrity issues.[54] The chapter examines the discussions over security held by the Board of Directors of SWIFT including details on technical security requirements.[55] It also looks at security reviews of the SWIFT system.[56] Provided here is an assessment of banks' growing awareness of computer network security, as machines became increasingly linked together in networks rather than being isolated machines, and an example of international co-operation between banks over that issue.

Chapter 5 looks at the first half of the 1980s. It begins by outlining the increased focus of central government on information technology in the private sector. This includes some thinking on the general implications of information technology for the economy by the Government's Central Policy Review Staff (CPRS), based in the Cabinet Office,[57] and thinking about specific implications for the financial sector by the Advisory Council for Applied Research and Development (ACARD).[58] The chapter then goes on to outline some specific efforts by individual banks to mitigate their new found reliance upon networking technology, for example at Midland Bank.[59] It then provides a snapshot outline from 1984 of the computer networks operated by both the Bank of Scotland and the Trustee Savings Bank, providing a detailed description of the number and types of networks and hardware these institutions utilised, as examples of large banking institutions outside of the group of the major clearers.[60] This chapter presents an overview of the increasing dependence on

---

[51] London Metropolitan Archive, File M32145X/1, 'Bankers' Automated Clearing Services Limited', 29 March 1973.

[52] LMA, File M32145X/6, 'Bankers' Automated Clearing Services Limited: Inspection Report 1978', 7 November 1978.

[53] LMA, File M32145X/6, 'Bankers' Automated Clearing Services Limited: Inspection Undertaken by Representatives of Coutts & Co. and Lloyds Bank Ltd', 19 November 1980.

[54] Barclays File 0328-0026, 'SWIFT – Problem RE. ST 200 Software', 12 December 1984, p. 1.

[55] See BoE, File 7A383/1, 'Minutes of 7th Meeting of the Board of Directors of SWIFT', 11 June 1974.

[56] See BoE, File 7A383/2, 'SRI Recommendations Contained in the Report "Status of the Security of SWIFT's Operations"', 30 May 1978, p. 1.

[57] The National Archives, File T390/698, 'CPRS note attached to Armstrong to Wass', 11 February 1980.

[58] TNA, File T390/698, 'Advisory Council for Applied Research and Development: Information Technology', August 1980, p. 21.

[59] HSBC Archives, Midland Bank, *Banking on Computers,* October 1981, p. 5.

[60] LMA, File MS32456/2, 'Existing Draft of Chapter for EEC Survey', 24 July 1984, p. 33.

the financial sector upon computer and network technology, the growing sophistication of this technology and a realisation from government that such technology in the private sector could have unforeseen impacts on the UK economy.

Chapter 6 details this work's third major case study, the Clearing House Automated Payment System (CHAPS), between its inception in 1972 and launch in 1984. The substantial amount of archival material available to draw upon means that this chapter is presented as three sub-chapters. The first of these outlines the substantial development period over the first half of the 1970s. It shows how from the preliminary planning of the project, before it was officially sanctioned, there was awareness from its developers, the London clearing banks, that security of the system would be integral to its success.[61] Key issues throughout this period for the banks include confidentiality and authentication in the new system.[62] The second sub-chapter concerns the period between approximately 1976 and 1980. It examines the detailed planning for the implementation of the system, including potential means via which criminals could manipulate CHAPS, including fraud.[63] It outlines the detailed security measures within the system and includes comments from the banks on the level of security they felt CHAPS provided.[64] The third sub-chapter takes the period from 1980 to 1984 and describes the security measures employed in the second iteration of CHAPS and the discussions between banks over prioritising such features.[65] It details an instance of alarm over the issuing of the system's source code and object code together to individual banks.[66] It also assesses some of the early failures of the CHAPS system.[67] Overall, this chapter provides an in-depth example on how computer and network security developed over the course of the 1970s and first half of the 1980s, including detailed discussion of key issues such as confidentiality and integrity of data, methods to ensure these qualities such as encryption and authentication measures, as well as system resilience and contingency planning.

Chapter 7 provides a broad overview of financial security cyber security over the last half of the 1980s. It discusses the appointment of the Committee on the Review of Banking Services Law, in 1987, which in part had the remit of examining the law and implications of financial services in relation to the security, reliability and availability of the new technology underpinning the sector.[68] It briefly considers early computer viruses, such as the Friday 13th virus, which emerged and spread in the late 1980s, and details the perspective of private sector banks on this relatively new

---

[61] See BoE, File 1A18/1, 'Summary of meetings between members of the 'CHAPS' working group and representatives of non-clearing banks', 13 November 1973.

[62] See Ibid.

[63] See BoE, File 11A70/4, 'Data Encryption', 5 June 1979, p. 1.

[64] See BoE, File 2A183/1, 'CHAPS', 31 October 1977, p. 2.

[65] See BoE, File 2A89/1, 'Note on the CHAPS 2 Concept', November 1980.

[66] BoE, File 2A89/3, 'Security of Gateway Software', 13 July 1983.

[67] BoE File 2A89/4, 'CHAPS Failure 20 August 1984', 23 August 1984.

[68] Professor R B Jack, *Banking Services: Law and Practice: Report by the Review Committee,* CM 622, 30 December 1988, p. 2.

phenomenon.[69] It also explores the security and contingency plans employed by some banks at the beginning of the 1990s.[70]

Questions

Three requirements dominated computer security major British banks' thinking and decision-making during the 1960s, 1970s and 1980s: defining and conceptualising computer security; identifying perceived threats to their computer security; and practically mitigating against those dangers. Debates were often as much principled and intellectual as they were grounded in practicality, certain subjects like encryption and its applications provoking protracted discussions before conclusions were reached.

Three research questions therefore drive the analysis in this work, attempting to gain deeper insight into the banks' three aforementioned priorities. How exactly did the London clearing banks, and their counterparts in the Bank of England, *understand* and *define* computer security in this period? What did these institutions perceive to be the main threats to this security? What practical measures did they enact to mitigate the risk they faced? Combined, these research questions provoke responses that can now be bolstered by the unprecedented detail found previously unexplored and newly released primary source material. These research questions seek to unpick computer security in this period from the perspective of the primary protagonists in the United Kingdom's financial sector. Answering these research questions therefore provides a new level of understanding of an area previously unexplored in such depth.

Research Methods & Sources

This research is written as a study of contemporary history. It explores a previously unstudied subject matter and employs hitherto overlooked archival evidence alongside that which has been recently released, allowing for new understanding to emerge from this in-depth study.

No significant contribution to the literature on financial sector cyber security in the UK has been grounded in such documentary evidence. No historical account such as the one presented here exists. For this reason, this book has attempted to gather as much available evidence as possible from British archives to offer a piece of research underpinned by reliable sources. Focus has primarily remained upon the United Kingdom's financial sector as the bulk of available evidence, for example on

---

[69] Channel 4 Dispatches, 11 October 1989.

[70] HSBC, *Electronic Banking News*, Issue 11, September 1992, p. 5.

the creation of BACS and CHAPS, shows how the London clearing banks were central in driving those processes. Where possible, and where allowed by the source material, comparisons and analysis of the UK with particularly the United States of America has been presented, though an entirely separate comparative book could be written on that subject, which is not within the scope of this work. Many of the folders and documents consulted have been released in the past decade, some more recently, and early access was also granted to a select few folders due for release in the years to come. The literature review above suggests that this book is the first time that the overwhelming majority of these documents have been used to inform work on computer and network security.

Most fruitful have been visits to the Bank of England Archive for material on their view of computer security across the sector; the London Metropolitan Archives for material concerning the Committee of London Clearing Bankers; and, from The National Archives at Kew, files were consulted which offered an insight into broader government understanding and encouragement of investment in technology by business, some specifically concerning the financial sector. Visits to individual bank archives, including to Barclays, HSBC for Midland Bank documents, Lloyds Bank, and the Royal Bank of Scotland have also provided substantive material for this book.

The advantage of access to the material outlined above, and the ability to combine this material in a single piece of research, is a new and unique grouping of evidence that is used to underpin a new and original contribution to the field. Nevertheless, several considerations must be considered. As a first attempt at writing such a history, it is difficult to understand what, if anything, is missing from the archival evidence. The relative lack of directly relevant secondary source material compounds this. Secondly, most archives and institutions have since 2010 been transitioning from the 30-year rule for document releases to the 20-year rule, so evidence is normally only readily available up to the late-1980s, which has been the case for the archives consulted for this research. Any consideration of the time after this period must rely upon interview evidence which may well not be as accurate as documentary evidence, and the sparse availability of public evidence. Thirdly, as the topic is clearly a sensitive one for financial institutions today, there are varying degrees of willingness to engage with academic researchers, and even then, there is only so much that employees can publicly reveal. Despite these potential drawbacks, a first attempt at analysing this material and presenting it in an accessible manner adds value to a field lacking even a general historical survey.

The significant amount of archival material available provides a unique perspective on the history of financial sector computer security in its burgeoning years of development. It represents a first attempt to shed light on how the London clearing banks first dealt with computer security issues. Even where errors and omissions may become clear with the passage of time and the opening of new archives, this work's reliance upon substantial archival documentation, ensures that its analysis is driven by consideration of the available facts as they are at the time of writing.

Overall, this work demonstrates that the roots of what would today be described as cyber security stretch further back than is commonly assumed. Computer security has been a consideration of major financial organisations since at least the early 1960s, and though the technology being discussed has evolved at speed, many of computer security's fundamental principles, particularly from banks' perspectives – including confidentiality, integrity and availability – remain at the forefront of "cyber" thinking today. Understanding the history of computer security in the UK financial sector in a new level of detail therefore provides deeper context to a contemporary issue of fundamental importance. Detailed for the first time here are the origins of computer security in the United Kingdom's financial sector.

Chapter 2
The London Clearing Banks and Computer Security: 1960–1977

Information technology revolutionised the United Kingdom's financial sector in the second half of the twentieth century. Beginning in the 1950s, and gathering pace throughout the 1960s and 1970s, the London clearing banks, responsible for facilitating financial settlements between institutions in the City of London, began harnessing the rapidly increasing power of computers for their operations. Tasks including branch accounting and cheque clearing were automated, made possible by vast room-sized computer installations and, as time passed, smaller individual computer terminals. Computer machinery became commercially viable soon after the Second World War and the banks took advantage, investing in this technology from an early stage.

The primary aim of this automation was utilitarian: to save on money and time primarily through lower staffing requirements, labour being relatively expensive in comparison to the processing power of computers. Machines could streamline the costs of bank operations but also make their undertaking more reliable and predictable by eliminating the manual, human involvement.

Driving automation in Britain's financial sector were the largest banks who possessed both the largest resources to invest in technology together with the greatest potential for savings given the scale of their operations. London's clearing banks, Barclays, National Westminster, Coutts (part of NatWest from 1969), Lloyds, Midland, and Williams and Glyn's (established in 1970), placed their trust in these new and mysterious electronic machines early in the post-war period. As an indication of the scale of their operations, these banks were collecting payments for roughly four million cheques per day by 1972 – enough to be four times taller than the Post Office Tower in London, or BT Tower since 1981, should their paper versions be stacked on top of each other.[1] While this investment offered the potential for significant financial savings, a level of risk accompanied automation given the dependency banks almost immediately placed on their new appliances.

---

[1] HSBC Archive (HSBC hereafter), File UK1793-0013, 'The Clearing System', January 1972, p. 1.

© Springer Nature Switzerland AG 2022
A. Sweetman, *Cyber and the City*, History of Computing,
https://doi.org/10.1007/978-3-031-07933-7_2

Security therefore became a key focus for these institutions. For example, dependency on these machines for updating branch balances meant that, should the banks' new hardware or software fail them, significant disruption could ensue as they attempted to manually complete a task whose scale and speed had been magnified by computer and communication technology. Malicious attempts to damage hardware or manipulate software were also concerns alongside its accidental breakdown. Banks began defining what computer security meant in immediate response to the assimilation of these machines into their processes, attempting to pinpoint the risks inherent in their computerised operations and outline practical means to alleviate the threats they faced.

Having first acquired computers in the very early 1960s, the banks' comprehension of computer security matured rapidly over that decade and the next. In this period, security mainly focused on the physical: both managing human access to machines and dealing with potential computer failure or damage, and banks developed contingency plans to guide recovery from any breach of security. Given the expeditious uptake of new and powerful technology, the banks had to learn quickly, and by the mid-1970s this knowledge aroused sufficient ambition for them to begin development of sector-wide infrastructure. Security was a built-in component of these financial communication systems from the outset, a consequence of the security awareness garnered from the development and management of their own internal systems. Computers had been bought to boost productivity and therefore profitability, and it took the banks only a short time to appreciate that such benefits could not be realised if their computer installations – be they within individual institutions or networked to link institutions – were not properly safeguarded.

Intertwined here are two key strands of history for the financial sector: firstly, the beginnings of systematic automation and the widespread embrace of new technology; and secondly, the origins of thinking and action on computer security. The first more general strand informs and underpins the second. Both are explored in some detail to provide vital context for understanding the significance of later developments in computer security that form the bulk of this book.

Outlined in this chapter is the progress of automation and security thinking covering the period 1960–1975. It outlines how individual banks took their first steps into purchasing computers for their operations and how they began to tackle the issue of security. Firstly, it looks at the role of World War II as a catalyst for this automation. Secondly, it details the banks' individual investments in computers in the early 1960s and the operations those machines were designed to automate. Thirdly, it considers the relationship between different actors with representative responsibility for the United Kingdom financial sector and its future, including government bodies in Whitehall, the Bank of England and the Committee of London Clearing Bankers (CLCB). It then concludes by illustrating how these actors first began to think about, define and manage computer security and distil the threats they felt they faced. By exploring these developments, this chapter traces the story of computer security in the United Kingdom's financial sector from its origins.

War and Automation

World War II acted as a direct catalyst for systematic automation in the United Kingdom's financial sector.

Some limited steps had been made in this direction prior to that conflict but none offered the benefits of scale in the same way that computers did. For example, in the early twentieth century there were attempts to establish the means for confidential communication. Amongst the first customers for *Enigma,* the cipher machine patented by Arthur Scherbius in 1918 invented to encrypt communications, were banks and businesses that held financially sensitive information and needed to communicate securely.[2]

Banks continued along this path during the inter-war years and explored the possibilities of data processing. For example, in 1929 Midland Bank established a centre for processing punched cards, early computer memory devices in the form of stiff paper segments containing holes, the patterns of which defined the information they held.[3] Also, in the 1930s, the Bank of England, the UK's central bank, invested in Hollerith punched card machines for both its Dividend Pay Office and Bullion Office, offering advanced functions for the time including calculation and alphabetisation.[4]

It was a result of the Second World War, however, that a more systematic attempt at automation began across the sector. Intensive technological development for the purposes of war meant that computer machinery was in a more advanced state by the mid-1940s and was more obviously applicable to the operations of the City of London's banks.

Two pivotal and interlinked reasons underpinned this drive for automation in the post-war period: firstly, cost savings, and the realisation that machines undertaking previously human, manual tasks could be more cost effective; and secondly, the rapid advancement and subsequent commercialisation of technology that had been developed during the conflict.

Cost and materials savings during the Second World War acted as an example of the benefits of automation: the Bank of England saved £6000 and 28,000 sheets of paper per year during the conflict as a direct result.[5] Also, a climate of rising costs, staff recruitment problems and the 'difficulties associated with increasing business in the existing branch premises using conventional means', given war time building restrictions, prompted action from Barclays Bank.[6] If wartime efficiencies could be

---

[2] Sinclair Mckay, 'The evolution of the Enigma machine', The Telegraph, 21/10/2014.

[3] Midland Bank, Banking on Computers, October 1981, p. 2.

[4] Ibid., p. 2.

[5] Bank of England Archive Display, 'Technology and the Bank of England: Early developments in automation and technology', viewed 26 January 2015.

[6] Barclays Archive (hereafter Barclays), File 0178-0004, 'Computers in Banking', February 1972, p. 1.

maintained during peacetime, the banks could more easily achieve the profitability so vital to their shareholders.

Commercial viability also played a key part in the banks' uptake of such technology. Computer development in the ten years after the war, according to Barclays, 'had progressed to the point' where computers were 'no longer being considered only as scientific instruments' but as 'commercially viable equipment for large scale operations.'[7] Increasing computer usage had aided the demystification of their abilities and intricacies.

Computers had evolved from an alien piece of high-technology machinery to practical pieces of engineering with the capability to solve tangible business challenges. In 1948, for example, Barclays began an investigation into 'the advantages and disadvantages of centralised book-keeping.'[8] By 1954 this enquiry had culminated in a pilot scheme in which the book-keeping of four London branches was carried out remotely at a centre in the City of London.[9]

Also, at this time teleprinters – essentially typewriters that could send and receive messages over telecommunication cables – were being installed in Barclays' branches as primitive computer terminals; a small punched card installation was set up in the bank's computer centre; and the bank's branches were linked to the computer centre by leased Post Office lines, transmission cables reserved for the use of the client.[10] Facilitating Barclays' embrace of technology was a change in how computers were viewed: as increasingly practical machines with problem-solving abilities rather than vast, abstract installations for tackling often larger, military-related issues. Banks were taking tentative but immediate steps in the direction of widespread automation.

The first of a series of three lectures at the Institute of Bankers on London's Lombard Street in November 1965 specifically referenced the impact of war on the advancement of computer technology. Taking the stage to discuss *The Actualities of Bank Automation*, DS Travers, an Assistant General Manager of Barclays, argued that banks, both in the UK and United States of America, were beginning to take the opportunities afforded to them by advances in data processing techniques which occurred during the Second World War:

> The need for new weapons ... had urged the scientists to develop information processing methods capable of handling the enormous data requirements of aircraft, air missile and atomic bomb design. The cold war of the 1950's between the United States and Russia, and the fears that remained after the Korean War, forced the United States into a vast programme to develop long-range missiles. The need for even higher-speed solutions in data processing became urgent. The work being done in the fields of nuclear physics and space technology on the H-Bomb and ballistic missiles programme was in danger of delay because of the inadequacies of the computer equipment then available. With the encourage-

---

[7] Ibid., p. 1.

[8] Barclays, File 0178-0004, 'Computers in Banking', February 1972, p. 1.

[9] Ibid., p. 1.

[10] Ibid., p. 1.

ment of almost unlimited dollars for research and development provided by the United States Department for Defense and a heavy research investment of their own, American manufacturers pressed on to design high-speed systems which could be applied not only to the military programme but, just as conveniently, to business routines.

Whether or not the aim, on both sides, of superior military strength was justified in any way is no concern of mine tonight. But a happier philosophy sees the business computers that are operating today, peacefully and unexplosively, in and around Lombard Street on non-militant matters, as a beneficial fall-out of the world's two greatest nations aiming for total annihilation capability.

In scientific research the general requirement is for intensive processing on a relatively small amount of information. More often than not in a business application it is just the opposite: the need is for only simple processing on a relatively large amount of information. In a nutshell, the manufacturers, wishing to satisfy the business market and confident as they might be of the computing capabilities of their computer – the central processors as they have come to be known – had to develop a new range of equipment to handle the input and output problems of the business world.[11]

Although a somewhat unexpected consequence of the Second World War, the banks embraced the general upgrade in the capability of technology available to businesses. Travers' optimistic interpretation of the technological fall-out from the war highlights the opportunities that such processing power offered commercial organisations. Provisioned with the requisite resources for investment, the major clearing banks in London had begun to contemplate how they could deploy this maturing technology to their benefit.

Travers also outlined the motivations of the banks for undertaking this process, which in his opinion were threefold: first, to 'achieve a reduction in the cost of work done'; second, 'to reduce the quantitative demands that they have had to make on the nation's available manpower'; and third, 'to check – or at least to delay – the rising premises costs which are unavoidable in a branch-based business like ours.'[12] Travers' second point would become increasingly clear as a driver for the banks, particularly in the automation of branch accounting – where employees actually helped deploy the technology which was aimed at reducing the number of employees required for branch operations. Articles in the national press highlighted the issue, as discussed later in this chapter, and Barclays referred specifically to staff costs in internal documents. Embedding computers into the day-to-day operations of banks had the potential to transform their activities. Rising long-term costs could be combatted through implementing new technology-based methods, and banks across the sector were all coming to the same realisation.

---

[11] Barclays, File 0080-2827, DS Travers, 'The Actualities of Bank Automation' in *Automation in Banking Lectures: The Institute of Bankers*, November 1965, pp. 10–11.
[12] Ibid., p. 4.

Committee of London Clearing Bankers

Banks began thinking strategically about automation in the mid-1950s. In 1955 the representative body of the clearing banks in the City, the Committee of London Clearing Bankers (CLCB), established an electronics sub-committee to 'discover first and foremost what the banks would require of the new electronic data processing techniques' and determine 'where the gaps in the integrated system of the future might lie.'[13] The sub-committee selected two areas for 'close and immediate' investigation: the 'automatic handling of clearings' and the 'use of computers in centralised bank book-keeping.'[14] In identifying these two bureaucracy-heavy exercises the CLCB was targeting activities with the most potential to be streamlined. Here was early recognition of the potential benefits of investment in information technology.

A relative dearth of automation experience within the UK banking sector meant that the initial activity of the CLCB's electronics sub-committee was focused on building partnerships and consulting with experts.

From 1955 to 1960 there was significant activity, including 'liaison with manufacturers and research bodies' in the United Kingdom, Europe and North America, resulting in a first major decision at the end of 1960: the adoption by the Committee of London Clearing Bankers of the American Bankers' Association (ABA) style E-13B characters as the 'common language for vouchers [cheques] passing through the banking system'.[15] The sub-committee, in favour of what had proved in America to be a viable system, rejected British and French alternative character styles.[16] These characters would be key to the automation process as they would be magnetically readable by machines.

In deciding whether to adopt the E-13B characters, the CLCB 'engaged the services of the National Physical Laboratory [NPL] to report on the technical qualities of three magnetic character codes'.[17] The NPL had been created in 1902 to 'bring scientific knowledge to bear practically upon our everyday industrial and commercial life' according to HRH The Prince of Wales, who noted at the time that this was perhaps the first example of the State taking part in scientific research.[18] For example, in 1966 at the National Physical Laboratory, Donald Davies developed the 'packet-switching' technique that still forms the basis of worldwide computer communications today: the way in which data sent across, for example, the Internet,

---

[13] Ibid., p. 2.

[14] Barclays, File 0080-2827, DS Travers, 'The Actualities of Bank Automation' in *Automation in Banking Lectures: The Institute of Bankers*, November 1965, p. 2.

[15] Ibid., p. 2.

[16] Lloyds Archive File 9595, JA Dunn, 'The Clearings' in *The History of Development and Automation Conference*, 11–13 November 1966, p. 19.

[17] Barclays, File 0080-2827, DS Travers, 'The Actualities of Bank Automation' in *Automation in Banking Lectures: The Institute of Bankers*, November 1965, p. 2.

[18] National Physical Laboratory, 'History', http://www.npl.co.uk/about/history/ [Accessed 10 November 2017].

such as emails, are dismantled into packets and then reassembled on reaching the recipient so as to allow for speedy and efficient transfer.[19] The CLCB humbly sought advice from those adept at working with information technology in order to fully capitalise upon benefits of that equipment.

The sub-committee also decided the standard for the position and contents of the code-line of cheques, as well as their sizes and paper quality, and collaborated with manufacturers to identify likely equipment requirements.[20] Released in August 1961, the allocation and arrangement of the characters in the Magnetic Ink Character Recognition (MICR) code line was also undertaken in co-ordination with the American Bankers' Association and required consultation and research to fit a serial number, sorting code number, account number, transaction code and amount into a cheque length of six inches.[21]

Such decisions marked the first steps towards automation in the United Kingdom's banking sector. Recognising that they did not possess the expertise required for making decisions about their technological future, the banks sought collaboration with those who did. Undeterred by their inexperience, they embraced this change, making the fundamental decision to pursue automation of their core operations, the potential benefits seemingly outweighing the risks or unforeseen consequences that might accompany wholesale change.

Computerisation in Banks

Systematic computerisation truly began in the early 1960s, driven by the capacity of new machines for processing large amounts of data and calculations. The question for the banks seemed to be *how* to automate their operations: a consensus already existed amongst them that investment in information technology was a positive step.

Similar optimism pervaded the political sphere. At this time, in one of the most quoted political speeches of the twentieth century, then Labour leader Harold Wilson announced at the Party's annual conference in 1963 that 'the Britain that is going to be forged in the white heat of this [technological] revolution will be no place for restrictive practices or outdated methods on either side of industry.'[22] Abundantly endowed with resources, the major City banks were in an advantageous position to utilise these technological advances at scale to drive growth and efficiency.

Computers had, according to one bank, 'emerged from the laboratory and the research establishment' in the late 1950s and early 1960s and 'begun to make

[19] National Physical Laboratory, 'NPL's History Highlights', http://www.npl.co.uk/upload/pdf/npl-history.pdf [Accessed 10 November 2017].

[20] Barclays, File 0178-0004, 'Computers in Banking', February 1972, p. 27.

[21] Lloyds, File 9595, JA Dunn, 'The Clearings' in *The History of Development and Automation Conference,* 11–13 November 1966, p. 19.

[22] Ben Pimlott, *Harold Wilson* (London: HarperCollins, 1992), p. 304.

inroads into the field of commercial accountancy' despite, at this stage, the 'speed of the electronics, the reliability and most of all the flexibility' leaving a 'good deal to be desired.'[23] Even given these supposed drawbacks, the banks acted promptly. A spending spree soon unfolded.

The clearing banks purchased their first computers in the early 1960s and Barclays was the first to place an order.[24] In 1959 it invested in an EMIDEC 1100 computer to maintain its branch accounts, which subsequently began operations at Drummond Street near Euston in London during 1961.[25]

The EMIDEC 1100 was a large rectangular machine, its main body resembling four modern-day fridge freezers attached to each other side-by-side. It was designed from the outset as a business machine and the first of its kind began operation for Boots, the chemists, on 5 September 1960.[26] Other commercial entities and government departments had also by this time ordered the same model.[27] Such powerful machines were capable of underpinning processes including stock control, payroll and accounting functions for organisations by acting as a hub in a primary computer centre with other, less powerful machines in branches and other premises linked to it by communication cables. Barclays believed that their EMIDEC machine was the first computer installation in the UK to be fed by data transferred over communications links, but they were aware that since March 1959 Bank of Scotland had been operating leased lines for use with teleprinters, the typewriter-like machine that could send and receive messages across communication cables, in conjunction with its centralised punched card centre.[28]

Barclays acquired a second EMIDEC machine eighteen months later.[29] Linked to the branches by leased Post Office telecommunications lines, input was prepared in the branches the computer served via paper tape and was transmitted 'overline' to the computer centre, while output was transmitted 'overline' to operate printers in branches.[30] The bank's EMIDEC machines served approximately 60 branches in the West End and Central London and the system as described here lasted, without major change, for almost a decade.[31]

National Westminster Bank ordered its first machine, a Ferranti Pegasus, in the second half of 1960 to batch-process its branch accounting.[32] The Pegasus was described as the 'first user friendly computer' and was equivalent in size to the

---

[23] Barclays Archive File 0178-0004, 'Computers in Banking', February 1972, p. 3.

[24] Ibid., p. 18.

[25] Ibid., p. 2.

[26] EMIDEC, 'EMIDEC Computer News 1', http://www.emidec.org.uk/emipicbr.pdf [Accessed 16 November 2017].

[27] Ibid.

[28] Barclays, File 0178-0004, 'Computers in Banking', February 1972, p. 20.

[29] Ibid., p. 2.

[30] Barclays Archive File 1683-0023, 'The Uses of Computers in Barclays Bank', May 1969, p. 1.

[31] Barclays, File 0178-0004, 'Computers in Banking', February 1972, p. 2.

[32] Ibid., p. 14.

EMIDEC, its main installation being approximately the size of three upright modern-day fridge freezers.[33] National Westminster built upon this in subsequent years by building up a large complex of IBM computers in London which retained the batch processing concept but also incorporated an 'enquiry' file which held balance positions for the previous day, allowing appropriate employees to access this information.[34] The National Provincial Bank, which merged with National Westminster in 1970, had also ordered their first computer in the second half of 1960, in their case a Ferranti ORION.[35]

Lloyds Bank placed an order for their first computer in the same month as National Westminster in 1960, opting for an IBM 305 RAMAC.[36] The RAMAC name was an abbreviation of the trade name for this system, a combination of Random Access and Method of Accounting.[37] Only six years after its purchase it was described as 'slow' and 'cumbrous' in comparison to newer standards, partly because it used older techniques such as electronic valves as opposed to transistors, diodes and printer circuitry used in the mid-late 1960s.[38] The IBM 305 was the first of its kind in terms of storage, being built around its disc file and using a movable recording head, as opposed to using magnetic tape for storage.[39] This meant that access to any account record could be gained directly without having to proceed from the beginning to end of the entire records of files as would have been the process with magnetic tape.[40]

Lloyds had security in mind from early on in their automation journey, and it represented a prime motivation for upgrading from their first computer to an IBM System 360. Until this point, disc file operations had been dependent upon the use of high density fixed disc files contained in relatively large cabinets, with no possibility of moving them to a place of safety or to another machine in case of an emergency. Lloyds had therefore found it necessary to introduce a system of periodic transfer of all records from the disc file to magnetic tape for security reasons. The new disc files on the 360 system were demountable and could be used either as fixed files, as was standard for Lloyds at this time, or on "grandfather", "father" and "son" techniques as was standard with magnetic tape.[41] As they could, therefore, be moved from one machine to another they provided Lloyds with greater security in their operations.

---

[33] Science Museum, 'The Pegasus Computer', https://blog.sciencemuseum.org.uk/the-pegasus-computer/ [Accessed 15 November 2017].

[34] Barclays, File 0178-0004, 'Computers in Banking', February 1972, p. 14.

[35] Barclays, File 0178-0004, 'Computers in Banking', February 1972, p. 14.

[36] Ibid., p. 14.

[37] Lloyds, File 9595, GB Hague, 'Advances in Technology' in *The History of Development and Automation Conference,* 11–13 November 1966, p. 32.

[38] Lloyds Archive File 9595, GB Hague, 'Advances in Technology' in *The History of Development and Automation Conference,* 11–13 November 1966, p. 32.

[39] Ibid., p. 32.

[40] Ibid., p. 32.

[41] Ibid., p. 33.

The grandfather, father and son technique was described as 'computer technicians' jargon' and was used to describe historic audit trails when updating a set of accounts.[42] Lloyds' security thinking was being dictated by the hardware they had already purchased, and they were alert to the risks involved in relying on these new machines for their operations.

Lloyds first began computer accounting in the autumn of 1961, beginning with their Pall Mall branch in London, and over the next two years they established a fully independent Computer Centre.[43] Pall Mall acted as Lloyds' test bed for automation and developments there eventually saw them loading the information of 56,000 bank accounts to their computer.[44] The company's first foray into deploying branch accounting began in 1963 with five outlets in London's West End.[45] Lloyds also created its Computer Systems Department in December of that year, its goal to persuade branch managers and staff of the effectiveness of these new systems whilst exploring how to adapt and implement the Pall Mall system further across its branch network.[46] Accounting at Lloyds' principal London branches was automated by the end of 1965, and these locations were given the 'full red carpet treatment' during roll-out, meaning that 12,000 accounts per month were transferred to the system at the peak of the process.[47]

Most progress in this early phase was smooth for the bank, but security requirements impacted their advancement. Specifically, a Lloyds employee recalled that time had to be spent considering the consequences of using new methods for undertaking pre-existing tasks: 'There was also one occasion when it was necessary to think very deeply about one of our routines and to decide how much it was worth fighting for.' The difference of opinion arose over ledger sheets and whether they should be kept overnight upstairs in an office, or taken in the "Book Safe". 'Much careful thought was given to ways and means of doing what traditional security measures required, but in the end, it was evident that it would be necessary to re-build or extend Book Safe accommodation at most branches we wanted to tackle,' a Lloyds report concluded. 'Obviously, you cannot lightly brush off questions of security – in the last resort you take responsibility for any risks in a routine which is novel and which you want to stick to.'[48] This was exactly what was eventually done.

Lloyds placed paramount importance upon security and recognised both its necessity and its consequences. It was not a given that they should have, but their awareness highlights the continuity in security thinking between the computer and

---

[42] Ibid., p. 33.

[43] Lloyds, File 9595, P.I. Burden, 'Computer Accounting: Branches Progress to Date' in *The History of Development and Automation Conference,* 11–13 November 1966, p. 1.

[44] Ibid., p. 1.

[45] Ibid., p. 1.

[46] Ibid., p. 1.

[47] Ibid., p. 2.

[48] Ibid., p. 2.

pre-computer era. Despite logistical difficulties, they saw risk management as simply a cost of doing business in this new way. It required planning and to some extent perseverance, but Lloyds did not let security concerns hinder their progress excessively.

Midland Bank also entered the automation revolution at the same time as its peers. By 1961 it had developed a programming team of seven staff and purchased an English Electric KDP 10, a machine 'designed to handle a wide variety of commercial data processing applications'.[49] In Midland's case, the KDP 10 was initially to process the current accounts of 60 branches, eventually being joined by two dedicated computer centres in the City of London and Birmingham that utilised the same type of machine, so that by 1966 the three centres were processing the work of 280 branches.[50] The Bank of England, the UK's central bank, also prized cost savings and enhanced reliability and had begun batch electronic data processing by the mid-1960s.[51]

Practicalities

Branch accounting was one of the first key operations that banks automated. It initially worked as a batch process in which account records were stored in numerical order according to their identification code, and the transactions were then sorted into account number order and updated by running through the accounts from beginning to end, applying the relevant transactions as accounts were reached.[52] Often this was done overnight, and there were significant cost advantages to restricting the number of full 'runs' through the accounts list.[53]

Real-time systems, which became increasingly widespread as time progressed, could be updated and information conveyed to branches throughout the day.[54] While real-time offered greater flexibility than batch processing, its cost was higher, it was more complex than the batch method and crucially it exacerbated uncertainty around 'system security' as the design of any real-time process had to allow the system to recover, in Barclays' opinion, 'from even temporary total failure without the loss or distortion of information.'[55]

Lloyds Bank provides an illustrative example of exactly how a branch was upgraded to automated accounting, the process comprising three stages: firstly, the

---

[49] *The New Scientist* (11/245), 27 July 1961, p. 236.

[50] Midland Bank, Banking on Computers, October 1981, p. 2.

[51] Bank of England, File 5A199/4, 'Computers and Auditing', 27 August 1975.

[52] Barclays, File 0178-0004, 'Computers in Banking', February 1972, p. 5.

[53] Ibid., p. 5.

[54] Ibid., p. 6.

[55] Ibid., p. 6.

creation of a cheque book library; secondly, the staff preparation of the branch preceding the transfer programme itself; and, thirdly, the settling in period.[56]

Following significant preparatory work, the initial phase involved an 'Instructress' from the Computer Department, assisted by one or more Departmental clerks and members of branch staff, allocating account numbers to each account.[57] To do this, the Instructress used specially prepared cards bearing pre-determined account numbers calculated by computer, and then supervised the preparation of a paper slip corresponding to each cheque issuing account, resulting in three personalised cheque books per customer and a means of indexing for each branch.[58]

The second stage involved the transfer itself, which at this point only concerned bank current accounts rather than, for example, savings accounts.[59] For each account, the computer had to be told specific details about its holders, including: the name and initials of each customer; their account number; the address to which their statement should be sent; and the date on which that statement should be dispatched.[60] This information was fed into the computer by paper tape, a data store produced taking the form of thin white paper whose punched holes represented its content and which was produced on an NCR 32W machine that had a keyboard similar to that of a typewriter.[61] Resulting from this process were records produced by the computer which could give an overview of an entire branch and its customers, the most important of which was the Strip Index – an alphabetical list of customers' names – against which appeared the their account numbers.[62] On the transfer day itself – always a Saturday – accounts were reconciled and ledgers were finalised, the balances then relisted on a paper tape machine together with each account number and fed into the computer to be matched up with account titles and provide an account balance for each customer name.[63] The completion of this stage marked the beginning of computer accounting in a branch.

Stage three involved Inspectors and Instructresses from the Lloyds' Computer Systems Department providing guidance to branch staff.[64] During this time the bank begun to seek and achieve reductions in branch staff, as soon as was 'reasonably possible' after the transfer.[65] In effect, the branch staff members who implemented computerised branch accounting were replacing themselves with machines as their

---

[56] Lloyds, File 9595, GA Peters, 'Computer Accounting Branches: Preparation and Changeover' in *The History of Development and Automation Conference,* 11–13 November 1966, p. 5.

[57] Ibid., p. 5.

[58] Ibid., p. 6.

[59] Ibid., p. 7.

[60] Ibid., p. 7.

[61] Ibid., p. 7.

[62] Ibid., p. 7.

[63] Ibid., p. 7.

[64] Ibid., p. 8.

[65] Ibid., p. 8.

employers sought a return on their investment and immediately pursued long-term cost savings.

Progression

Consolidation was the theme of the mid-to-late 1960s for the London clearing banks and automation. Broadly, these institutions were either implementing or planning for the introduction of automated branch accounting and cheque clearing, whilst also considering the expansion of their automated offerings.

Having made progress in computerising its branch accounting, Barclays' next significant move was to automate its cheque clearing process. Cheque clearing as described here was the movement of a cheque from the bank it was deposited at to the bank it was drawn from, and the requisite amount of money moving in the opposite direction. In the early 1960s Barclays had to cope with receiving, scrutinising and then sorting into branches for dispatch up to one and a half million cheques per day.[66] To reduce the pressure of such an enormous undertaking the first automatic cheque sorters were introduced into their Clearing Department in 1961, and by 1964 automation had permeated the operation further, when Barclays introduced the ability to record complete transaction details on magnetic tapes and pass these tapes over to the Computer Centre, thereby eliminating the need for branches to manually input the details of these cheques.[67]

Also, by the mid-1960s the number of customers who received statements from computer branches had grown and was steadily increasing, while lots of banks' 'foreign work' was also being automated: travellers' cheques; registrar's work; standing order payments, staff pay and statistics; and head office accounting routines.[68]

Each of the London clearing banks had 'opened or laid plans to open computer centres for processing customers' accounts', and by 1965 most had taken steps towards either partially or fully automating their clearing process or were preparing to do so.[69]

Facilitating this work were often computer centres housing state of the art equipment. These centres tended to be set up in London or at banks' head offices if outside of the capital, and two of the big five clearing banks had opened provincial processing centres by 1965.[70] Others of the big five London clearing banks preferred to concentrate large volumes of work on processing depots in one centre,

---

[66] Barclays, File 1683-0023, 'The Uses of Computers in Barclays Bank', May 1969, p. 1.

[67] Barclays, File 0178-0004, 'Computers in Banking', February 1972, p. 2.

[68] Barclays, File 0080-2827, DS Travers, 'The Actualities of Bank Automation' in *Automation in Banking Lectures: The Institute of Bankers*, November 1965, p. 7.

[69] Ibid., p. 1.

[70] Ibid., p. 7.

relying on telegraphic networks to collect and transmit the transaction information, sometimes over long distances.[71]

By May 1966 a more advanced system for Barclays' Lombard Street Local Head Office had been developed and installed, using IBM System 360 Model 30 computers.[72] These computers replaced IBM 1401 equipment and permitted 'more streamlined operations with optimised sorting routes' whilst also providing an audit trail so that inter-bank and inter-branch settlement could occur.[73]

Barclays pushed further ahead with automation as the 1960s ended. A comprehensive system for managing book-keeping of its branches began operation in April 1967 at the bank's Greater London Computer Centre (GLCC) on one IBM System 360 Model 50 and over the next two years the project was implemented in a series of phases, to ensure that the capacity of the Centre remained adequate as new branches were added to the system and its load therefore increased.[74] Barclays felt that it was 'probably true to say that the current GLCC batch updating operation … is among the best examples of this technique in the world' at that point.[75]

By the end of 1971 their GLCC was handling just under 2.5 million accounts on three computers and, in connection with this operation, IBM designed and produced, primarily 'at the insistence of Barclays', a special terminal – the IBM 3940 – for the UK market, some 500 of which were installed by Barclays alone in the London area in 1972, Lloyds Bank also purchasing the terminal soon after.[76]

Such equipment was required to underpin a swathe of facilities now offered by the clearing banks. By 1969 the Barclays' activities included, but were not limited to: branch accounting, direct debiting, staff salaries and statistics, clearing operations, foreign branch accounting, customers' payrolls, simulation techniques and econometric model building.[77]

Banks continued to be receptive to advances in the hardware and software available to them and were prepared to invest in the "state of the art". Burroughs Corporation had introduced the TC500 branch computer terminal in 1967, a 'considerable technical advance' on anything available at the time, and Barclays soon installed them in around 2000 of its branches.[78] Until the release of the TC500, Barclays had ambitions to extend automation to all branches as their 'ultimate goal' but had not been able to formulate any workable plans to go any further than the 200 branches already automated.[79]

---

[71] Ibid., p. 7.

[72] Barclays, File 0178-0004, 'Computers in Banking', February 1972, p. 2.

[73] Barclays, File 1683-0023, 'The Uses of Computers in Barclays Bank', May 1969, p. 1.

[74] Barclays, File 0178-0004, 'Computers in Banking', February 1972, p. 4.

[75] Ibid., p. 4.

[76] Ibid., p. 4.

[77] Barclays, File 1683-0023, 'The Uses of Computers in Barclays Bank', May 1969, p. 2.

[78] Barclays, File 0178-0004, 'Computers in Banking', February 1972, p. 6.

[79] Barclays, File 1683-0003, 'Burroughs Project: Notes on Managers' Meeting', 1968, p. 1.

The TC500 was a small, powerful desk-sized computer, the total installation being approximately 4 feet wide and two and a half feet tall.[80] It possessed two keyboards, of similar appearance to modern computer keyboards, the left-hand side one being alphabetical and the right-hand one being an abbreviated numerical keyboard.[81] The machines' in-built printer was 15 inches wide, its platen split at 7.5 inches so that one could be used for "waste" such as calculations and workings not required in other tasks and the other could be used for different activities, such as enquires, reports or file preparation.[82] Thanks to recent technical developments spur lines could link these terminals to Post Office trunk communication lines, using a modem to facilitate communication.[83] Such advancements, and the affordability and compact nature of the TC500, meant that banks could invest in significant numbers of this machine and place them in each of their branches across the country.

At the same time, Burroughs also launched their B8500 computer which met Barclays' requirements for real-time processing, and was based upon previously developed hardware and software for military applications used in its B5500 machine.[84]

Future Ambition

Automation in the bank not only changed the nature of banking operations in the short-term but also altered the banks' thinking about their medium and longer-term futures. Ambition for advancement was in plentiful supply and the banks identified that following their investment in computer technology, the ability to link these computers together for communication purposes could have a revolutionary impact. Already bank computer centres were operating where a single computer served several branches linked to it by telegraph line. It was suggested that the 'most explosive developments' could occur in the telecommunication field in the upcoming few years. Barclays noted that in the United States it had been forecast by the Western Union who, together with the Bell System and International Telephone and Telegraph, owned almost the whole of the telegraph network there, that whereas only 1% of computer installations were then linked to communications systems, the figure would rise to 60% in ten years' time.[85]

---

[80] Ibid., p. 3.

[81] Barclays, File 1683-0024, 'Commentary for TC500 Film', 1968, p. 1.

[82] Barclays, File 1683-0003, 'Burroughs Project: Notes on Managers' Meeting', 1968, p. 3.

[83] Ibid., p. 3.

[84] Barclays, File 0178-0004, 'Computers in Banking', February 1972, p. 6.

[85] Barclays, File 0080-2827, DS Travers, 'The Actualities of Bank Automation' in *Automation in Banking Lectures: The Institute of Bankers*, November 1965, p. 12.

Hunger for such development clearly existed, and despite the potential challenges involved in the uptake of new communications technology, a sense of excitement existed about what could be achieved. As would increasingly occur as time passed, the UK banks looked to America to learn about where the future of technology could take them. It seemed that telecommunications combined with computer technology, in the view of at least one of the banks, offered the most dramatic potential.

The banks were soon conscious of how they would have to adapt to changing user needs and expectations as technology became progressively more affordable for consumers. 'Further ahead of us, and as more and more of our customers install their own computers, lies the prospect of closer integration of bank and customer accounting', Barclays identified, acknowledging that some individuals had alluded to this as 'computer talking to computer' and that the prospect existed of new competitive services being developed by their competitors.[86] They realised that 'the needs of small as well as big customers' had to be kept at the forefront of their thinking.[87] Despite the sector as a whole sharing the drive to automate their workings, there also existed a perception that at some point the services they offered as a result of new technology could become a competitive marketplace.

Difficulties

The process of automation was not always as smooth as the banks would have liked. Although they were willing to invest heavily in cutting-edge technology, manufacturers at the front-line of computer development often struggled to fulfil the ambitions of their financial sector clients. For example, Barclays' preparations for Decimalisation in 1971 were hampered by delays in production at the computer manufacturer. Its plans for Decimalisation without incurring heavy re-equipment costs for conventional machines were centred upon the use of a Willesden-based B.8500 multi-processor computer which would operate in real-time: processing each transaction or enquiry as soon as it had been transmitted by one of the branch TC500 terminals.

Barclays' plans received their first setback in 1968 our when Burroughs advised that, in view of development delays and the Decimalisation deadline, the bank should change its B.8500 order to two slightly smaller, but technically superior, B.6500 systems. This was done and supplemented by an order for a third B.6500 for installation at Wythenshawe, which it deemed necessary due to its merger with Martins Bank.

Production of the B.6500 computers fell behind schedule, along with the development of the necessary operating control programs. Barclays was therefore forced

---

[86] Ibid., p. 6.

[87] Ibid., p. 6.

to meet Decimalisation with only a third of its total number of accounts automated. The Burroughs TC500 mitigated the bank's issues, its flexibility making allowing for a different program to be loaded into the terminal in the form of punched paper tape and for branches to use this for decimal operation immediately.

Burroughs' inability to deliver prompted Barclays, in early 1970, to install two IBM 360/65 computers at its Wythenshawe Computer Centre to maintain momentum in its automation programme. This new system used the same basic account processing programs as the Greater London Computer Centre but was served by Burroughs TC500 terminals instead of the IBM 3940 terminals currently in use in the London Area. The revised date for the Wythenshawe system's "go live" was in May 1971 and Barclays did, in fact, meet this commitment two weeks early.

The bank was decided in early 1971, in the face of continued delays from Burroughs, to enlist the aid of Computer Analysts and Programmers Ltd. to design and run a series of acceptance tests which the B.6500, by now up-graded to a B.6700, duly passed in May of that year. Given these delays and the changed circumstances it was decided that it was right to concentrate upon the single objective of early automation of all branches on a batch up-dating system similar to that of GLCC and Wythenshawe and the more ambitious concepts of real time working were temporarily shelved.[88]

Working at the cutting edge of new technological developments clearly had its drawbacks. Even given the hunger of the banks for new hardware and software, they were liable to being hamstrung by the actual producers of this new and rapidly advancing underlying technology. Driving the process of computerisation was a desire for efficiency: the ability to work faster and at greater scale by automating labour-intensive processes. In order to achieve this, it had to be able to rely upon manufacturers to fulfil their promises and provide robust, reliable and capable hardware and software.

Efforts to connect computers over networks had also begun. By the early 1970s, most branches of the UK's clearing banks were served by computers.[89] Lloyds Bank was developing a network of cash machines that would utilise the power of encryption – specifically Horst Feistel's "Lucifer", a cryptographic algorithm with the ability scramble messages – in order to secure the process of computers validating these cash machine transactions.[90] Midland Bank at this time decided to develop a 'full on-line network to each of the 1750 branches' it maintained, a project that was completed in August 1974.[91] Technological advancement in the sector was beginning to focus upon connectivity during this period.

---

[88] Barclays, File 0178-0004, 'Computers in Banking', February 1972, pp. 6–8.

[89] HSBC Archive, File UK1793-0013, 'Banks and Automation', March 1972, p. 1.

[90] Gordon Corera, *Intercept: The Secret History of Computers and Spies* (London: Weidenfeld & Nicolson, 2015), pp. 104–105.

[91] Midland Bank, Banking on Computers, October 1981, p. 2.

The Bank of England's Computers

Vast mainframe computer installations increasingly underpinned the running of the Bank of England's operations over the course of the 1960s.

In October 1963, the very month in which Harold Wilson gave his rousing "white heat" conference speech at Scarborough, the Bank began considering whether computer system may offer advantages over its current punched card equipment. The Heads of Departments of the Balance of Payments, Bullion, Dealing and Accounts and Payments offices studied the possibilities and it quickly became apparent that two computers were required; their initial proposed budget of '£150,000/ £200,000' soon appeared severely inadequate.[92]

A Bank of England memo written in 1965 outlined that institutions' perception of the long-term potential for savings: 'computer methods offer the opportunity of increased productivity and efficiency and ultimately savings in staff'.[93] Such potential was difficult to ignore, although it was highlighted that the introduction of these machines was likely to have a 'disturbing effect' on the staff, given that part of the aim was to save on labour. An 'air of mystery' still surrounded computers, the Bank observed, compounding this effect.[94]

Nevertheless, the Bank fully embraced this new technology. 'Computers are unquestionably the tools of future', the same 1965 memo philosophised.[95] How apparent this would become as the decades advanced. Accompanying these tools was a need to ensure that those with malicious intent did not misuse the efficiency and productivity benefits these new machines offered.

By 1969 it operated three mainframe computers: three configurations of International Computers Limited (ICL) 1900 series machines which each operated for 70–80 h per week.[96] An ICL 1904E was installed in February 1968 in the Bank's Head Office building in Threadneedle Street in London and provided a service for all Departments. The only exception was the Accountant's Department, which was serviced by two ICL 1903s at the Bank's New Change site.[97] These new installations offered 'many advantages in cost and efficiency' over upgrading their previous ICL 1301 computer.[98] Two of these computers, the 1903s, were single program computers operating to full capacity for two shifts on five days per week. The other, the 1904E, was a multi-program computer also operating on the same basis. It was noted that the 1904E was only utilising approximately one third of its overall

---

[92] BoE, File 5A199/4, 'Computers for Head Office Work: Background', 18 June 1965.

[93] Ibid.

[94] BoE, File 5A199/4, 'Computers in the Bank', 27 December 1965.

[95] BoE, File 5A199/4, 'Computers for Head Office Work: Background', 18 June 1965.

[96] BoE, File 7A386/1, 'The Use of Computers at the Bank of England', 24 January 1969.

[97] Ibid.

[98] BoE, File 5A199/4, 'Extract from the meeting of the Committee of Treasury: 3 March 1965', 12 March 1965.

capacity.[99] Visible, however, was the centrality of these machines to the Bank's operations in specific departments.

Installed in March and April 1966, by August that year the two ICL 1903 machines were undertaking dividend preparation work for the Accountant's Department at the Bank.[100] Before the 1903s took over this operation, following some brief experimentation with machinery and the ICL 1301 computer, the process had been an expensive one: two record types needed to be maintained, on top of the main stock register, and all dividend calculations had to be done clerically by means of interest and tax tables.[101] Recalculation was also required should the income tax rate change.[102] In spite of the initial need to convert magnetic tape files from the width and format of those used by the ICL 1301 to those used by the ICL 1903s, the economies found in terms of time and number of staff outweighed the inconvenience.

As the advantages offered by computers became more explicit, the number and type of operations being computerised in the Bank of England expanded. By 1967, the largest stock that the Bank managed – 3.5% War Stock, a UK Government bond issued in 1932 – comprising 650,000 accounts – was transferred to the computer register. Shortly after, a further 21 other stocks were transferred to magnetic tape and all new issues were set up under the computer system.[103] The following year, nearly 70% of the 2.6 million accounts on the Bank's registers were being dealt with by the system.[104] Computerisation offered a level of efficiency that humans simply could not surpass for this amount of administration.

As well as improving existing processes within the Bank, computers also facilitated new thinking. Forecasting was an area in which at least one part of the Bank benefitted. Electronic computers offered the ability to predict future trends based on the data in these newly computerised functions. For example, a small Mathematical Analysis Section of the Economic Intelligence Department of the Bank had written programs to produce security yield curves and to calculate seasonal adjustments.[105] Not only were computers transforming current functions but they were also opening the possibility of new ones.

By 1969 however, the Bank was beginning to have trouble in recruiting people to operate their advanced hardware and software. In particular, the Bank struggled with 'selection and training of staff' and 'remuneration of computer staff,' due to the incompatibility of rates paid by the Bank to rates paid outside.[106] The private sector could simply afford to pay higher salaries to those with sought after skills.

---

[99] BoE File 7A386/1, 'The Use of Computers at the Bank of England', 24 January 1969.

[100] BoE File 7A386/1, 'Bank of England Quarterly Bulletin', September 1968.

[101] Ibid.

[102] Ibid.

[103] Ibid.

[104] BoE, File 7A386/1, 'Bank of England Quarterly Bulletin', September 1968.

[105] BoE, File 7A386/1, 'The Use of Computers at the Bank of England', 24 January 1969.

[106] Ibid.

Broader uncertainty also existed as to 'the determination of the role of the computer in the general organisation.'[107] The Bank was clearly thinking deeply about technological advancement. However, significant investment in these machines required justification and planning, not only because of the financial cost but also due to the potential impact upon working practices.

Nevertheless, the Bank was predicting the general expansion of its computer activities over the following five years with progress expected in, amongst other areas: record keeping and processing; establishment of data banks for advanced analytics and forecasting; and the 'adoption of "online" "real time" techniques, incorporating automatic data transmission and "on line" file interrogation facilities.'[108] The Bank had a clear idea of how their functions could be optimised by the growing benefits of computers. Included in this was the potential to link computers together and transfer confidential information between them.

Managing this incorporation of computers in the Bank was undertaken through a combination of high-level oversight, considering broader strategic development, in parallel with day-to-day decision-making by the departments directly involved. As of June 1968, a high level inter-departmental committee, chaired by the Deputy Governor, was created to offer 'direction to the process of putting appropriate parts of the Bank's work to computers.'[109] Until 1969, the process of computerisation had been governed by 'largely practical considerations, such as the need to replace ageing accounting machines and punched card equipment'.[110] With practical solutions established, the Bank could begin to adopt a more strategic view of how computers could improve their overall function.

Bank of England & Private Sector

Alongside computerising their own operations, the Bank recognised that taking a longer-term view of technological modernisation for the sector involved needing to 'co-operate with the commercial banks in their automation plans.'[111] The Bank felt it could lead by example and facilitate the relationships between its private sector counterparts.

One way they did this was by sharing understanding. Knowledge accumulated by the Bank was shared, through staff. For example, an Assistant Secretary of the Bank of England was a member of the Systems and Development Committee set up by the Committee of London Clearing Bankers.[112] A Deputy Chief Cashier of the

---

[107] Ibid.

[108] Ibid.

[109] Ibid.

[110] BoE, File 7A386/1, 'The Use of Computers at the Bank of England', 24 January 1969.

[111] Ibid.

[112] Ibid.

Bank was a member of the steering committee of the Inter-Bank Research Organisation; the Bank's Chief Accountant was Chairman of a committee sponsored by the London Stock Exchange which considered how modern data processing methods could be used in stocks and shares dealing and transfers; and the Bank of England were members of the British Computer Society and National Computing Centre.[113] These bureaucratic measures facilitated the information sharing, though arguably the private sector banks were some years ahead in their computerisation progress.

By the early 1970s the perception that their private sector counterparts were outpacing them was prevalent within the Bank of England. A draft Bank memo to computer experts working for other central banks, including those of France, Canada, Italy, Germany and Japan, in September 1971 stated that the private sector was visibly leading the way in terms of technological development compared to central banks generally.[114] Far greater resources in the commercial banks meant they could more readily procure the newest technology. In 1975, for example, Midland Bank agreed to purchase new equipment for two of its computer centres at Brent in North London and Bootle on Merseyside, including two Burroughs 700 dual processor systems, at a combined cost of £12.9 million.[115] Surviving in the private sector meant needing to innovate through investment in new technology whilst justifying its utility to the company.

The Bank's worries were not unfounded. The biggest London clearing banks were investing immense resources in their computerisation. A Barclays memo from 1973 emphasised this: 'Barclays Bank is one of the largest computer users, for commercial purposes, in the world. The only comparable investment to be found in Great Britain, outside Government, is probably that of the National Westminster Bank.' The Bank noted that the relative scale of its operations against other substantial users was indicated by a recent publication from HMSO [Her Majesty's Stationery Office] where the classification "large" was employed for those spending more than £500,000 per annum on data processing, which was 'only a few per cent of the Bank's 1972 computing costs'.[116] Optimistic about its impacts, private sector banks were charging forward with spending on computer machinery as they saw it to be profitable and dependable for their large-scale operations. They had a vision of the future that involved a far less labour-intensive and far more technology-enabled financial sector in the United Kingdom, and were beginning to build this future through investment.

---

[113] Ibid.

[114] BoE, File 7A386/2, 'Basle Meeting-September 1971: Guidance to "Computer Experts"', 31 August 1971.

[115] HSBC Archives, File UK0009-0017, 'Board Meeting Minutes', 5 December 1975.

[116] Barclays, File 0178-0001, Computer Analysts and Programmers Ltd., 'Barclays Bank Computing Strategy: Interim Report to Management', 1973, p. 5.

Whitehall

Whitehall adapted incrementally to the new computer age, both through its machinery of government mechanisms and its actual facilities.

Harold Wilson's Labour government, following their election in 1964, created the Ministry of Technology, often abbreviated as "Mintech". Wilson noted later that he saw Mintech as needing to be a 'Ministry of Industry' with a 'very direct responsibility for increasing productivity and efficiency'.[117] Set up in 1965 and based inside Mintech was the Government Computer Advisory Unit (GCAU).[118] Developed 'from a former unit in the Treasury' as part of the Government's attempt to extend the use of computers across industry, its remit was limited to 'objective technical appraisals'[119] as part of vetting 'any proposals for a computer purchase involving public monies.'[120] In June 1966 the National Computing Centre was also founded as a non-profit making body primarily to disseminate information about computer programmes and training to new users.[121]

Central government also offered a level of practical support to the financial sector, although this was to the Bank of England as opposed to the private sector companies. The Bank made annual use of the War Office's I.B.M. computer for the seasonal adjustment of banking figures through the Central Statistical Office, the forerunner of the Office for National Statistics.[122] Senior officials within the Bank suggested that it might be appropriate for its employees to attend a series of events to learn about computers, perhaps, they speculated, presented by a leading academic, similar to a three-day demonstration given to Members of the House of Commons on computer usage by Elliott Automation.[123] To counteract the dearth of specialist technical skills within its staff, it was also proposed that 'the more promising younger men from all Departments' could be given more extensive knowledge and advanced training to equip them for the long-term.[124] Seemingly in reaction to the pace of private sector modernisation, the Bank sought to plan for its long-term prosperity.

Within the City there was concern about a lack of communication between it and central government. An Inter-Bank Research Organisation (IBRO) report from 1972 said that 'partly owing to the United Kingdom's market-orientated financial system,

---

[117] Harold Wilson, *The Labour Government, 1964–70* (London: Weidenfeld & Nicolson, 1971), p. xix.

[118] Wayne Sandholtz, *High-Tech Europe: The Politics of International Cooperation* (Berkeley, University of California Press, 1992), p. 78.

[119] Hansard, HC Deb 27 April 1965 vol 711 cc196-7, http://hansard.millbanksystems.com/commons/1965/apr/27/computer-advisory-unit [Accessed 1 February 2016].

[120] BoE File 5A199/4, 'Computers in the Bank', 27 December 1965.

[121] Ibid.

[122] Ibid.

[123] BoE File 5A199/4, 'Computers in the Bank', 27 December 1965.

[124] Ibid.

in which the City and the government have tended to deal with each other at arms' length, and 'partly owing to the arrangement whereby the main channel of communication has been through the Bank of England, few people at the working level in Whitehall and the City know one another or have much insight into one another's work.'[125] Though acknowledging that matters had improved in recent years due to one or two exchanges of staff, and some increase in 'social contact', the IBRO firmly believed this was not enough to solve the problem.

There was a dislocation, both parties feeling that they could mutually benefit from a closer relationship and a more detailed understanding of each other's capabilities, which IBRO detailed. 'Indeed, despite good will on both sides, the communication gap tends to be self-reinforcing. Whitehall officials from three different departments told us that they would welcome initiatives from the City … But many City people are not in close enough contact with government to know what kind of proposals might be feasible and how to present them in a manner that would enable Whitehall officials to deal with them constructively,' IBRO surmised. Perhaps unsurprisingly the organisation also noted that it had met 'several people in the City who have genuinely felt that, if only they could have been consulted about the practical effects of decisions made in the Treasury or the DTI [Department of Trade and Industry], they could have helped the officials concerned to make better decisions.' Siding with their City colleagues, IBRO noted that it was Whitehall official who did not know who to consult, or, 'quite possibly, what questions to ask … The arms-length relationship prevails.'[126] Despite the closely aligned interests of the City and Whitehall there seemed to be little practical co-operation between the two.

There was skepticism as to whether the Bank of England could help reconcile this situation, according to the IBRO report: 'many people in the City and in Whitehall appear to doubt whether it is realistic to expect the Bank of England to continue to act as the main channel of communication between the two.'[127] Advances in automation occurred in spite of the relationship between the City and Whitehall, rather than because of it. This reinforces the view that driving this process of modernisation was a desire for profitability and greater efficiency on behalf of the banks, as opposed to gaining favour with the government by listening to its encouragement.

The Actualities of Automation

While ambition for technology-driven change existed in abundance within the clearing banks, there was also an awareness of the adverse impacts that automation, could have. Those in leadership positions at the banks saw automation as an almost

---

[125] London Metropolitan Archives, File MS32157x/1, 'The Future of London As An International Financial Centre', IBRO Report 117, October 1972, p. 41.

[126] Ibid., p. 41.

[127] LMA, MS32157x/1, 'The Future of London As An International Financial Centre', IBRO Report 117, October 1972, p. 41.

entirely positive process, even a necessity. No more so was this the case than for managers and directors concerned with their business's profitability. Nevertheless, there were several realities that had to be confronted. As early as 1965, only a small number of years after the beginning of the computer revolution in the City, DS Travers, Assistant General Manager of Barclays, listed some of what he described as the 'actualities of automation' in his previously mentioned lecture to the Institute of Bankers: 'keeping the staff and customers informed of what is going on; proper training for the job; getting the pay and promotion structure right; seeing that shift work, which is recognised as being inevitable at computer centres is well planned and appropriately rewarded; demonstrating to young bank people who are selected to work in automation that they can have a really successful future in this field.'[128] Listed here are some of the fundamental aspects to the automation process. Fears of staff had to be assuaged, their understanding deepened and their potential future career paths thoroughly explained.

The banks were likely aware of precedents being set for automation having a negative impact on employment, exemplified by an article that appeared in *The Times* just over a year prior to Travers' lecture. 'The largest New York bank, Chase Manhattan, reported recently that its payroll had fallen in 1963 for the second year in succession', the article declared, 'in spite of an increase in the number of its branches, many more cheques passing through them, and a general growth of business at all levels.'[129] The bank's report cited the 'continued expansion of the bank's use of electronic data processing' as the main reason for the decrease in size of its payroll.[130]

A similar article had appeared in that same newspaper a few months prior, in March 1964, entitled *Automation: Cause of Unemployment?* and authored by Maurice Laing, the President of the British Employers' Confederation. Examining the impact of automation on employment in America, Laing described how the 'alarming and unprecedented combination of prosperity and unemployment' had been 'widely attributed to the rapid advance of automation'.[131] The article also referred to claims that 'unlike earlier technological revolutions' this one was failing to create additional jobs for those displaced.[132]

Moreover, in a 1962 booklet distributed to customers of branches being served by computer, Barclays explicitly referred to its increasing wage bill as a difficulty. It stated that a 'very large proportion of the Bank's operating expenses is taken up in meeting the ever-increasing staff salary bill, and in providing premises and

---

[128] Barclays, File 0080-2827, DS Travers, 'The Actualities of Bank Automation' in *Automation in Banking Lectures: The Institute of Bankers*, November 1965, p. 18.

[129] Barclays, File 1023-1053, Newspaper Cutting, 'Office Workers Threatened by Automation', *The Times*, 6 June 1964.

[130] Barclays Archive File 1023-1053, Newspaper Cutting, New York Correspondent, 'Office Workers Threatened by Automation', *The Times*, 6 June 1964.

[131] Barclays Archive File 1023-1053, Newspaper Cutting, Maurice Laing, 'Automation: Cause of Unemployment?', *The Times*, 31 March 1964.

[132] Ibid.

equipment for the staff do to the work.' Moreover, it followed that if the bank continued using the established system, and costs continued to rise, 'it might well be that in a few years' time we should be unable to provide an adequate banking service at a cost which could reasonably be expected.'[133] It seems likely that among the lower and middle echelons of staff within the London clearing banks there may have existed some justified fears over the future of their jobs. Computers were fundamentally altering bank operations and a crucial part of this was a decreased demand for staff.

Recognition of these potentially far-reaching consequences persisted. In 1972 the Governor of the Bank of England, Leslie O'Brien, said in a speech that 'computers, allied to modern management techniques such as clerical work measurement and methods study, are capable of making radical changes in work processes leading to substantial staff savings', noting that rising labour costs seemed inevitable.[134] The Inter-Bank Research Organisation (IBRO) also noted that questions about distribution and total employment levels in the financial services industry were arising.[135] A great irony existed, in that serious thought and work had been put into automation by staff of the banks, even though the longer-term aim of this automation was to drastically reduce staff costs for these institutions.

Security & Vulnerability

Outweighing the realities of automation and the potential for unemployment was a level of nervousness about security. Particularly marked from the middle of the 1960s onwards, banks were acutely aware of the risks they now found themselves vulnerable to having started becoming dependent upon computers for crucial aspects of their work. Recognition rapidly grew that employing machinery in their operations to undertake previously manual tasks meant that oversight of those activities also had to account for new dangers. Automating tasks meant having to find new ways of overseeing their security.

Speaking in a 1965 lecture entitled *The Way Ahead*, RL Hopps, Assistant General Manager at National Provincial Bank, said 'Some of the developments I have mentioned will call for some revision in the method of auditing branches linked to computers. Thus far inspectors have had to carry out their audit on the basis of print-outs, balance lists, etc. provided by the computer.'[136] Hopps expanded: 'In the future, however, more and more data will be retained in machine language form and not printed out. When that happens, inspectors will have to carry out their audit *through*

---

[133] Barclays, File 0235-0020, 'Computer Accounting', 1962, p. 2.

[134] LMA, File MS32157x/1, Leslie O'Brien quoted in 'The Future of London as an International Financial Centre', IBRO Report 117, October 1972, p. 31.

[135] Ibid.

[136] Barclays Archive File 0080-2827, RL Hopps, 'The Way Ahead', in *Automation in Banking Lectures: The Institute of Bankers*, November 1965, p. 57.

the computer, using special programmes written for this purpose.'[137] Computers had the potential to effect fundamental change on banks' internal operations. In this case, new measures had to be employed to ensure that historical activity on such machines could be examined in detail.

Whilst this could have a positive impact upon the security of such institutions, Hopps also identified some potential risks arising from these new auditing methods: 'security of data may be jeopardised when it is displayed on screens, and it may therefore be helpful to mention ways in which security can be achieved.' His thinking included that computers could be programmed so as to only show confidential data on 'specified consoles under the control of authorised people'. Another possible solution was for the 'interrogator to insert a key into the console which initiates the signal' so that only those people with keys receive confidential data.[138] The banks were optimistic and open-minded, particularly to finding solutions to new problems rather than rejecting change outright. New methods were embraced, likely because the potential benefits were recognised to be significant, and so security emerged on their agendas as a manageable reality. Confronted by this burgeoning risk, the banks had to find creative ways to manage it.

Computer failure was amongst the first and most obvious key vulnerabilities that these machines opened the banks up to. The Bank of England recognised that if work was to be concentrated on a single computer then arrangements needed to be made for contingency in the form of standby facilities.[139] Necessity forced the banks to consider contingency plans in case an unforeseen issue rendered their computers useless. The focus here was on availability: banks needed to replicate this quality of paper-based systems so that they would not have to cease potentially time-sensitive operations in the event of machine failure, whether this occurred deliberately or not.

Securing access to the information these machines processed and the media they were stored upon soon became a consideration. New Government Stock Regulations in 1965 clarified the legality of keeping the Bank of England's stock registers on magnetic tape.[140] Controls were outlined for certain processes in the Bank: 'dual control of certain documents, e.g., the custody of magnetic tape registers, programmes.'[141] Every transfer was to be accurately recorded in the register, no alterations to the register were to be made without the support of a sufficiently authenticated document and all paper certificates or dividend warrants were to be kept under 'proper control' and duly accounted for.[142] The nature of information being stored in physical formats meant that computer security had to take into

---

[137] Ibid., p. 57.

[138] Ibid., p. 57.

[139] BoE, File 5A199/4, 'Computers in the Bank', 27 December 1965.

[140] Bank of England, 'Quarterly Bulletin: 1968, Q3', http://www.bankofengland.co.uk/archive/Documents/historicpubs/qb/1968/qb68q3262270.pdf [Accessed 19 February 2016].

[141] BoE, File 5A199/4, 'Register on Magnetic Tape: Security', 13 October 1965.

[142] Ibid.

account both physical and technical measures for securing the computers them-selves and their external stores of data.

Clear lines of accountability were also drawn for staff working closely with com-puters: each Head of Department was to 'ensure, so far as is practicable, that his system is secure against fraud, both internal and external'.[143] It was the duty of the staff to 'carry out the system strictly.'[144] These techniques were implemented to mitigate risk by employing a level of oversight, much needed as the capability of these computers grew. Managing the human interaction with these machines was the purpose of these control measures. Preventing unauthorised access required safeguards of this kind.

Mitigating Risk

Banks came to recognise that the new risks they faced could not be eliminated com-pletely. Instead, they had to act to manage these risks, minimise their exposure to them and understand how they could most easily recover. This would be crucial as the scale of investment by the banks reached unprecedented levels. In 1970, for example, Barclays claimed that it had 'the largest private computer investment' in the United Kingdom and that it led the field in the 'application of modern equipment to commercial problems.'[145] Investment on such a scale would not be worthwhile if it was easily undermined as a result of insufficient protection for its new systems, whether against fault or malicious attempts to damage or manipulate it.

Banks therefore demanded high standards around specific areas of security that created complexity but reflected an awareness of why security was so crucial to the success of their businesses. Such 'onerous' complexity in banking computer appli-cations arose from two factors, according to Barclays, the first of which was the 'sheer size' of operations stemming from the 'completeness' of new systems, given that even the 'one-in-a-hundred case' occurred too frequently to leave to manual undertaking and so automation procedures were even created for such outliers.[146] The second factor creating complexity, according to Barclays, was security: 'there is a need for high security against data loss, which goes beyond what was necessary, and therefore achieved in most other big systems (e.g. in airline and military applications).'[147] The bank believed, therefore, that major banking computer sys-tems required a degree of innovation, not only in the design of the banking work but also in the basic software function of data management and security.

---

[143] Ibid.

[144] Ibid.

[145] Barclays, File 1682-0023, 'Barclays – Careers in Computing', 1970, p. 5.

[146] Barclays, File 0178-0001, Computer Analysts and Programmers Ltd., 'Barclays Bank Computing Strategy: Interim Report to Management', 1973, p. 5.

[147] Ibid., p. 5.

Data loss was more of a worry than in earlier airline and military computer systems and required new thinking. Banks had a clear idea of their security requirements, framed by their recognition that customer trust had been historically
important to them and would continue to be so. Computer security was not just for
its own sake, but a core requirement of their role and function as guardians of sensitive financial information.

Computer security for banks in the 1970s was a comprised heavily of physical
measures designed to manage access and others to bolster the resilience of important sites against interruption or damage. An instructive example is provided by the
development of Midland Bank's South Yorkshire Computer Centre.

First, contingency took the form of an Uninterruptable Power Supply System to
power the computers and air-conditioning.[148] As its name suggests, in the event of
failure batteries would maintain power until the standby generators were brought
into action.

Secondly, a high level of physical security was described as 'fundamental'.[149]
This would be achieved through perimeter fences, closed circuit television cameras
and reinforced concrete structures with no windows for high security areas.[150] The
Centre also operated with restricted access measures, and internal doors had card
access locks with differing levels of security for various areas.[151] A monitoring system comprised of three minicomputers, smaller machines with less power than
mainframe computers, was also developed to control and record access to these
areas.[152] In this case, Midland certainly seemed aware of the risks they faced, and
primarily combated the issue through access monitoring and restriction. Relatively
old techniques were being used to secure spaces as opposed to the technology itself.

Contingency planning caused some anxiety within individual institutions, especially so as operations expanded to include multiple computer processing centres.
Barclays, for example, cited particular scenarios that troubled them, including its in
ability, as of 1973, to transfer its most important work, at short notice, from one
computer centre to another. The bank wanted to 'lessen' this vulnerability as quickly
as possible. Recognising that there were multiple potential causes of interruption of
their operations for an extended period, including fire, a labour dispute at a crucial
third party electricity or telecommunications supplier, the bank began to distinguish
between acts by a small group, for which technology could provide some mitigation, and larger national issues against which it could not. And the bank knew just
how important it was to keep details of the security and transfer arrangements secret.

Barclays also recognised how crucial the time period of transfer was. They estimated that an interval of 24 hours before processing was continued elsewhere would

---

[148] HSBC Archives, 'Computer Services Division News: South Yorkshire Computer Centre',
December 1978.
[149] Ibid.
[150] Ibid.
[151] Ibid.
[152] Ibid.

be 'inconvenient but not disastrous for current applications', and that in an emergency it looked like the equipment in a centre could be replaced in approximately eight weeks, if not less, primarily due to the significant capacity to do so by their mainframe suppliers IBM. 'Thus 24 hours and 8 weeks appears to bracket the current problem. If the Bank has, or embarks upon, systems of a greater urgency, it would be prudent to provide alternative forms of back-up, which might involve manual operation by staff unlikely to be involved in the same local dispute or cause of stoppage', was Barclays' conclusion.[153] New thinking had to be done about recovering from some of the potential scenarios outlined above. There was almost the same requirement of action regardless of whether the action was deliberate, such as strike action, an issue for the UK in the 1960s and 1970s – and another irony given banks' motivation for investment in computers being savings on staff costs – or accidental damage such as fire.

One underpinning assumption in the banks' thinking, and the strategic advice given to them by external consultants, was lowering risk to an acceptable level. For example, Computer Analysts and Programmers (CAP) advised Barclays that they could counteract the risk posed by physical damage to their hardware by operating multiple processing centres: 'It is clearly essential, from the security point of view, that the Bank should maintain its current position of distributing computing facilities over several separate centres. It is also essential that any computer systems which are regarded as critical must be capable of being transferred from one computer to another.'[154] Extra capacity could lower the risk of computers becoming unavailable and therefore their operations being interrupted. It also alluded to the need for banks to prioritise between services which were critical and those less so. CAP outlined two key factors which influenced their report: firstly, that there was concern about the 'vulnerability of the Bank's business to accidental or malicious damage at a computer centre', the branch accounting system being the most critical; and secondly that Barclays intended to develop a wide variety of communications-based systems each likely to bring its own network needs, its own computer terminals and its own security requirements.[155] Both the practicalities of computer security and the strategic thinking around it became increasingly specific as these machines underpinned a greater amount of banking activities.

As computer technology became increasingly powerful, banks further sought expert advice from consultants as to capabilities and new mitigation measures. Computer Analysts and Programmers Ltd. (CAP) was one such company, whose expertise covered 'all aspects of computing systems', offering advice and implementation services as well as selling their own products, and was co-founder of the CAP group of companies, at the time Europe's 'largest independent computer

---

[153] Barclays, File 0178-0001, Computer Analysts and Programmers Ltd., 'Barclays Bank Computing Strategy: Interim Report to Management', 1973, p. 17.

[154] Ibid., p. 17.

[155] Barclays Archive File 0178-0003, Computer Analysts and Programmers Ltd., 'Barclays Bank Computing Strategy: Interim Report to Management – Appendix D', 1973, p. 7.

software house.'[156] Their work included implementation of large scale systems for computer users, including 'advanced technology projects' in such fields as avionics and process control, employing over 400 professional staff by mid-1976.[157] They outlined a detailed scenario for Barclays and some steps for transferring data between computer centres in case of an emergency. Under certain conditions, CAP assessed, it would be possible to transfer data and programs between computer centres by connecting them via suitable telecommunications links. It was also possible to connect terminals to those links in such a way that they could have access to at least on computer centre. CAP explained that this formation was often described as a 'computing grid', a facility which was still 'rare in business' but existed in 'military commands' and 'scientific centres.' Construction of such a facility would be technically difficult and transferability in a bank was made more onerous by the volume of data and 'the need for high reliability and accuracy in the communications system.' The consultants expanded on the challenges, making reference to the Advanced Research Projects Agency, or ARPA, the organisation responsible for supporting the evolution of packet switched networking and ultimately the Internet:

> The problem essentially consists of transferring the variable data (e.g. a day's waste, such as workings out), the master files and the programs. If desired these can all be moved by wire as is done in the well-known ARPA grid between scientific institutions in America. However we suggest a simpler and safer mechanism … Most of the variable data already arrives by write and it would be possible to divert this, via switching nodes, to any given centre. The centres and nodes would have to be over-connected (i.e. incorporate some redundancy) in order to allow for the loss or failure of particular lines.
>
> The master files can be extremely large and, as a routine safety precaution, copies are already removed regularly from the computer centres. We suggest that all the Bank's major computers should standardise on the same media for master files (e.g. IBM 3330 disk packs). Copies of the files could then be moved daily in a van to some other centre. Programs would not be moved physically because they can be extremely sensitive to minor differences in the machines (e.g. levels of operating system in use). We do not believe that centres can always keep in step as exact replicas of each other. Instead we propose that all "transferable" suites of programs should be kept at each centre and it would be that centre's responsibility to ensure that the suite would run correctly on their machine. Every suite would have a single maintenance team who would be responsible for updating the centres with authorised modifications to the programs.[158]

Technological solutions, in this case telecommunication connections were being incorporated alongside physical measures in order to fully deal with new risks associated with concentrated collections of hardware.

Though receptive to such advice, there was also the need for banks to continually reassess their computer security methods and overarching ideas. For example, CAP advised Barclays that their solutions would need to adapt as time progressed: 'The

[156] *New Civil Engineer* (NCE), July 1973.

[157] *The New Scientist,* (70/2001), 20 May 1976,

[158] Barclays, File 0178-0001, Computer Analysts and Programmers Ltd., 'Barclays Bank Computing Strategy: Interim Report to Management', 1973, p. 17.

solution is described as partial for several reasons. First, it must be remembered that security is a continuous endeavour,' the consultants noted. 'Having taken certain steps it is necessary to anticipate how a potential saboteur or other person might be clever enough to overcome them and then one proceeds again.'

Second, CAP said, further safety could be achieved by extending transferability so that certain applications had no "home" base but were moved back and forth weekly, or even daily, potentially reducing the risk or feasibility of 'industrial espionage'. However, transfers of that frequency could prove problematic for output and reliability. Thirdly, CAP said, 'we have not explored the full implications of security in the Bank's computing centres or the possibilities and dangers which will arise through the greater use of telecommunications. Yet we cannot but contrast the apparently limited precautions now employed with those existing elsewhere (e.g. Bank of America).' In this case, it seemed that another of CAP's clients were further advanced in their information security capabilities.

Before implementing a full grid, or network, CAP suggested that local storage devices at terminals, such as magnetic tape cassettes, could provide a convenient interim solution for branch accounting data collection, despite them being relatively novel. Procedures could also be employed at branches to reduce the impact of computer failures, CAP said, but it would be necessary to understand this type of contingency planning as an ongoing activity – one which could be overseen by a dedicated Contingency Manager who would be responsible for priorities and planning, but also co-ordinating actions 'when such a disaster occurs.'[159] Understanding that security would be a "continuous endeavour" was clearly seen as important in the eyes of Barclays' advisers. Alongside this was the realisation that the risks faced were diverse: from industrial action to computer failure, the deliberate and the non-deliberate, non-technical and technical.

Computer Analysts and Programmers Ltd. were also proponents of the idea of risk reduction as opposed to risk elimination. They declared Barclays' operations as 'vulnerable to the disablement of a major computer centre, from whatever cause' and that this vulnerability covered not only the loss of processing power of a computer centre, but also the loss of its communications facilities or critical data stored in the centre.[160] CAP recommended that Barclays make it a 'prime requirement' to reduce this vulnerability to an 'acceptable level'.[161] They also wrote that five principles should be borne in mind as Barclays' computer security thinking progressed: distribution of work; standby capacity; transferability of work; external security of information; and contingency planning.[162]

---

[159] Barclays, File 0178-0001, Computer Analysts and Programmers Ltd., 'Barclays Bank Computing Strategy: Interim Report to Management', 1973, p. 19.

[160] Barclays, File 0178-0003, Computer Analysts and Programmers Ltd., 'Barclays Bank Computing Strategy: Interim Report to Management – Appendix D', 1973, p. 13.

[161] Barclays, File 0178-0003, Computer Analysts and Programmers Ltd., 'Barclays Bank Computing Strategy: Interim Report to Management – Appendix D', 1973, p. 13.

[162] Ibid., p. 14.

Computer security thinking in the London clearing banks had truly begun in the decade and a half to the mid-1970s. The expansion of computing installations and the creation of multiple computing centres prompted the banks' thinking to continually evolve, though they were comfortable with seeking advice from experts. Much of their thoughts and action had revolved around resilience, or recovering from inevitable incidents, and security against damage or failure, primarily focusing on keeping people out of proximity to computer hardware. By the late 1970s, however, banks' viewpoint shifted and they began to consider increasingly technical threats, as computers became increasingly linked together in networks, and therefore the ability to breach security without having to approach the machines themselves.

The Threat from Outsiders

By the mid-1970s concerns pivoted towards safeguarding computer systems against outside actors who wished to view or intercept confidential data without authorisation. This threat had evolved out of the worry that those with a significant degree of technical knowledge could fraudulently use these machines and exploit the very advantages they offered.

Although prompted by advancements in technology, the major banks recognised how crucial confidentiality had always been to their operations. 'The overriding need to maintain confidentiality when dealing with their customers' affairs has long been enshrined in accepted banking practice, a 1976 note by the British Bankers' Association read, 'and, as major users of computers, the banks have a special interest in this issue.'[163] Confidentiality of communications was recognised as a crucial part of the banker-customer relationship and one that had to be monitored and managed as banking operations modernised with new technology.

In 1975, senior figures at the Bank of England spotted the potential vulnerabilities that were opening because of computerisation. Sir Alastair Pilkington, of the Merseyside glass manufacturers of the same name, at this point a director of the Bank, enquired to the Bank's Audit Committee about the vulnerability of the its 'computer configurations' to 'fraudulent use by persons of high intellect with a knowledge of electronic engineering'.[164] Sir Alastair even thought that a "redteam" – an internal attempt to uncover vulnerabilities – of the system may prove useful, asking whether consideration had been given to utilising the services of a 'highly qualified technician' to 'examine ways and means of manipulating the systems in operation at the Bank for dishonest purposes.'[165]

---

[163] HSBC, File UK0200-1024A, 'BBA Chief Executive to Jordan', 1 November 1976, p. 1.

[164] BoE File 5A199/6, 'Extract from Audit Committee Minutes 30.1.75', 30 January 1975. For an overview of the historical significance of TEMPEST, see Ashley Sweetman, 'TEMPEST and the Bank of England', *Intelligence & National Security*, 33/7 (2018), pp. 1084–1091.

[165] Ibid.

Attendees of the Audit Committee agreed that every effort should be made to keep up with the latest thinking in this burgeoning area and that 'constant vigilance' was required. Relevant articles on the subject in technical or other journals were to be copied for dissemination and consideration at future meetings.[166] It had taken a senior business figure to advance the thinking about the risks posed by new computer systems.

However, Sir Alistair's concerns were echoed by similar worries from secretive experts within central government. Only 2 months on from the meeting at which Sir Alastair expressed his concern, a Secret-classified document was issued in the Bank entitled 'Security of Data' which included a specific threat warning. The document announced that the Management Services Department would now undertake responsibility for the security of the Bank's data following agreement between the Chief of that department and the Chief Cashier. Security, here, was defined as 'measures necessary to protect the Bank from its information being "leaked" radiated or emitted from computer cables, outside telephone lines, VDUs [Visual Display Units, or computer monitors] or other peripherals.'[167]

Previously the Bank had assumed 'little hazard' in these areas because VDU emissions were only detectable within 300 yards. With the Bank's computers operating amongst the 'electronic "noise"' emitted from the rest of the City and the measure of protection provided by the Bank's building itself, the Bank may have had reasonable justification for not showing immediate concern. Such a specific proposed threat was, however, explained later in the memo: 'We have been informed by a unit of the Ministry of Defence, in the strictest confidence, that equipment is available (capable of being operated from a mini-van) which could "home-in" on to a device and record data passing through it.' Most concerning to the Bank was 'that a display of data on a VDU could be picked up "in clear"'.[168]

As opposed to the "insider threat" of a rogue individual misusing the system, the very specific threat outlined here was one to confidentiality of data from outsiders. In theory, malicious actors could replicate unencrypted versions of computer monitors outside the building and see them exactly as their rightful operator could. The threat landscape was beginning to widen. No longer was the vulnerability of misuse the primary concern; external malicious actors with the potential technical ability to gain unauthorised access to privileged information were becoming an increasing threat.

The Bank suddenly had to enquire whether they had possible exposure to information leakage and what corrective action was required. For this, they contacted the department who informed them of such a threat: the 'Communications Electronic Security Group [CESG] of the M.O.D [Ministry of Defence]', who were only contactable by letter, not telephone.[169] CESG is the UK government's National Technical

---

[166] BoE, File 5A199/6, 'Extract from Audit Committee Minutes 30.1.75', 30 January 1975.

[167] BoE, File 5A199/6, 'Security of Data', 18 March 1975.

[168] Ibid.

[169] BoE, File 5A199/6, 'Security of Data', 18 March 1975.

Authority for Information Assurance, based within Government Communications Headquarters (GCHQ) and since 2016 part of the National Cyber Security Centre (NCSC). It advises organisations, including the public sector, suppliers to government and companies maintaining the UK's critical national infrastructure on how to protect their information and information systems against threats.[170] The Bank had reason to believe, therefore, in the credibility of this threat.

Three months on, in June 1975, the Bank was still showing significant concern. In the time between then and the March memo, personnel security and the security of their premises had been re-examined.[171] Nevertheless, one area of concern remained: data, and particularly the electronic theft thereof as opposed to the theft of physical data storage devices.[172] Again, the potential for a small van and detector equipment outside was mentioned with particular reference to the Bank's Gold & Fixed Exchange Office whose computer application was in trial stage and therefore potentially insecure. Of particular concern to the Bank was that the data potentially picked up from a screen in the Gold & Fixed Exchange Department would be 'in clear' and could be 'understood by anyone interested in the subject.'[173]

A memo noted that the Bank had been in touch with Air Vice-Marshal Foden, Director of CESG in the MoD, to gain his expert opinion on whether the Bank had a problem. Nevertheless, CESG were most concerned that protocol was followed and as such the Bank were asked to 'formally request the help of the Security Service [MI5] … [who] would then call on the C.E.S. Group for their technical assistance.'[174] It was suggested that the Bank should mention that Air Vice-Marshal Foden had, on receipt of their inquiry, steered them in the direction of the Security Service.[175]

A further handwritten note from 24 July noted that the Bank had been in touch with CESG who had responded asking for the following detail: the volume of classified material involved; the level of classified material involved; the site of the equipment and the type of the equipment, to which the Management Services Department were drafting a reply.[176] The security issue was also discussed at a further meeting of the Audit Committee on 24 July 1975, in which the Committee expressed its concern that the Post Office and manufacturers should 'minimise the dangers of security leakages in computer configurations.'[177] Having received credible notice of a threat, from an organisation with the legitimacy of CESG, officials at the Bank clearly understood the potential consequences of a security breach. Such vulnerabilities were new and directly as a result of investment in computers.

---

[170] CESG, 'About Us', https://www.cesg.gov.uk/articles/cesg-information-security-arm-gchq [Accessed 19 February 2016].

[171] BoE, File 5A199/6, 'Computer Systems – Security of Bank Data', 10 June 1975.

[172] Ibid.

[173] Ibid.

[174] Ibid.

[175] Ibid.

[176] BoE, File 5A199/6, 'Security', 25 July 1975.

[177] BoE, File 5A199/6, 'Extract from Audit Committee Minutes', 24 July 1975.

Internal Auditing: Learning from America

As the perception of threat rose, the Bank of England began to think about processes for the internal auditing of their systems. Whilst the UK was relatively advanced in the computerisation of its financial sector, the United States kept pace, and in some cases led by example, to the extent that UK auditing officials were sent to the United States to learn from their counterparts in the Federal Reserve Bank.

This had happened in 1967 when the findings from the visit of the Bank of England's Auditor and its '3rd Auditor Computers' to the US 'relieved' the problems being encountered in the UK.[178] The Bank decided to do similar for these 'next generation of systems' – namely on-line, real-time systems – and sent two representatives to the United States in 1975. They had enquired with I.B.M (U.K.) and several users in the UK 'but with little positive result': IBM themselves had 'no experience' on which they could draw.[179]

The trip of 'Miss Marshall' and 'D.J. Scrivens' to North America in 1975 was successful in spite of their particularly quaint complaints over their budget constraints: having to eat breakfast in 'a drugstore and other meals ... in relatively inexpensive restaurants'; the 'not exactly lavish' hospitality of the Federal Reserve Bank of New York; and only being 'lunched once and dined once' during the stay.[180] Insight was gained, however, into the overall audit processes of the banks visited. Underlined in the project report by its reader were the two words 'encryption techniques' in the sentence 'there is no evidence of malpractice through tampering or wire tapping but encryption techniques are being studied in order to keep "one step ahead" of would-be infiltrators.'[181] This added protection was clearly something that appealed to the worried Bank officials. Learning from their counterparts across the Atlantic was of great use.

However, some two years later, in January 1977, the issue of emissions from Visual Display Units was still on the agenda for the Bank's Audit Committee. Discussions between the Bank and the Security Services resulted in a suggestion that 'protection might be afforded in the form of a box around' VDUs. This suggestion, however, was rejected within the Bank at Deputy Chief Cashier level, possibly on grounds of cost.[182] Here the trade-off between cost and security is explicit. Security at all costs was not the aim of the Bank, but creating sufficient disincentive effects at a compromised cost was more in line with their thinking.

Seemingly still unsatisfied with the issue come September 1978, however, the Computer Services Division (CSD) within the Bank attempted to summarise the

---

[178] BoE, File 5A199/6, 'Computers and Auditing', 27 August 1975.

[179] Ibid.

[180] BoE File 5A199/6, 'Miss R.A. Marshall and D.J. Scrivens to New York/Washington/Kansas – November 1975', 20 November 1975.

[181] Ibid.

[182] BoE, File 5A199/6, 'Audit Committee', 21 January 1977.

situation and find a way to progress. R.A.J. Middleton of the CSD wrote that this really was a question of 'risk analysis' and that after such an analysis it seemed that additional security measures were not warranted at this time.[183] Middleton outlined his own personal scepticism: 'I have doubted whether someone could really beam in on to particular VDUs within the walls of the Bank, there being so many VDUs in the Bank and elsewhere in this area of the City.'[184] Despite this contention, he conceded that there had been significant developments in technology in the last couple of years and that perhaps 'micro-processor developments have made eavesdropping equipment smaller (and possibly more difficult to detect)' as well as 'more sophisticated and therefore more able to distinguish particular radiation from background noise'.[185] Admitting that this was speculation rather than fact, Middleton suggested that perhaps the 'best thing' was to 'go round the course once again with the CESG.'[186] It can be inferred that the issue was a recurring one, to which no satisfactory solution, within the acceptable range of cost, was available. It seems that the Bank wished to understand more definitively just how realistic or remote the threat of radiation emanation was before deciding the level of protection the Bank needed against it. Proportionality was key to their thinking.

The Banker-Customer Relationship

Despite the rapid pace and development of technology during this period the fundamental concerns for the banks when implementing new uses of computer equipment remained relatively unchanged. This is illustrated by internal discussions at Barclays Bank that in 1976 was conducting a pilot scheme for storing profiles of correspondent banks on a computer located at a computer bureau in the United States.[187] Computer terminals at Barclays' premises that were linked by telephone lines could then print these profiles.[188] The bank planned on utilising this new facility for extracting a variety of significant information related to countries, currencies or analysis of individual banking groups and were seeking permission to load data on the rest of its correspondent banks to the system as well as information about 400 potential corporate customers.[189] Although an attractive proposition, accompanying this endeavour was some risk.

Barclays was concerned about confidentiality of the data stored and transferred in this function. Precisely, they were worried about the sensitivity of data

---

[183] BoE, File 5A199/6, 'Security – Radiation from VDUs', 11 September 1978.

[184] Ibid.

[185] Ibid.

[186] Ibid.

[187] Barclays, File 0080-6198, 'Group Data Banks', 29 November 1976, p. 1.

[188] Ibid., p. 1.

[189] Ibid., p. 1.

concerning their corporate customers, of which a 'considerable' amount was confidential in the 'usual banker and customer' relationship.[190] The bank felt that a leak of this data could, at best, embarrass the relationship and at worst cause 'considerable financial loss' either to Barclays itself, its customer or to both.[191] Although the bank understood that government departments both in the United Kingdom and United States of America used the system, Barclays admitted to having no knowledge of the sensitivity of such data, and moreover felt that the security level at the computer centre, the location they deemed to be of highest risk, could not be accurately assessed.[192]

Debate within Barclays around the idea of a Group Data Bank highlights the competing agendas around technological development within the financial sector. The Computer Services and Inspection Departments of Barclays Bank International advised against continuing with the data bank method, yet the Business Development office regard the establishment of a data bank as an essential part of their strategy.[193] For the former, the bureau system failed on a number of essential factors, including: the secrecy around the operational controls within the computer centre which the bank was precluded by contract from obtaining any information on; vulnerability to employees at the bureau who for political, ethical or financial reasons could manipulate or leak information; the inability of Barclays to test the effectiveness of the security password system at the bureau; and that the sensitive data could not be completely enciphered and could fall into the wrong hands through incorrect routing of a transmission.[194] Confidentiality was deemed crucial in such a system and the degree of separation between Barclays' security-focused departments and this facility was causing some problems. These concerns illuminate the continuity in thinking around security even as technology was changing. The banks still had a duty to its customer, and had to maintain the trust in this relationship for both parties to wish to continue such a relationship into the future.

Code of Conduct

An internal exchange of views at the Bank of England in late 1977 was concerned with the security of electronic data processing techniques, prompted by an exceptionally busy day of activity. Approximately 8500 market transfers had to be conducted on 10 October 1977, and with time pressures mounting, the Bank was faced with the dilemma of either telling the Market that it could not cope or involving

---

[190] Barclays, File 0080-6198, 'Group Data Banks', 29 November 1976, p. 1.

[191] Ibid., p. 1.

[192] Ibid., p. 1.

[193] Ibid., p. 1.

[194] Ibid., p. 1.

extra staff to aid its operations.[195] In what the Bank described as this 'emergency situation', having already had to switch all normal resources to deal with the level of activity, it became essential to draft in staff from the Chief Accountant's Planning Office (CAPO) who were issued with around 40 computer usage badges.[196] These badges were held in a safe overnight and given to the same holders in the morning, until they were withdrawn at midday on completion of the work.[197] Print-outs were available showing the activities actually undertaken by the users of these badges during operations.[198]

Access to live programs was the primary issue of controversy here. The Accountant's Department stressed that it took separate steps to prevent unauthorised access of CAPO Staff to live programs and in these circumstances the 'risks in terms of security' would have been 'the same' as for staff working on transfers in their normal daily work.[199] It was the opinion of the Accountant's Department, therefore, that there was no requirement for exceptional verification or enquiry regarding the work carried out in these exceptional circumstances, particularly given that examination of the accounts involved, as was usual, could be subject to an independent check to ensure that transfers were correct.[200]

Despite these reassurances the Audit Division in the Bank of England replied in strong terms. Although clarifying that they did not 'demur' at the solution chosen to solve 'the very difficult problem' they were particularly uneasy with the principles, the precedent created and the possible need for additional control procedures to be introduced.[201]

The Audit Division were particularly concerned with the prospect of fraud which they felt the actions of the Accountant's Department may have perpetuated. Their grievances, worth quoting at length, reveal their worries and perception of the threat of fraud in some detail: 'There are two fundamental elements necessary to facilitate fraud (or other malpractice), namely, knowledge (combined with adequate skill) and opportunity to use that knowledge to ill-effect. On this, and on the general desirability of not allowing programmers direct access to a live system, I suspect that there is no significant difference between us.' This combination of knowledge and opportunity could be applied to various forms of criminality, but was a helpful way for the Bank to begin thinking about the risk of computer fraud it faced.

Such fraud could manifest itself in two primary ways, in the view of the Audit Division. 'Malpractice on the part of programmers is usually regarded as encompassing either the addition of fraudulent coding or the suppression of built-in checking processes (or both).' It was deemed unlikely, though possible, that a programmer

[195] BoE, File 5A199/6, 'Accountant's Department to The Auditor', 12 October 1977, p. 1.

[196] BoE, File 5A199/6, 'Accountant's Department to The Auditor', 12 October 1977, p. 1.

[197] Ibid., p. 1.

[198] Ibid., p. 1.

[199] Ibid., p. 1.

[200] Ibid., p. 2.

[201] BoE, File 5A199/6, 'E.D.P.: Security', 24 October 1977, p. 1

could in this instance have planned ahead, assuming the eventual opportunity for access would occur. 'The introduction of fraudulent code becomes more attractive and the possibility cannot be ruled out with safety – this despite the many checks imposed by programmers and others engaged in processing program amendments. On these grounds we would not regard any future use of programmers in this way with such equanimity; and we recognise but regret the need to employ this particular solution on this occasion.'[202] Although cautious in their approach, the Audit Division of the Bank was seeking to improve the level of control it had over access to program code. They categorically disagreed with the assertion of the Accountant's Department that security would have been the same as normal.[203] They sought far greater reassurance and specific discussion about overseeing inputs by programmers and their overall system of controlling access of personnel to computer equipment. While in this case it seems that any worst-case scenarios had been avoided, the Bank's internal audit function was caught by surprise by the necessary quick-thinking in the face of an exceptionally high requirement for electronic data processing, and sought clarification and greater oversight as a result.

Conclusion

The Inter-Bank Research Organisation (IBRO), writing in 1972, felt that the automation that had occurred in the financial sector over the previous decade had been transformational:

> It is not altogether fanciful to suppose that … the computer may be bringing about a technological revolution in the financial services industry, parallel in some respects with that being brought about by containerisation in the docks. Not only is more work being done by fewer people, but work previously divided between different places and different specialisms can increasingly be handled as a single operation. Without pressing too far the parallel with containerisation, it is clear that these developments are very relevant to London's future as an international financial centre.[204]

An intensive period of roughly a decade of investment in computing power by banks in the financial sector had revolutionised the industry. A relatively short space of time had seen incredible pace of change, from the banks purchasing their first computers at the beginning of the 1960s to an increasingly wide array of services being automated by the early and mid-1970s. Computing had become integral to the way that London's financial services market operated. It was now interwoven with the city's success in the global financial market.

This revolutionary change had been driven from the outset by the private sector banks. Whilst Whitehall and the Bank of England looked favourably upon such

---

[202] BoE File 5A199/6, 'E.D.P.: Security', 24 October 1977, p. 1

[203] Ibid., p. 1

[204] LMA, File MS32157x/1, 'The Future of London as an International Financial Centre', IBRO Report 117, October 1972, p. 30.

investment, the process of automation was market-driven. The London clearing banks were acutely aware of the potential long-term cost and efficiency savings and felt that these savings justified substantial short-term outlay. Ambition was in plentiful supply, and the banks embraced this technological change with enthusiasm.

If security was not at the forefront of thinking for the banks when they purchased their first machines in the early 1960s, it certainly had become a priority in the following decade. 'The subject [of computer security] has become as popular as sex in the last few years', said Adrian Norman, a computer security consultant, in 1979.[205] While Norman was choosing his language to garner attention, the financial sector had certainly been forced to think in new ways about minimising risks in their business operations.

Computer security grew in complexity over the period. It began mainly as a requirement for physically managing access to new machines. It also encompassed the need to maintain reliability – even against non-malicious actions – and grew to include the need for contingency planning as vast mainframe installations at computer centres began to underpin a wider array of services. Dependency on these machines created a new normality in the UK financial sector and the firms concerned realised relatively quickly that the security of these installations had to be understood and managed. Investment in computers was for the long-term, so the issue of security would also remain.

Dealing with this increasingly complex subject also meant that banks grew in confidence. As this book outlines, in the following decades ambition grew further and further to the extent that banks began to collaborate on sector-wide financial infrastructure, underpinned by computer and communications technology, with security addressed from the outset. Facilitating the transfer of payment instructions and even direct financial transfers, computer security took on renewed importance in a different order of magnitude as the bigger projects of the 1970s and 1980s evolved.

The 1960s and 1970s had pioneering decades for banks with regards to technology. While major decisions were being made, there was also an element of being beginners when it came to computers. This was nicely summarised by Ann Bassett, a clerk-telephonist at Wolverhampton Trustee Savings Bank's (TSB) Head Office, who in 1974 penned 'Ode to a Computer' in a dentist's waiting room. Quoted in Lloyds' internal newsletter, reflecting on an air conditioning failure at the Head Office:

> One Friday in June 'twas so hot.
> The Computer said, "No. I cannot
> Work out any more sums.
> 'Til the Engineer comes.
> Or the temperature falls quite a lot.[206]

---

[205] Ibid.

[206] Lloyds, *Banknotes,* Issue 28, September 1974, p. 3.

Computer security would become an increasingly critical subject in the late 1970s and early 1980s, but in the decades immediately following World War II, it had been a new and evolving subject to tackle, from warnings to the Bank of England from the intelligence services to the temperamentally of new machines.

Chapter 3
BACS: 1971–1980

Bankers' Automated Clearing Services (BACS) was one of the first major co-ordinated attempts at automation in the United Kingdom's financial sector. Created as the Interbank Computer Bureau in 1968, the organisation became BACS in 1971 and was owned jointly by the five largest London clearing banks at that time: Barclays, Lloyds, Midland, National Westminster and Williams & Glyn's.[1] Settling between each other large volumes of credits and cheques for huge sums of money, the clearing banks sought a more efficient and reliable means of undertaking this process, and so collaborated in the creation of an automated system to meet their needs. Introducing transfers into the banking system in entirely computer readable form was the chosen method.[2]

Full participation in BACS entitled the clearing banks to sponsor their corporate customers to have direct input into the system, and so by the late 1970s the banks involved included the five owners listed above plus the Bank of England, Co-operative Bank, Coutts, Bank of Scotland, Clydesdale Bank and the Royal Bank of Scotland.[3] Uptake was relatively rapid: 620,000 entries passed through BACS each day by the end of 1971.[4] Approximately 1500 users, comprised of the banks and their sponsored customers, were using the system by 1975.[5] By 1979 this figure had risen to 4000.[6] A further rise to 6451 users had occurred by 1981.[7]

---

[1] Lloyds Archive (hereafter Lloyds), File 10131, 'BACS Summary', July 1979, p. 1.

[2] HSBC, File UK1793-0013, 'Banks and Automation', *Bank Education Service*, March 1972, p. 1.

[3] Lloyds, File 10131, 'BACS Summary', July 1979, pp. 1–2.

[4] HSBC Archive (hereafter HSBC), File UK1793-0013, 'Banks and Automation', March 1972, p. 16.

[5] London Metropolitan Archive (hereafter LMA), File M32145X/3, 'Inspection undertaken by representatives of National Westminster Bank Limited and Williams and Glyn's Bank Limited', 3 October 1975, p. 1.

[6] Barclays Archive (hereafter Barclays), File 0080-2165, 'Annual Report – Financial Year 1979', 2 January 1980, p. 2.

[7] Barclays, File 0156-0019, 'BACS – Annual Report 1981' 19 January 1982, p. 4.

© Springer Nature Switzerland AG 2022
A. Sweetman, *Cyber and the City*, History of Computing,
https://doi.org/10.1007/978-3-031-07933-7_3

BACS continued to be a vital component of the technological infrastructure underpinning United Kingdom's financial sector well into the twenty-first century.[8] Today it still offers 'schemes behind the clearing and settlement of UK automated payment methods', primarily Direct Debit – authorisation by customers to their banks to collect certain amounts of money from their accounts, normally through regular payments – and BACS Direct Credit – which allows organisations to pay directly into a bank or building society account.[9] In 2015 alone, 6 billion payments were made in this way – with a total of 110 billion having been completed since its inception.[10] This level of reliance on BACS has been bolstered and even amplified in large part due to its reliability, the certainty that it undertakes its operations in a confidential and secure way, with settlement services functioning when required and in the exact way intended. From its inception, the London clearing banks knew just how important these qualities would be to their new service.

A manual element still existed in the clearing process even once BACS was launched. When first created in the early 1970s, BACS physically accepted from its user banks magnetic tapes. These tapes contained instructions for transactions, either to pay or collect, referred to as Bank Credits and Direct Debits.[11] On completion of this process, its role was to then communicate the net settlements that had to be made between the clearing banks to conclude the clearing operation.[12] So-called 'omnibus tapes' detailing all transactions were then produced for individual banks to feed through their own data processing systems in order to post the entries to the relevant accounts.[13] The process worked on a three-day cycle: on day one, details of credits and debits were sent to BACS on magnetic tape; the data was sorted overnight into credits and debits for each bank, and on day two magnetic tapes containing this information were sent out; on day three the banks processed this information and updated their accounts.[14] By the early 1980s the transactions files were accepted on a variety of physical media including magnetic tape, cassette tape and 8-inch Diskette.[15] However, telecommunications links to BACS were also available by this time, including leased lines, the Public Switched Telephone Network (PSTN) and

---

[8] Bacs, 'Bacs corporate information', http://www.bacs.co.uk/Bacs/Corporate/CorporateOverview/Pages/Overview.aspx [24 February 2016].

[9] Ibid.

[10] Ibid.

[11] LMA, File M32145X/3, 'Inspection undertaken by representatives of National Westminster Bank Limited and Williams and Glyn's Bank Limited', 3 October 1975, p. 1.

[12] Royal Bank of Scotland Archives (hereafter RBS), File NWB/1372, Theresa May & John Presland, 'UK Bank Clearing Systems and Related Arrangements', *Inter-Bank Research Organisation*, October 1984, p. 29.

[13] LMA, File M32145X/3, 'Inspection undertaken by representatives of National Westminster Bank Limited and Williams and Glyn's Bank Limited', 3 October 1975, p. 1.

[14] LMA, File MS 32456/2, 'EEC Survey on Information Technology in Credit Institutions: Draft UK Chapter', 24 June 1984, p. 20.

[15] RBS, File NWB/1372, Theresa May & John Presland, 'UK Bank Clearing Systems and Related Arrangements', *Inter-Bank Research Organisation*, October 1984, p. 29.

Switch Stream, previously known as the Packet-Switching Service.[16] Computer and later network technology could power a significant increase in the volume and scale of BACS' clearing operations. The key types of transactions that BACS conducted in this initial period included salary payments, payments of trade bills by organisations and direct debits, for example from insurance companies and local authorities.[17]

Motivated by a desire for greater efficiency in carrying out their core clearing and settlement function, the clearing banks knew that computers and networking technology could offer the benefits they sought. Relatively new software and hardware would be tasked with shouldering the strain of this automated cheque clearing service. BACS' 30,000 square foot computer hall, based at Edgware in London, became the nerve centre of this effort, containing the core computer equipment that underpinned this new service.[18] Playing the supporting role was a BACS office based in the City that acted as a more convenient drop-off and pick-up point than Edgware for banks and their storage media containing transaction details.[19] While this hardware and software boasted the potential for significant improvements in the way that the clearing banks did business with each other, it also had to be relied upon heavily from the outset, meaning it had to be professionally managed, and crucially, protected.

Presented in this chapter is the story of how BACS, owned and operated by London's pre-eminent banking institutions, dealt with computer security of its service from its origins until the early 1980s. Recently released and previously unexplored archival material allows for a snapshot of BACS' security thinking and action from the early 1970s to the early 1980s. Available documents, in particular a succession of security assessments of BACS' operations from 1973 to 1980, illuminate in detail the company's management of computer security in its formative years.

BACS' definition of security came to be based around resilience. Key to this was recognition that the service's operations may well be disrupted, deliberately or not, but that, crucially, there were contingency plans in place and a clear path to timely recovery. Security for the clearing banks also meant reliability, being available when required. It also meant the confidentiality of the information transmitted across the system and its integrity, being processed accurately and as intended without alteration during transmission. Strong security, BACS felt, would engender trust in this new service and could ultimately help it prosper as an efficient automated means of carrying out the clearing and settlement service in the UK financial sector. Considerable regard was paid to security throughout this early period in BACS' existence, driven by this aim to engender and maintain trust in it, the vital quality it required when dealing with such sizeable operations and transfers of monetary value.

---

[16] Ibid., p. 29.

[17] HSBC, File UK 0200-1024A, 'BACS', May 1978, p. 3.

[18] HSBC, File UK0200-1024A, 'BACS', March 1978, p. 1.

[19] LMA, File M32145X/3, 'Inspection undertaken by representatives of National Westminster Bank Limited and Williams and Glyn's Bank Limited', 3 October 1975, p. 1.

BACS perceived destructive intent to be a key threat to its service's security. Inspection reports commonly referred to the ability of an individual to be able to access its premises including crucial areas within its buildings, and a perennial issue through the period covered in this chapter was the persistent reference to needing a contingency site in case of disaster. Intruders into BACS' premises, as well as individuals working within it, also represented a threat to security if they were able to transmit unauthorised messages and payments across the system. Alongside this the clearing banks shared significant concern over the confidentiality of private and sensitive customer information, conveying apprehension about some of its processes including the transfer of computer storage media like magnetic tapes and disks between its City centre and Edgware.

Focusing on the physical security of its computer installation and premises was a core component of BACS' tactics for dealing with computer and network security. Over time the service implemented more purely technical means of protection and risk mitigation, such as logs of activity taking place on computer terminals. However, significant importance was placed on managing access, including controlling entry to the computer centre building itself, the computer hall within it and to individual computer terminals. A contingency site was eventually appropriated for use in a disaster scenario, but this took some time. It is perhaps unsurprising that in this first co-ordinated attempt at large scale automation, security was still sought through more traditional measures.

Security was a primary consideration in the creation of BACS for its owners. From its earliest days BACS thought deeply about computer security, considering it crucial to the service's success. This progress is explored and analysed here.

"What Are the Advantages?"

Promotional literature for BACS from 1978 posed the above question. Alongside references to efficiency, the brochure put forward two key benefits: 'security' and 'reliability'.[20] Security was inherent as a result of BACS' processes, namely 'handling a single tape instead of many pieces of paper' and also copying to micro-film, a physical store which could hold reproductions of items in photographic form, all items passing through BACS.[21] Reliability of operations was ensured, BACS argued, by five key features: 'round-the-clock' maintenance of computers; provision of 'ample stand-by computer capacity'; an alternative electricity supply; 'strict' security of premises; and 'sophisticated' fire-warning and fire-fighting installations.[22]

These boasts of a secure and reliable operation provide an insight into the computer security priorities of the clearing banks in charge of BACS. How true these

---

[20] HSBC, File UK 0200-1024A, 'BACS', May 1978, p. 9.

[21] Ibid., p. 9.

[22] Ibid., p. 9.

statements were is open for debate, especially when accounting for this literature's purpose of helping to persuade businesses to use BACS' services. They do provide a rough outline of the way BACS conceptualised computer security during this period. Discussion between BACS' owner banks about proportionate protection measures had begun far earlier than the publication of the promotional brochure.

Rotating Inspections

BACS saw strong and thorough computer security as intrinsic to its success from the earliest days in its creation. Maintaining user confidence in the concept of the new system was one aspect, as was the need to provide reassurance that the hardware and software that underpinned the new service were capable of withstanding the pressure placed upon it. As opposed to eliminating all risk, which the banks seemingly realised from the outset was an unrealistic goal, they saw their task as running BACS with an acceptable level of risk involved. Realising that managing this risk would be crucial to its development, BACS developed a system in the early 1970s of carrying out inspections of itself by its shareholding banks, at first at half-yearly intervals and later annually. Different combinations of two of the banks undertook these inspections which offer an insight into just how security in BACS was managed.

Immediately visible in the inspection reports from the early 1970s and recurring as the decade progressed is how physical protection of BACS' premises was the cornerstone of its computer security. Part of the threat that the company felt it faced was that of an intruder, or multiples intruders, gaining access to its computer installation with malicious intent. Inspectors in 1973 evaluated external security and control of access to BACS' main site at Edgware Road as being of a 'high standard'.[23] To bolster this, strengthening of window locks was being undertaken and in order to 'counteract the vulnerability' posed by the roof area, a feasibility study for installing a closed circuit television network was being undertaken, with a view to monitoring approaches to the external walls of the building.[24] For BACS, security of their computer network began by trying to prevent unauthorised access to the physical premises in which key equipment was located.

Concern did exist over procedures for fire and bomb drills suggesting that the potential for a large-scale destructive attack, or accident, were seen as realistic emergency scenarios. 'The basic fire fighting equipment is sophisticated', the 1973 security report found, but there existed 'considerable gaps' in the implementation of procedures for dealing with such situations and there did not appear to be any published rules for bomb alerts.[25] Although seemingly uncertain, the report noted that

---

[23] LMA, File M32145X/1, 'Bankers' Automated Clearing Services Limited', 29 March 1973, p. 3.
[24] Ibid., p. 3.
[25] Ibid., p. 3.

'apparently' no fire or bomb drills had been undertaken since the move to Edgware.[26] Whilst acknowledging that security of the installation required 'very careful thought' to be given to such procedures, the inspectors, in this instance from Lloyds Bank and Midland Bank, stressed the need for immediate action on this issue.[27] Such statements suggest that BACS' inspectors saw one of the primary threats to the service to be destruction of its key equipment and injury, or worse, to staff. As opposed to fearing that individuals could access the system and take advantage of the speed at which it could transmit payment for personal gain or to cause disruption, apprehension was aroused by the potential for some form of catastrophic or violent attack.

The inspectors went on to discuss contingency measures in case this destructive eventuality arose, emphasising just how much of a reality BACS' operators felt this project to be. 'The lack of off-site back up facilities', said the 1973 inspection report, 'should receive careful consideration in case there is a complete catastrophe at the Centre.'[28] It was recommended that a comprehensive backup lodged in a remote security area should include source program libraries, systems documentation, including both existing systems and those under development, and programme documentation, including operations instructions, all updated at 'frequent intervals.'[29] Creating such a facility would mean that if an emergency situation arose at the BACS site in Edgware then the company would be more readily able to deal with and recover from such an incident. Already BACS' thinking was framed by the idea of resilience rather than total prevention of any form of incident.

Operations Security

BACS also devoted its energy to ensuring that its operating procedures were designed to minimise the risk of prohibited activity. One example of this was the testing of a new method being developed for receiving magnetic tapes at the Edgware premises. This new system would use a Visual Display Unit (VDU) and while the system was under test an agreement had been made by the management of BACS for 'hands-on testing', meaning direct intervention by the programmer at the terminal.[30] In the 1973 inspection it was noted that such a situation was not normally permitted but that inspectors had been assured the tests would take place 'under strict control' and only when there was no 'live work' being processed.[31] BACS'

---

[26] Ibid., p. 3.

[27] Ibid., p. 3.

[28] LMA File, M32145X/1, 'Bankers' Automated Clearing Services Limited', 29 March 1973, p. 2.

[29] Ibid., p. 9.

[30] Ibid., p. 4.

[31] Ibid., p. 4.

inspectors felt that this direct access left the system's software vulnerable to unpermitted alterations.

Manipulation or alteration of software was also seen as a key risk when changes were made during live running of the system. It was noted that there were no documented procedures for 'the verification of amendments made' to programmes in an emergency during live running; and, in order to overcome this 'serious shortcoming in the area of data security', it was recommended that an Incident Report should be created and disseminated each time an amendment was made, detailing the corrective action taken.[32] On the following day, this report, along with the Console Log, logging user activities on a terminal, and the Compilation Listing, explaining how the computer had processed the software and helping to identify what went wrong, of the amended program was to be passed to the Systems & Programming Liaison and Co-ordination Controller, who would enter details of the occurrence into a log book and quote the Incident Report number, briefly describing the failure and the action taken.[33]

The Co-ordination Controller would then investigate the action taken to rectify the fault, examining the Console Log and the patches inserted into the program to 'ascertain whether the action taken was correct, whether it had the desired effect' and whether any subsequent action was required.[34] The log book was then to be initialled to indicate that the corrective action had been checked and found satisfactory and this evidence was to be retained.[35] The Inspection team noted that it was a 'matter of concern' that this problem area still proved unsatisfactory in 1973 despite numerous attempts on their behalf to lobby BACS to take action.[36] Given the likely difference in technical understanding between those making the programme alterations and those with bureaucratic oversight, keeping track of changes being made was key to maintaining an understanding of the computer system. Access to the computers and their software in this way, combined with the ability to manipulate it, put the individual in charge of making amendments in a powerful position whilst simultaneously putting BACS in a vulnerable one. Control and oversight in this area would be crucial to allaying the company's fears of manipulation of its service.

BACS' operational security was further discussed in the 1973 inspection, this time focussing on storage of data, often using magnetic tape. Only files containing the non-confidential data of BACS' users were stored at the 'City Tape Reception Centre' as it was not considered 'entirely secure'.[37] Although it was hoped that a 'satisfactory solution' would be found in the near future, the inspectors requested that 'various other files of customer confidential information and microfilm' should

---

[32] Ibid., p. 8.

[33] LMA File, M32145X/1, 'Bankers' Automated Clearing Services Limited', 29 March 1973, pp. 8–9.

[34] Ibid., pp. 8–9.

[35] Ibid., pp. 8–9.

[36] Ibid., pp. 8–9.

[37] Ibid., p. 4.

be stored off-site 'as a matter of urgency.'[38] Confidentiality of user information, historically crucial to the trust relationship between banker and customer, now had to be dealt with in a system based on technology rather than simply human interaction. Priority was given to the issue, as any breach of this confidentiality could ultimately lead in the breakdown of trust and the disintegration of relationship between BACS' ownership and its users.

Neither were the inspectors satisfied with the security of the arrangements for transporting magnetic tapes containing confidential data between the City and Edgware. Causing concern was the way in which the driver or messenger would load the tapes into his van alone, leaving the van unattended and loaded, albeit locked, during this process.[39] Transferring these physical data stores, in the opinion of the inspectors, was not being treated with as much respect as required in terms of security, given the potential for confidential data to be lost or taken and the resulting reputational damage that could ensue.

A potential solution to mitigate the risk involved in the handling of these tapes soon emerged. Customer banks delivered both original and duplicate tapes to BACS' City Centre and it was suggested in 1974 that both sets subsequently be transferred at different times to the Edgware branch in separate vans in order to manage the risk of both sets of tapes being damaged or stolen. This was not ultimately introduced, however, and it was recognised that a risk, 'albeit remote', still existed in this process.[40] Back-up copies of tapes were, from 1975, held at Bow Bells House in the City of London.[41] BACS' goal here was pragmatic: the aim was not to eliminate entirely any risk involved but to reduce it to a level acceptable for all parties.

A system was also introduced to minimise the risk of fraudulent tape inputs. To ensure the authenticity of the transaction data held on the magnetic tapes delivered to it, in 1974 BACS piloted and then rolled out to all new users a system of 'User Input Cards', whereby the customer submitted with each tape a punched and laminated card which could be read by the badge reader incorporated within the Visual Display Units installed at the Tape Reception areas to manage incoming media.[42] BACS would accept no tape without a pre-issued identity card, provided to users and computer bureaux through their sponsoring clearing banks.[43] Each card assigned to a user or computer bureau was identifiable to its owner through a unique number, printed on the card in both clear and coded form.[44] Each card was then checked

---

[38] Ibid., p. 4.

[39] Ibid., pp. 4–5.

[40] LMA, File M32145X/3, 'Inspection undertaken by representatives of National Westminster Bank Limited and Williams and Glyn's Bank Limited', 3 October 1975, p. 8.

[41] Ibid., pp. 7–8.

[42] Ibid., p. 7.

[43] BoE, File 7A386/4, 'Electronic Fund Transfer Systems', 30 January 1979.

[44] Ibid.

against information recorded on the magnetic tape it accompanied.[45] False payment instructions could lead to incorrect calculations being made and banks ultimately transferring incorrect sums of money to each other in the settlement process. Whilst rectifiable, BACS recognised that such an occurrence could be detrimental to its reputation and ultimately the trust that customers held in the system, and them, therefore acting to decrease the likelihood of this eventuality arising.

Access Control

Unauthorised access to information was also a problem *within* the BACS building at Edgware. Given the leasing out of excess computer time to organisations like the Department of Environment and the BBC, non-BACS personnel could enter the computer complex and in theory access confidential information given that the librarian was found to have left the Internal Tape Library unoccupied at certain moments.[46] An electronic security system known as MASTIFF was investigated, which didn't physically prevent access but provided warning of unauthorised access to certain areas, and could therefore limit access to the Microfilm and magnetic tape libraries by holding individuals in a "lobby", greatly enhancing security.[47] As an interim measure it was suggested that the outside door handles of the Microfilm storage room be removed, permitting entrance only via another controlled space.[48] Although noted that a security risk would persist should no solution be found, construction costs of MASTIFF were seen as prohibitively high and so further investigations were made into the feasibility of the project without the "lobby".[49] Investment in security at BACS had to be proportionate to the risk that was being managed and so the trade-off between cost and protection in this case resulted in the idea being dismissed.

Methods were also evaluated for recording access to computers and the programmes running on them to increase the likelihood of quickly spotting attempted fraud. In 1973, urgent consideration was recommended in regards to the Console Log held in systems, the log of all use and access, to check for 'fraudulent input' and 'misuse of computer facilities'.[50] An examination or check was proposed but given the 'various methods of discrediting the integrity of the print-out' referred to, other methods of improving the security in this 'vital area' were to be explored.[51]

---

[45] Ibid.

[46] LMA, File M32145X/1, 'Bankers' Automated Clearing Services Limited', 29 March 1973, p. 2.

[47] LMA, File M32145X/1, 'Bankers' Automated Clearing Services Limited', 29 March 1973, p. 6.

[48] Ibid., p. 6.

[49] LMA, File M32145X/2, 'Bankers' Automated Clearing Services Limited: Inspection Security Review', 2 August 1974, p. 7.

[50] LMA. File M32145X/1, 'Bankers' Automated Clearing Services Limited', 29 March 1973, p. 6.

[51] Ibid., pp. 6–7.

Given the relative speed with which computers were able to process information in BACS, the company saw it as vital that activity was recorded in order to be able to have some level of oversight, albeit after the event.

1974: Progress?

Security was such a concern for the Committee of London Clearing Bankers (CLCB), the clearing banks' representative body, that it felt its own security committee should have some link to BACS' Board on relevant issues. The CLCB's Security Sub-committee wrote in July 1973 that while it appreciated the position of the Board of BACS in relation to the shareholding Banks, the Members of the Security Committee nevertheless felt that they could not entirely relinquish there responsibilities regarding 'two specific matters: the security of the building and the periodical inspection report.' They Committee also 'wished to feel free to take up with BACS any other matters of security' as and when they arose.[52] It was therefore agreed that before replying to the Chairman of BACS, the Committee should report its views to the Chief Executive Officers. Security was evolving into an issue to be discussed at board level and therefore assumed importance relative to other traditional business issues such as financial results.

Perhaps the CLCB's concerns were justified, as the story of 1973/74 for BACS' computer security was one of inaction, without major tangible progress despite language which suggested the eminence of security as a concern for the company.

Some advancement was made by 1974 on fire and bomb drills and procedures, with notices regarding action to be taken in such circumstances displayed within the centre and new staff being given training on emergency breathing equipment.[53] Measures had been developed for dealing with suspicious letters and packages and the inspectors were satisfied that this process was now at 'an acceptable standard'.[54] The potential disruption to the computer service in the event of a destructive attack could be considerable and BACS seemingly felt it was important to be thoroughly prepared in this area of security, as a large interruption in the service at this relatively early point in its existence could be fatal.

However, progress on the external security of BACS' premises remained stagnant between 1973 and 1974. The roof as a vulnerability and closed circuit television (CCTV) as a solution were both still acknowledged, but no decision had yet been made regarding installation.[55] There was a sense that CCTV could be a favourable system of protection especially since it had been enhanced to give an audible

---

[52] LMA, File MS32041/6, 'Security-BACS Ltd', p. 4.

[53] LMA, File, M32145X/2, 'Bankers' Automated Clearing Services Limited: Inspection Security Review', 2 August 1974, p. 4.

[54] Ibid., p. 4.

[55] Ibid., p. 5.

warning if there was movement on the monitor screens, negating the need for keeping a continual watch on screens.[56] Some small measure of 'indirect protection' for the vulnerable roof area came from Post Office Security Guards of a nearby area patrolling the vicinity.[57] Despite the importance placed on this issue by the inspectors, actions had not yet been taken to prove it.

Similar inaction blighted the effort to find a suitable contingency centre to operate in the case of disaster at Edgware. The 1974 inspection report stated that investigations had been made into the 'different solutions' available to the company in the event of a catastrophe with regards to standby facilities, and the suggested solution was a second computer centre, a proposal for which had been submitted to the Chief Executive Officers' Committee of the Committee of London Clearing Bankers.[58] Were this to be rejected, the report said that other alternatives would be reappraised, but the inspectors would not countenance any solution that suggested a return to paper-based operations in which paper documents needed to be printed and handled by the banks for their clearing operations.[59] Contingency plans were at the forefront of the banks' minds, but again it seemed that the cost involved had to be balanced against the level of risk and therefore the benefit involved of having a remote back-up computer centre, in this case delaying the decision-making progress.

Little progress had been made on remote storage of back-up files since the previous inspection report. BACS told the inspectors that 'efforts to store the confidential files at a Bank Computer Centre' had 'not proved successful and the commercial data storage centres were not at convenient sites.'[60]

Confidentiality of information, however, remained a constant worry for BACS. In the 1974 inspection report a reference was made to BACS having drawn up a more comprehensive contract with their legal advisers for parties who wished to purchase excess computer processing time from the banks, in particular to cover 'the confidentiality of information' and reserving the right to refuse admittance.[61] Also outlined were plans for the development of 'interrogation programs' into the computer system in 1974 as well as a program for examining the console log of machines' activities, with the view to establishing formal processes for internal audit.[62] Whilst it extended great energy on managing the security of the premises against intruders, BACS was also pushing for greater control over access for those with legitimate reasons to be within the building. Through a combination of technical and physical security it could monitor access to and usage of its computers, providing it with an opportunity to spot those using them illegitimately.

---

[56] Ibid., p. 5.

[57] Ibid., p. 5.

[58] LMA, File M32145X/2, 'Bankers' Automated Clearing Services Limited: Inspection Security Review', 2 August 1974, p. 4.

[59] Ibid., p. 4.

[60] Ibid., p. 6.

[61] Ibid., p. 4.

[62] Ibid., p. 2.

Contingency Centre

Described as the 'Achilles heel of the operation' by 1975, it was noted that should BACS' computers become inoperable, then due to a lack of a dedicated standby site – because of the prohibitive cost of a mainframe computer installation purely for standby purposes – the banks would simply be 'thrown back on to whatever alternative arrangements they themselves could make,' as no alternative processing power was available.[63] Standby processing capacity did exist at the Edgware premises but the 'growth of peak volume' in BACS' operations was eroding its usefulness.[64] It was thought that a 'satisfactory solution' was unlikely to be found in the short term.[65] Anxiety over the lack of adequate standby facilities for BACS was growing as time progressed, yet still no acceptable resolution was found.

BACS knew that continued expansion only intensified the need for a remote back-up site. 'We strongly emphasise the lack of contingency arrangements and suggest the various alternatives continue to be explored until a satisfactory solution is found', the 1975 inspectors stressed, 'particularly in view of the steady increase in the number of Users and the possible extensions of the Company's field of operations.'[66] Given how quickly BACS' reputation could be undermined by its security there existed a sense that the existing standby arrangements were insufficient.

Awareness

Regardless of the persistent unease around the lack of a standby data processing facility, the general outlook towards the security in the service was positive. In 1975 the inspection report described a 'good general level of security awareness' among BACS' employees and 'an acceptably high degree of protection' afforded by the various measures of securing the premises.[67] Physical security was seemingly well understood by those working at the site and the level of risk faced was deemed acceptable. This was partly due to the location and nature of the Edgware site, which stood on a site shared with the Post Office who themselves employed Group 4 Security Company to monitor road access to their premises during the day and patrol the sight at night, including the roads at the sides and back of the BACS premises, providing BACS with some degree of protection. The inspection recognised

---

[63] LMA, File M32145X/3, 'Inspection undertaken by representatives of National Westminster Bank Limited and Williams and Glyn's Bank Limited', 3 October 1975, p. 3.

[64] Ibid., p. 3.

[65] Ibid., p. 3.

[66] Ibid., p. 3.

[67] Ibid., p. 4.

that the roof area was 'still vulnerable to someone utterly determined to obtain access to it'. Consideration to 'external television cameras' covering the walls and roof area was considered by the company but not felt worthwhile.[68] Some level of security was afforded by convenience rather than by specific measures employed by BACS. It seems that the company was willing to utilise the protection provided by its neighbours' security functions, deeming them proportionate to the threat the building faced.

Given the provision of numerous measures for internal access to rooms and to individual computer terminals themselves, perhaps the company felt that an intruder to the premises was now less of a danger. However, further considerations about the physical security of the building were made: 'At present the only exterior door away from the security-controlled main entrance which is not alarm-protected is that giving access to the staff recreation area at the rear of the premises', the report read. The area was sealed off from the remainder of the BACS complex, except for an 'alarmed fire exit into the area from a first floor corridor adjacent to the Chairman's suite'. During parts of the day, the external door to the recreation area was found to be unlocked, potentially allowing 'unauthorised persons to obtain entry', although they would not be able to access other parts of the building. Providing securable ground floor access to the recreation area from the main part of the building was a consideration, as was providing 'alarm cover for the outer door' which would only then be opened in the event of social functions held in the recreation area to which visitors were invited. In those instances, it was thought that the internal door would be secure while the outer doors were off the alarm system.[69]

The inspectors concurred that it would seem beneficial to alarm-protect this door in line with existing arrangements for the rest of the building.[70] Relatively straightforward measures, unrelated to computer technology itself and actually more traditional general security solutions were contributing to the security of BACS' computer-based service. With no contingency site in the case of a complete system failure, protecting its premises from anyone with destructive intentions assumed a high degree of importance.

Access Controlled?

Since the service's inception, close attention had been paid to ensuring that only authorised individuals could use computers linked to the BACS installation within its Edgware premises. These measures, however, were not entirely infallible.

---

[68] LMA, File M32145X/3, 'Inspection undertaken by representatives of National Westminster Bank Limited and Williams and Glyn's Bank Limited', 3 October 1975, p. 4.

[69] Ibid., p. 4.

[70] Ibid., p. 4.

Internal security came, for employees, in the form of wearing Polaroid Identity Cards with different coloured backgrounds denoting the various sections of the staff, though this was not wholly effective unless everyone displayed their card while on duty.[71] Different background colours indicated who was permitted to enter the operational and control areas of the centre.[72] Management of entry to the computer complex at BACS provides an example of computer centre access control measures. A standard key card was required to access the computer complex, but although tape libraries were marked with signs stating 'No admittance to unauthorised staff', there was no physical barrier, with protection being obtained by 'unofficial querying' of staff who weren't recognisable. The tape library was also 'occasionally left unattended' and as non-BACS staff were authorised to enter the computer complex when computer time was sold to others for use, the 1975 security report recommended that access controls were introduced to the library and 'other discreet areas.' Following a previous inspection an electronic system known as MASTIFF was being investigated for such a purposes, but the constructions costs of the full system, which 'held unauthorised personnel in a lobby', were prohibitively high. 'Security risk will remain' for as long as there is no method of 'prevention/warning of access to the library ... and other areas with the computer complex', although a few alterations could be made to accommodate the disk library where access would only be permitted via the control room area.[73]

The physical storage used by computers meant that solutions for managing the security of new systems had to include both physical measures alongside the technical. Managing people and spaces was a core tenet of computer security for BACS in the mid-1970s.

Technical means for managing the risk of computer usage were also employed to some degree. For computer users at BACS' Edgware site, an International Computers Limited (ICL) software package was introduced in 1975, initially on a test basis, to automatically log all commands fed into a console and analyse the contents of the file at a later date through a separate programme.[74] Although helpful, it contained weaknesses such as not having sequence numbers for commands and messages that could highlight anomalous entries.[75] Nevertheless, it offered a level of accountability and oversight and showed that BACS' owners were aware of the potential threats they faced.

---

[71] LMA, File M32145X/3, 'Inspection undertaken by representatives of National Westminster Bank Limited and Williams and Glyn's Bank Limited', 3 October 1975, p. 4.

[72] Ibid., p. 4.

[73] Ibid., p. 7.

[74] Ibid., p. 5.

[75] Ibid., p. 5.

Growth & Security

By the middle of the 1970s BACS' understanding and management of its security had evolved to account for the increased popularity and success of the service. BACS' user base had grown and continued to do so, primarily through the addition of non-bank users: in 1976, for example, BACS' fifth year of operation, it processed 261 million items and made a gross profit of £994,000 compared to 198.6 million items and £318,000 in 1973.[76] Accompanying this was an increasingly professionalised operation and greater integration into the UK'S financial sector.

BACS' contingency arrangements caused particular consternation in this light. The 1977 inspection report outlined the worries in no uncertain terms: 'It is not impossible that a major disaster could render the Edgware Centre unusable for a considerable period of time. In this event the onus would be on the users to provide whatever facilities they could to cope with the items presently processed by BACS.' Despite such a stark warning, it was understood that 'no arrangements whatsoever' had been made to deal with such a situation. This state of affairs was regularly highlights in the annual inspection report and was considered at length by the Board of the Company. Nevertheless, by 1977 'no acceptable solution' had been formulated. 'Lack of provision of this most basic level of contingency arrangement is considered to be the most significant weakness in the present BACS operations,' the report concluded.[77]

Six years on from its launch and still BACS had found no adequate solution to this vulnerability. Further, the Committee of London Clearing Bankers (CLCB) in 1974 had encouraged BACS' customers to write programs that could enable them to produce vouchers, or paper equivalents, in case of an emergency, but it was understood that this had 'by and large' not occurred and so the majority of customer users of BACS would also be 'thrown into a state of complete chaos' if an emergency situation occurred.[78] If BACS were to be disrupted or rendered entirely inoperable then it was vulnerable to potential loss of business given the level of disruption that could ensue in the underprepared banks.

In the 1977 report's recommendations, the contingency issue was reiterated, and the inspectors stressed the need to try and comprehend the potential impact of a disaster scenario, perhaps to make the banks realise explicitly what a worst-case scenario could look like. 'Procedures do not presently exist for coping with the extreme disruptive problems which would arise in the event of the prolonged unavailability of the processing facilities housed within the Edgware Computing

---

[76] LMA, File M32145X/4, 'Inspection Undertaken by Representatives of Williams & Glyn's Bank Limited and Barclays Bank Limited', 22 April 1977, p. 2 and Barclays, File 0300-0957, 'Bankers Automated Clearing Services Limited: Report & Accounts 1977', 17 January 1978, pp. 4–7.

[77] LMA, File M32145X/4, 'Inspection Undertaken by Representatives of Williams & Glyn's Bank Limited and Barclays Bank Limited', 22 April 1977, p. 9.

[78] LMA, File M32145X/4, 'Inspection Undertaken by Representatives of Williams & Glyn's Bank Limited and Barclays Bank Limited', 22 April 1977, p. 9.

Centre,' the report said. It provided a strong recommendation that the effects of such a situation should be considered and 'adequate contingency arrangements be provided and documented.'[79] The contingency centre issue had maintained its place as the prime security-related concern for BACS and the threat of destruction, or attempted sabotage of the main computer installation, was still deemed to be realistic. With customer banks seemingly heavily reliant upon the service and with little in the way of contingency in its absence, BACS, willingly or not, accepted much of the burden of danger. Whilst the company had some appetite for risk where the cost of mitigation was deemed excessive, their appetite was limited, though their actions, or inaction, in this area did not necessarily make that apparent.

Through the Roof?

Greater granularity on physical security measures and access control to BACS premises were included in the security reports towards the late 1970s. For example, recommendations for reducing the vulnerability of external air vents and night-time security and supervision were included.[80] It was deemed that the 'surrounding geography' of the site was such that it would 'not be difficult' to gain access to the rear of the centre via an adjacent housing estate.[81] Reference was also made to how easily an intruder, once they gained access to the site, could easily find their way onto the roof, 'without doubt the most vulnerable aspect of the centre.'[82] Investigations were being made into a 'microwave detection' system for use along the sides and rear of the centre so that an effective monitoring and detection system could be implemented.[83] BACS was keen to ensure that its first line of defence, access to its site, was both effective in its direct use but also acted as a disincentive to those with malicious intentions.

Security within the centre also remained important. Intruder access to sensitive areas within the premises was seen by BACS as a serious concern that had to be mitigated. It was identified that the keys to the 'bulk eraser' and two 'Kybe tape cleaners' were freely available to the library staff, making it possible that a 'disgruntled' library employee could erase data from tapes without authorisation.[84] While this may not have had as significant an impact as fraudulently entered transactions, this offered the potential for severe disruption and delay in the service.

---

[79] Ibid., p. 5.

[80] Ibid, p. 13.

[81] Ibid., p. 12.

[82] Ibid., p. 12.

[83] LMA, File M32145X/4, 'Inspection Undertaken by Representatives of Williams & Glyn's Bank Limited and Barclays Bank Limited', 22 April 1977, p. 12.

[84] Ibid, p. 22.

Having seemingly become dissatisfied with the system of identity cards for employees and visitors to the centre, BACS devoted resources to upgrading this measure. The 1977 inspection report described a recently implemented new security system for identity management in BACS' main building for staff and guests, providing a 'much enhanced level of restricted and controlled access to the centre'.[85] It was accepted that the new system was in an 'embryonic stage' and would require operational modifications as time passed.[86] It was also noted that several members of staff were not found to be wearing their identity cards at all times.[87]

Particularly pressing for BACS was the protection of its main Computer Hall, housing the core hardware that powered the system. Controlling access to this area was thought crucial although the company spotted potential flaws in its own procedures for entry. Access to the Computer Hall could be gained by using a magnetic key card at any of the entrances. Visitors or staff who did not hold key cards were required to enter via Air-Lock doors adjacent to the Reception Area. Entry through the first set of doors was remotely controlled from within the Air-Lock by a member of staff situated there for that purpose when a bell was sounded by the visitor from outside this first set of doors. Somebody who had gained unauthorised access to the centre via reception could 'easily and quickly gain access to the Air-Lock, and subsequently the Computer Hall.'[88] BACS did not attempt to achieve the highest possible level of security, attempting to eliminate the risk of any kind of attack, but focused its energies on decreasing the likelihood of what it saw to be the most probable means of attack or disruption. An intruder, once inside the Computer Hall, had the potential either to commit fraud or disruption by using the system itself or to sabotage the service's software or hardware.

Controlling access to these sensitive areas formed a significant part of BACS' strategy for minimising the security risks its computer installation faced. If flaws in these access procedures could be exploited, the system and therefore the company were vulnerable.

Assuming Greater Importance

Recognition of BACS' growing role in the UK financial sector was forthcoming in the 1978 inspection report. In the previous year BACS had processed 296 million items at a gross profit of £1,218,000, an increase from 261 million and £994,000 respectively from 1976.[89] The number of users had also grown, reaching 2812 in

---

[85] Ibid., p. 4.

[86] Ibid., p. 4.

[87] Ibid., p. 10.

[88] Ibid., p. 12.

[89] LMA, File M32145X/5, 'Bankers' Automated Clearing Services Limited: Inspection Report 1978', 7 November 1978, p. 3.

1977, more than three times as many as the 936 users of the system only four years earlier.[90]

Whilst the 1978 report surmised that the system was run in a 'satisfactory and professional manner' the report also acknowledged that from an audit perspective there were numerous problems that needed to be addressed, 'particularly in light of the increasing importance of the operation.'[91] Alongside BACS' growth, the actual computer premises itself had assumed greater significance since the UK concentrators of SWIFT, the hardware controlling the onward transmission of that system's payment instructions, had become operational at Edgware in the course of 1977/78.[92]

Physical protection of the premises at Edgware therefore maintained and even grew in importance from BACS' perspective. Despite this, the 1978 inspection noted how security appeared stronger than it was: on 'first impression', the general facilities for physical security at BACS 'are good, but unfortunately there are a number of loop-holes that, if breached, would not prevent nor detect unauthorised entrance.' Numerous 'good' features existed in the building's security, but 'the increasing importance of the building and its contents', in the report's view, demanded a further evaluation of all aspects of the building's security. The inspector's noted how it was 'particularly pleasing, however, that regular night security visits were made by various members of management which clearly demonstrates the concern that line management has for the installation.[93] Specifically, there was concern that only the ground floor windows had been fitted with anti-bandit glass while the first floor windows remained vulnerable, and the accessibility of the roof persisted as a concern.[94] The threat from either lone or multiple intruders was at the forefront of the minds of BACS' security staff.

Potential weaknesses also remained in the security procedures inside the Edgware building itself. In 1978 it was noted that the security of entrances to the Computer Room at Edgware Road was 'inconsistent' and that the inability of the guard to monitor both key-card doors made undetected access to the Room 'very easy'.[95] During the day a security guard monitored access through the main entrance and during the evening and night this entrance was unmanned.[96] There were also two entrances to the computer room that were unmanned but covered by CCTV during the day, monitored from the main entrance.[97] These measures reduced the level of risk that an intruder posed, but not to a level at which BACS' owner banks felt comfortable.

---

[90] Ibid., p. 3.

[91] Ibid., p. 1.

[92] Ibid., p. 3.

[93] Ibid., p. 5.

[94] LMA, File M32145X/5, 'Bankers' Automated Clearing Services Limited: Inspection Report 1978', 7 November 1978, p. 10.

[95] Ibid., p. 10.

[96] Ibid., p. 10.

[97] Ibid., p. 10.

Technicality & Security

Featuring heavily in BACS inspection reports in the late 1970s were computer-based security and contingency measures. For example, it was established that all BACS' software was not adequately backed up at the remote security store and also that it was 'difficult to assess the extent to which unauthorised access to live data files can be made'.[98] Any emergency amendments that programmers made to ICL software still appeared not to be subjected to any formalised checking procedure.[99] Similarly there was no procedure to ensure the new version of an amended program that had been tested by the System Department was the one actually passed on to the Operations team for implementation; neither were test logs maintained by system analysts or programmers.[100] Also, the inspectors noted that untrained Operators were allowed to operate the computer systems unsupervised on occasions.[101] Again present here was concern that those with the technical know-how could manipulate their access privileges and alter the system, without even needing to obfuscate their actions given the apparent lack of oversight.

The increasingly technical nature of the BACS security reports fostered concern over the rotational basis on which member Banks carried out the review. It had been the pattern that representatives from two banks would undertake each annual review – for example, Barclays Bank Limited and Williams & Glyn's Bank Limited in 1977, Barclays Bank Limited and Coutts & Co in 1978. The internal audit function of BACS said that not all member banks had adequate knowledge of ICL hardware or software, or details of the programs, and highlighted the differing opinions and expertise of various inspection teams that led to poor progression in anything but the fundamental issues.[102] The audit team proposed that it should be they who inherit the review of all aspects of BACS' operation.

Accordingly in early 1979 a Systems Audit Section was set up comprising three auditors and a senior member of one of the shareholding bank's Inspection Departments.[103] A key area of its responsibilities was the existing Electronic Funds Transfer services, namely the BACS service, and it would be responsible for linking a rotating auditing programme with the ongoing annual inspection programme.[104] It was also tasked with the 'progressing to implementation' of accepted changes arising from the annual internal inspection and participation in and audit clearance of any new systems.[105] BACS was taking a long-term approach to security, creating its

---

[98] Ibid., p. 15.

[99] Ibid, p. 17.

[100] Ibid., pp. 17–18.

[101] Ibid., p. 12.

[102] Ibid., p. 20.

[103] Barclays, File 0080-2165, 'BACS Annual Report – Financial Year 1979', 2 January 1980, p. 9.

[104] Ibid., p. 9.

[105] Ibid., p. 9.

own oversight function to ensure that in any future developments, procedures would be put in place from the outset to manage its usage.

Investment in Security

While the inspection reports continued the perennial issue of contingency planning persisted. 'The situation in respect of a major disaster, rendering the Centre inoperable for a lengthy period, remains critical', the 1978 report said, noting that it was 'imperative' that suitable contingency plans were drawn up to cope with such a situation.[106] Barclays' employees noted in a report to their board in 1978 that BACS' board was 'continuing to develop plans for contingency arrangements' which was becoming increasingly necessary as more work was becoming concentrated at Edgware.[107] A change in tone in the language can be seen, greater urgency being placed on finding a solution. Such an escalation in concern was perhaps part of a deliberate attempt to persuade the company of the case for a significant financial investment in a remote back-up site.

If the increasingly concerned language was a concerted attempt to reach a solution on a contingency centre, then it should be deemed a success. Come 1980 and BACS had finally managed to solve one of their longest standing security issues.

Opened at Acton, West London, BACS finally had provision for a remote centre in case its primary Edgware site was victim of a destructive attack. Almost immediately BACS concluded that this centre's physical security should be protected equally as well as the main installation in case of a simultaneous attack.[108] In its annual report BACS specifically referred to the 'growing scale of customer dependence on electronic funds transfer' and therefore the need for a contingency processing centre.[109]

At the time of the 1980 inspection the Acton site had 18 months left on its lease, in which time BACS' 'advanced plans' for establishing another contingency centre based at Dunstable were planned to come to fruition, the hope being that the Dunstable site would become operational once the Acton lease had expired.[110] The permanent back-up centre at Dunstable would be installed on the ground floor of a newly-built, 42,000 square foot industrial warehouse in Bedfordshire, on the Woodside Industrial Estate.[111] Earlier that year it had been estimated that the

---

[106] LMA, File M32145X/5, 'Bankers' Automated Clearing Services Limited: Inspection Report 1978', 7 November 1978, p. 5.

[107] Barclays, File 0300-0957, 'Report to Board on BACS', 15 February 1978, p. 5.

[108] LMA, File M32145X/6, 'Bankers Automated Clearing Services Limited: Inspection Undertaken by Representatives of Coutts & Co and Lloyds Bank Ltd', 19 November 1980, p. 4.

[109] Barclays, File 0080-2165, 'Annual Report – Financial Year 1979', 2 January 1980, p. 2.

[110] LMA, File M32145X/6, 'Bankers Automated Clearing Services Limited: Inspection Undertaken by Representatives of Coutts & Co and Lloyds Bank Ltd', 19 November 1980, p. 32.

[111] Barclays, File 0080-2165, 'Contingency Plan – BACS', 19 September 1980, pp. 1–2.

conversion of the premises would cost between £3.5 million and £4 million, representing a substantial investment in contingency for the long-term.[112] An updated figure of £5 million for the renovation was estimated in 1980 and noting that a 45-year lease had been taken on the new warehouse, BACS explained how the Dunstable site would initially provide a contingency service but in the longer term become a second operational centre for dealing with the growth in the volumes of business processed by the company.[113]

For this reason it was 'not realistic to suppose that any large sum of money' should be spent on improving security at Acton, despite, for example, there being no back-up power supply at the site and there being some deficiencies in its physical security.[114] This was a significant step forward for BACS, however, which had been concerned over a period of years about the potential for some form of destructive attack at their facilities.

Defending Two Fronts

Such an attack was still seen as a realistic prospect by the end of the decade and mitigations were planned with this in mind. For example, perimeter defences at both the Edgware and Acton sites were described as inadequate.[115] BACS felt that its installations constituted 'prime targets for subversive organisations by the very nature of its position in the banking industry.'[116] To this end, a specialist security officer was appointed to make recommendations on such issues; however, the bank inspectors were, by 1980, still very concerned by the vulnerability of the premises to a determined intruder.[117]

Most concerning in terms of the so-called "insider threat", the potential for an authorised, internal member of staff to use the system for unintended purposes, was the almost unrestricted computer access for numerous sections of workers who were situated within the Computer Hall at Edgware Road. Staff working within Computer Operations, Disk and Tape Library, Data Preparation and the Society for Worldwide Interbank Financial Telecommunication (SWIFT) all had access to the equipment and so it was suggested that the Hall should be re-designed to tailor access to the above areas.[118] Of great concern was unauthorised access to sensitive confidential information and the potential misuse of it.

---

[112] Ibid., p. 1.

[113] Barclays File 0156-0017, 'BACS Annual Report – 1980', 20 January 1981, p. 9.

[114] LMA, File M32145X/6, 'Bankers Automated Clearing Services Limited: Inspection Undertaken by Representatives of Coutts & Co and Lloyds Bank Ltd', 19 November 1980, p. 32.

[115] Ibid., pp. 10–11.

[116] Ibid., p. 10.

[117] Ibid., p. 10.

[118] LMA, File M32145X/6, 'Bankers Automated Clearing Services Limited: Inspection Undertaken by Representatives of Coutts & Co and Lloyds Bank Ltd', 19 November 1980, p. 13.

For the first time in 1980, however, this access to information was mentioned in the context of 'on-line data transmission'. Data was sent between Scottish Banks and BACS via an on-line system and loss of privacy due to a fault was an explicit concern.[119] If an addressee bank was prevented from receiving data due to a fault then the data was to be re-routed to another bank, hence the concern over confidentiality. Specifically, BACS wanted written confirmation from the Scottish Banks that absolved them from any liability.[120] This scenario involved diversion as opposed to interception, but it had the potential to be damaging to BACS' reputation with its customer banks.

Another specific complaint was one recognisable in contemporary computer security: poor password protection. Passwords to the MAXIMOP system, an operating system run on the ICL mainframe computers, had not been changed since the inception of the system.[121] These passwords were also displayed on the master console.[122] Providing such easy access to 'source programs' and 'programs under test' worried the inspectors greatly.[123] Basic lack of understanding of their uses was one of the main issues.

Concluding the 1980 report, the inspectors suggested that there was 'little point' in the banks continuing to inspect BACS in the same way given the creation of a Systems Audit Department whose work they would be duplicating.[124]

The inspectors suggested a new standing committee be created instead of the rotational system currently in place, in order to utilise the benefits of continuity.[125] It was envisaged that one of the committee's first tasks would be to 'define the standards of security required at BACS.'[126] For roughly its first decade in existence, its standards had been high, even if its actions had sometimes not kept pace with its rhetoric.

Developing Trust

Behind all of BACS' thought and endeavour around computer security was one fundamental goal: to instil and maintain the trust and confidence of its users in the system. The major London clearing banks which owned BACS were acutely aware of this requirement from the outset. Growing the volumes of transfer made through

---

[119] Ibid., p. 16.

[120] Ibid., p. 16.

[121] Ibid., p. 24.

[122] Ibid., p. 24.

[123] Ibid., p. 24.

[124] Ibid., p. 36.

[125] LMA, File M32145X/6, 'Bankers Automated Clearing Services Limited: Inspection Undertaken by Representatives of Coutts & Co and Lloyds Bank Ltd', 19 November 1980, p. 36.

[126] Ibid., p. 36.

the service and increasing the number of customers required the system to appear secure and dependable.

Security for BACS became understood as an attempt to manage the level of risk. The goal was not to eliminate all potential dangers, and there was a realisation that this was impossible to achieve, but the banks involved in the ownership and inspection of BACS pragmatically sought to minimise the risk of damage or disruption to an acceptable level. The company also thought about security through the lens of resilience. Significant discussion was had around the need for a remote contingency centre should some catastrophic event occur at its primary Edgware site. Based on their assumption that they could not entirely cut out risk from their operations, the logical conclusion in their thinking was that they had to be able to recover from such an event quickly and with the minimum of disruption. It took some time to finalise investment in a back-up computer centre, but it happened nonetheless.

Achieving this acceptable level of risk was done through a mixture of physical and technical measures. It concerned access to premises, access to spaces, access to hardware and ultimately access to information. Physical protection for BACS was as crucial to their computer security as measures to monitor and control usage of computer terminals. Despite a willingness to continually evolve its security practices, particularly through inspections by its shareholder banks, measures for controlling security were proportionate. The battle between cost and the level of protection of certain methods of security certainly existed. However, as the system grew and its headquarters also began to house the hardware of other parts of financial sector infrastructure, it realised the increasing significance of its site and discussed security there accordingly.

BACS' perceived the key threat to its security to come from intruders to where its computer installation, and later its backup installation, were held. It seems that the most anxiety was provoked by the potential for some form of destructive attack which physically damaged or destroyed its hardware. The potential also existed for fraudulent input into the system which BACS seemed concerned about due to the potential disruption involved. Given the physical nature of the storage media it accepted information on, the threat was both a relatively new one in that these magnetic tapes could be processed by a powerful machine but also relatively traditional in that they could be stolen, broken or misplaced. BACS had to manage this hybrid kind of security throughout its existence.

The London clearing banks who owned and operated BACS, despite this being their first major co-ordinated attempt at automated data processing, were aware of the significance of security from the outset. The company's own assessments of its progress, success and failures in this area highlight the focus and attention paid to the issue as well as a number of specific factors including the threats which they felt they were most vulnerable to. Over the course of the 1970s, the banks had placed great energy into understanding and managing BACS' security, paving the path for the service to rapidly grow and expand. Its early success, and continuation as a core constituent of the UK's financial sector infrastructure, can at least in part be attributed to the thoughtfulness and care for security during its formative years.

Chapter 4
SWIFT: 1972–1984

'The international banking and financial community clearly has entered into a period of evolutionary change', remarked Charles Reuterskiold in early 1982.[1] Reuterskiold was the General Manager of the Society for Worldwide Interbank Financial Telecommunication, or SWIFT, which had been launched five years earlier. 'International banking and financial services, markets and structures are changing', he continued, identifying the new requirements, challenges and opportunities that this change offered the sector.[2] Writing in a publication called *The World of Banking*, Reuterskiold was musing on what the future held for both the new SWIFT network and the global financial sector. International collaboration between banks had led to tangible technological progress in financial market infrastructure but also fuelled a step-change in their ambition and vision for modernisation.

National projects had begun to arise in the previous decade and started the process of connecting financial institutions within cities, states and countries. For example, in the early 1970s, the SIBOL project was designed to link up all Swedish banks in an electronic interbank connection; the CHIPS cheque-clearing system was under development in New York; a Japanese project for a teleprocessing link between all domestic banks was ongoing; the Bank of Italy was connecting its branches via telecommunication links; 97 California banks were part of the SCOPE project for effecting payments by teleprocessing transfers instead of by cheque; and the COPE project grouped together five Atlanta banks with similar objectives to SCOPE.[3] Other industries also operated large-scale automated systems including both SITA, the airline companies' worldwide system for seat reservations, and LACES, London airport's apparatus for customs authorities, air freight companies

---

[1] Lloyds, File 10133, Charles Reuterskiold, 'S.W.I.F.T: the next 10 years', *The World of Banking*, March-April 1982, p. 6.

[2] Ibid., p. 6.

[3] BoE, File 7A386/3, 'Summary note on an international technique for effecting international payments', 23 June 1972.

© Springer Nature Switzerland AG 2022
A. Sweetman, *Cyber and the City*, History of Computing,
https://doi.org/10.1007/978-3-031-07933-7_4

and customs agents.[4] Banks and businesses in other industries were capitalising on the power of new hardware and software to transform their business operations. Computers possessed the requisite power to underpin increasingly complex operations.

SWIFT's creation was primarily driven by the desire for standardisation, so that financial institutions across the world had a common means of communication. Communicating at greater speed and with greater certainty, whilst doing so at a lower cost, were three of the benefits that SWIFT proposed to offer. Accompanying this new service were new computer security risks, such as deliberate attempts to utilise the system's benefit of rapid communication to send false payment instructions, or simply attempts to damage and break the hardware or software underpinning the service. However, a consensus emerged within SWIFT from early in its development that the benefits outweighed the vulnerabilities faced. SWIFT saw its task to be the minimisation of risk that if faced as owners, and its users faced, to a mutually acceptable level.

A reputation for well-understood and well-managed security could have a significant impact on the service's reputation, SWIFT believed, instilling trust in its operation and ultimately contributing to its future prosperity. Computer security therefore took on paramount importance in the development of SWIFT. The Society's Board gave it substantive thought, from almost half a decade prior to its launch and continuously thereafter. They oversaw the management of security as it transformed from ideas and concepts to practical reality. Far from being an afterthought or addendum, computer security was a key tenet of SWIFT's creation, one that persisted throughout the period covered here.

SWIFT's overseers broadly understood security of their system through the lens of confidentiality, integrity and availability. With potentially market-sensitive payment instructions being sent across the new service, the Board saw confidentiality of these communications as vitally important. They also needed to engender trust in the system by reassuring users that messages sent across it were unaltered during transmission and received exactly as intended. Furthermore, they felt that high levels of availability of the system would be crucial to its success, both for practical reasons but also for instilling confidence in its user base. Achieving a perfect level of security was never explicitly the aim, but SWIFT wished to make it as difficult as possible for its security to be breached. Creating disincentives and barriers significant enough to prevent would-be attackers was how SWIFT saw its job.

Security also took on a somewhat dual meaning. It was about certainty and reliability, as well as the minimising of risk. SWIFT saw plenty of deliberate threats to this, including fraudulent messages being sent or private communications being read, but there were also un-deliberate threats such as computer failure or accidental alteration of messages which could result in an equally damaging eventuality. The system in its entirety was extremely new: both the concepts involved and the

---

[4] Ibid.

technology it was dependent upon. To develop trust and confidence in SWIFT, security had to be at the forefront of both its thinking and its offer to users.

Computer and network security for SWIFT was a hybrid of both physical security and technical security. On the physical side, it was about managing access to machines linked to the network, managing the access of individuals to computer terminals and the overall security of buildings housing its most vital equipment. Also employed were numerous technical measures, including sequence numbers for instructions sent across the system, log-in procedures and cryptographic measures such as the scrambling of messages to ensure their confidentiality. Both types of security were seen by SWIFT as crucial areas to manage.

Authentication also became a core part of SWIFT's computer security thinking. Users had to be sure of the authenticity of the instructions they received, as acting on them meant the transfer of significant amounts of money. Using cryptography to ensure that communications were being legitimately made with peer banks, and by computer users with the permission to do so, was important to SWIFT establishing itself as a trusted piece of infrastructure.

Security was a core component of SWIFT's overall values. Ample, but not unlimited, financial support was provided for combating the risks it faced. SWIFT understood that it needed to be protected, but that spending had to be proportionate to achieving an acceptable level of risk rather than simply pushing to make the system as secure as possible.

As well as being a factor that required continuous oversight, security was a motivation for the system's development. Technology could both increase the security of these operations, employing some of the methods mentioned above, or, in certain circumstances, it could undermine the security of communications if the technology carrying this information was exploited.

Outlined here is the story of SWIFT's management of computer security covering the period before and during its creation to some years after its launch. Previously unexplored archival evidence allows for a snapshot of SWIFT's development of approximately a decade, from the early 1970s to the early 1980s, providing an insight into how the society defined computer security, what they saw as the main threats to this security and how they acted to manage these threats.

Motivation

Banking institutions in Britain and globally had been investing significant amounts of money in new computer and communication technology since the early 1960s as detailed in Chap. 2, but by the middle of the 1970s there had been little co-ordination above city or country level. Even within the financial sector achieving consistency in new technology-based applications was a challenge. Modernisation of operations continued apace, but planning had certainly not yet coalesced globally. Charles Reuterskiold, General Manager of SWIFT, commented on this disjointed development, noting that in the 1960s, the expansion of international banking operations generated an expansion of private bank communications networks. 'By the end of that decade, there were many different private bank networks with each using formats, media and data processing procedures specific to each bank's requirements', meaning that networks were 'rarely compatible with each other, and in no case were they interactive, one system with another.' Private "intra-bank" networks began the process 'and they made – and still make – substantial contributions to increasing the speed and quality of banking and financial services' both nationally and internationally, in Reuterskiold's view.[5] Lack of co-ordination between banking institutions up to this point meant that the advantages of automation had not diffused in a uniform manner across the international financial system. Compounding this was a lack of standardisation across the sector, each bank using their own choices of data processing software, hardware and techniques.

Reuterskiold expanded on how this acted as a prompt to the international financial sector for increasingly joined-up thinking. The great majority of international banking operations typically involved two, three or more different banks in the execution of a transaction. 'Private bank networks, although international in scope, could only bring the benefits of automated handling to that portion of the total transaction chain involving the bank operating the private network,' in Reuterskiold's view. As the volume and complexity of international banking transactions continued to grow throughout the 1960s, a small group of European and North American banks began seeking ways to 'rationalise and automate' interbank transaction processing and transmission in order to 'cope with the ever-rising volume' of international business.[6]

The result of the European and American banks' thinking was SWIFT. No more thoroughly was the SWIFT concept explained than by Reuterskiold himself: 'S.W.I.F.T. is a non-profit, co-operative society owned by members and shareholding banks that use the Society's services. It links member banks around the world through a specially-designed data processing and transmission network.' The Society owned and operated data processing facilities connected to international data communication lines leased from national or commercial communications carriers, and its purpose was – and remains – to provide automated international transaction processing and transmission services among and between member banks.[7]

By 1971 a group of 68 banks in ten European countries and the United States were working together to examine the feasibility of an international message switching system. Initially called the 'Message Switching Project (MSP)', it was later renamed SWIFT, and would be launched some six years later.[8] Ambition existed in abundance, the task of SWIFT's planners being to turn this concept into reality.

---

[5] Lloyds, File 10133, Charles Reuterskiold, 'S.W.I.F.T: the next 10 years', *The World of Banking*, March-April 1982, p. 7.

[6] Lloyds, File 10133, Charles Reuterskiold, 'S.W.I.F.T: the next 10 years', *The World of Banking*, March-April 1982, p. 7.

[7] Ibid., p. 6.

[8] Barclays, File 0080-4134, 'Society for Worldwide Interbank Financial Telecommunications', June 1975, pp. 1–2.

SWIFT: Case Study in International Collaboration

In 1977 the Society for Worldwide Interbank Financial Telecommunication (SWIFT) became fully operational. With an initial membership of 518 commercial banks across 22 countries in Europe and North America, the members had created a 'shared worldwide data processing and communications link and a common language for international financial transactions.'[9]

SWIFT was set to speed up international transfers considerably. Payment instructions would be sent from commercial banks to a central national concentrator or "switching centre" in each country by leased or Public Switched Network lines at high speed and from there to an international concentrator.[10] Here, instructions were sorted and passed to the concentrator in the country of destination, then onto the recipient bank.[11] Prior to this, payment instructions had primarily been sent by mail (80%) and Telex (20%).[12] This new system brought the international financial services market into closer accord by allowing rapid communication between banks globally. Like the development of Bankers' Automated Clearing Services (BACS) in the UK the subject of Chap. 3, the advantages offered by SWIFT meant that banks who signed up to the service became dependent upon it relatively quickly.

Security, as well as being a risk that had to be managed in the new SWIFT system, was also partly motivation for its creation. In a speech given at Barclays Bank International's Computer Conference in June 1975 by computer project managers from Barclays in the UK, security was explicitly cited as a key driver for the project alongside three other perceived advantages: greater speed compared to international mail; cheaper costs than the charges involved with using the telex network; and standardisation of message formats meaning the eventual possibility of greater automation of different types of transactions.[13] 'The majority of messages will be sent over private lines', the speech announced, meaning 'much greater security than the present network', especially when combined with data security techniques to ensure the message hadn't been altered during transfer, which were not possible with the telex network.[14] New technology could therefore be used to ensure that the integrity of messages sent over the network was intact. This was important when sending instructions for the payment of substantial sums of money across a wide geographical area.

---

[9] SWIFT, 'SWIFT History', https://www.swift.com/about_swift/company_information/swift_history# [Accessed 10 December 2015].

[10] BoE, File 7A386/3, 'Summary note on an international technique for effecting international payments', 23 June 1972; HSBC, 'Computer Services Division: SWIFT Project', January 1977.

[11] Ibid.

[12] HSBC, 'Computer Services Division: SWIFT Project', January 1977.

[13] Barclays, File 0080-4134, 'Society for Worldwide Interbank Financial Telecommunications', June 1975, p. 1.

[14] Ibid., p. 1.

From the outset, the banks involved in SWIFT recognised the importance of security and its role in engendering trust in the new service. Seven key requirements were set out at its creation, three of these being the need to make it continuously available, reliable and secure, highlighting an understanding of the need for certainty of performance for future success.[15] SWIFT described the need to offer 'an exceptionally high standard of security in keeping with the value of the transactions' that the system would process and transmit.[16] The prior experiences of the banks involved, with various measures of automation in their own countries, seemingly contributed to the understanding that being secure would be vital were SWIFT to fulfil its potential. For the banks to fully embrace this new system, they would have to sufficiently trust it to securely transmit payment instructions involving huge sums of money.

Scoping the Project

Consideration of computer security in this new international system was initiated well in advance of its launch. Logica Limited, the technology consulting firm, were tasked by the original 68 banks with undertaking a review of the 'technical and economic aspects' of a potential system.[17] Their preliminary report was delivered on 17 March 1972, roughly five years before SWIFT's inauguration.[18] The banks had a clear view of their aim in creating the new system, that its primary function would be the 'transmission of international payments and related messages'.[19] It would provide a 'private communication service' to enable user banks to transmit international payment messages between each other.[20] Sending or receiving such messages would then result in banks transferring money to one another as required.

A key part of the Logica scoping exercise was an assessment of the security requirements for SWIFT. Firstly, it explicitly outlined the inherent risks of communications systems based upon technology like this: 'Messages in a communications network are vulnerable to accidental alteration due to faults in the system equipment or communication lines, and to fraudulent manipulation.'[21] Logica recognised that the convenience of being able to send messages directly over the network could potentially be undermined by either deliberate action or non-deliberate faults in the

---

[15] Lloyds, File 10133, Charles Reuterskiold, 'S.W.I.F.T: the next 10 years', *The World of Banking*, March-April 1982, p. 8.

[16] Ibid, p. 8.

[17] BoE, File 7A386/3, 'Logica: The Banks' International Message Switching Project', 17 March 1972, p. 1.

[18] Ibid., p. 1.

[19] Ibid., p. 1.

[20] Ibid., p. 2.

[21] Ibid., p. 13.

hardware powering this new system. They acknowledged that for the system to prosper, both the confidentiality and integrity of messages could not be violated.

Also outlined were three core measures that SWIFT could use to manage its computer security. The first concerned message sequencing. 'The MSP [Message Switching Project, the preliminary name for SWIFT] System will protect messages against loss or duplication', the Logica report proposed, 'by ensuring that all messages are sequentially identified and individually acknowledged at each system node.'[22] Whilst this was foremost a means of avoiding errors in transmission, it also meant that messages could be sorted into their correct order, allowing for both the auditing of messages and for fraudulent or unauthorised messages to be spotted straightforwardly.

Secondly, Logica identified that this purpose-built system would be inherently safer than the public switched telex network, the network of teleprinters able to send text-based messages to each other using a series of standards and exchanges, because of enforced terminal access restrictions, message sequence controls and error checking procedures planned for the MSP. Such procedures attempted to mitigate the risk of anybody with malicious intent gaining unauthorised access to the service and sending unsanctioned messages. Logica added that terminal log-in and log-out procedures, together with automatic fault detection and reporting on the leased telecommunications lines, would more securely establish the authority of connected terminals and allow security personnel to identify any abnormalities.[23]

Thirdly, an appreciation of the need for authentication was explicit from Logica's report. The potential for fraud existed in their opinion, so it had to be ensured that those using computer terminals to enter payment instructions were those authorised to do so, rather than imposters. 'Messages are exposed to potential fraud within the banks and during transmission through the system', the Logica reported noted, whilst also observing that 'procedures' would be in place to 'discourage and detect attempts to manipulate messages within the system.'[24]

This report served to make the banks involved in the project aware of security from the outset, both the threats they faced and specific measures to guard against them. With security concerns being explored at a very early stage in the life of SWIFT, the system could be designed with such threats and mitigations in mind. Transmitting potentially sensitive payment instructions across the globe via a communications network powered by relatively new hardware and software was a potentially risky challenge, one that the service's owners had to undertake with consistency and certainty in order to satisfy its users.

---

[22] BoE File 7A386/3, 'Logica: The Banks' International Message Switching Project', 17 March 1972, p. 13.

[23] Ibid.

[24] Ibid., p. 13.

Security in Development

In 1973, the Society of owners comprising SWIFT was established by a group of 239 European and North American banks.[25] The Logica report from the previous year had initiated a continuous discussion about SWIFT's development in general and its security measures in particular. As the project became a reality, so the prospect of security the service required action.

For example, at the Seventh Meeting of the Board of Directors of SWIFT on 11 June 1974, the work of the Fraud Prevention and Security Working Group which had met only days before was discussed in some detail.[26] The primary problems in this area were seen to be 'security of line[s] for miscarriage of text' and 'unauthorized entry into the system.'[27] The parties involved needed to know that the payment instructions they received were legitimate and unchanged from the time they were sent.

Unequivocally stated by the Board was SWIFT's responsibility for security of messages from concentrator to concentrator. They were to be transmitted in 'unreadable form' by 'making use of cyphering and/or scrambling techniques.'[28] These unmanned concentrators were to be protected carefully although the switches, which *would* be manned, required 'even more attention'.[29] Although initially the case that two people were to be present to effect access to the concentrators, at the UK concentrator this became diminished soon after SWIFT became operational, as it became understood that it was common for only one authorised person to be available.[30]

In the opinion of its Board of Directors, SWIFT's biggest security 'headache' was to ensure the 'identification and authorization' of system users, a difficulty to which it was thought there would 'never be a perfect solution'.[31] However, there were some possible measures.

SWIFT's Fraud Prevention and Security Working Group outlined how banks using teleprinters or telex on leased lines could protect messages by 'scrambling' them using their own key.[32] Banks connecting their terminals on dial-up lines across the Post Office's Packet Switching Network (PSN) could utilise a specific bank to

---

[25] Lloyds, File 10133, 'Society for Worldwide Interbank Financial Telecommunications: Facts about S.W.I.F.T.', 15 April 1982, p. 1.

[26] BoE, File 7A383/1, 'Minutes of 7th Meeting of the Board of Directors of SWIFT', 11 June 1974, p. 4.

[27] Ibid., p. 4.

[28] Ibid., p. 4.

[29] Ibid., p. 4.

[30] LMA, File M32145X/5, 'Bankers' Automated Clearing Services Limited: Inspection Report 1978', 7 November 1978.

[31] BoE, File 7A383/1, 'Minutes of 7th Meeting of the Board of Directors of SWIFT', 11 June 1974, p. 4.

[32] Ibid., p. 4.

SWIFT encryption key.[33] It was noted that it was possible to 'cypher' messages from members' processors to SWIFT concentrators even though the types of cypher used would not be the same as SWIFT's.[34] It was decided by SWIFT that it should seek advice from military institutions with experience in cyphering and that the Working Group also study the American CHIPS cheque-clearing system for guidance.[35] Such solutions were still at this point hypothetical, as it would be three years until SWIFT was eventually launched. Highlighted here, however, is how acutely aware the banks within the Society were of the need to maintain the integrity and confidentiality of messages.

As time progressed this hypothetical thinking on security evolved into clearer comprehension. For example, by 1974 the member countries of SWIFT had developed and communicated exactly what they understood security to mean. Noted in the minutes of a SWIFT Board Meeting by the General Manager, Charles Reuterskiold, were its three distinct categories: 'identification and authorisation for use of the system by senders and receivers; 'detection and correction' of transmission errors; and 'privacy of the network including prevention of third party monitoring or interference with' SWIFT traffic.[36] Defining computer security and prioritising certain values helped guide decision-making thereafter, ensuring that methods directly helping to achieve these qualities were employed in the new system.

Security and Cryptography

In April 1975, the SWIFT Board decided that some form of encryption, scrambling messages to make them unintelligible to anybody monitoring communication lines, would need to be utilised within the system. Privacy of messages could be achieved using this technique. The view was 'overwhelmingly *for* crypto equipment' but a second vote won by 12 votes to nine decided that such protection be used only on the main international lines.[37] Thus, it was accepted that an extra approximately 10,500,000 Belgian Francs be invested in the installation of crypto equipment on all these main lines.[38] This was to be included in the SWIFT User Handbook alongside other mandatory security measures previously mooted: standard log-in procedures;

---

[33] Ibid., p. 4.

[34] BoE, File 7A383/1, 'Minutes of 7th Meeting of the Board of Directors of SWIFT', 11 June 1974, p. 4.

[35] Ibid., p. 4.

[36] BoE, File 7A383/1, 'Minutes of 8th Meeting of the Board of Directors of SWIFT', 17 October 1974, p. 6.

[37] BoE, File 7A383/1, 'Minutes of 10th Meeting of the Board of Directors of SWIFT', 1 April 1975, p. 5.

[38] Ibid., p. 5.

input and output sequence numbers; and a standard authenticator provided by SWIFT.[39]

The authenticator, or 'super test key', was described in some detail to the SWIFT board.[40] To work, it required a private number unique to the sending and receiving banks, together with a common algorithm provided by SWIFT. Once processed by a computer or 'intelligent terminal' a resultant test key was produced and then used to encrypt communications. The Swift Interface Device (SID), a computer terminal that was a requirement of banks as a condition of membership, provided this facility, and at this point it was anticipated that the authenticator would be incorporated in the SID at no cost to the user.[41] Specifically aimed at being able to identify the legitimacy of users, and therefore the validity of their communications, this method could provide reassurance for users that SWIFT was a reliable system for international funds transfer. Acting upon false payment messages could have marked financial consequences for the banks involved, an eventuality that SWIFT was taking great efforts to avoid.

In April 1975, approximately two years prior to SWIFT's launch, a policy statement of intent about security included six key summary points. The first two were mandatory procedures to be adapted by users: the log-in procedure and the use of Input Sequence Numbers and Output Sequence Numbers.[42] The second two directly concerned encryption, outlining that SWIFT was not responsible for line protection between the user banks and the national concentrators, but that 'crypto equipment' would be installed on all main international lines.[43] The fifth point stated that it would be mandatory for banks utilising computer-based terminals to make use of the standard authenticator provided by SWIFT, and the sixth outlined that banks not utilising computer based terminals could continue to use bilaterally agreed test keys between each other, until SWIFT developed a low-cost device for manual users to use the authenticator.[44] Accepted unanimously, this policy statement was included in the SWIFT User Handbook.[45]

A comprehensive plan had been developed, some two years before the system eventually went live. Security was being built in from the beginning, with methods enacted in response to specific threats that SWIFT had identified and prioritised. Measures that had been proposed by Logica some three years earlier were now fully embedded into security plans, and a clear definition of what "good security" looked like had been established. Implementing these security measures was now SWIFT's challenge.

---

[39] Ibid., p. 5.

[40] Ibid., p. 4.

[41] BoE, File 7A383/1, 'Minutes of 10th Meeting of the Board of Directors of SWIFT', 1 April 1975, p. 5.

[42] Ibid., p. 5.

[43] Ibid., p. 5.

[44] Ibid., p. 5.

[45] Ibid., p. 5.

Discussion & Dissent

Included in this challenge was the task of assuaging dissenting voices on certain methods of security. In particular, the issue of encryption aroused heated debate. Reporting back from the Board's 12th meeting in Helsinki on 12 June 1975, David Robinson, Divisional Director of the Management Services Division of Williams & Glyn's Bank who had represented the UK at the meeting, wrote to Derek Balmforth, the SWIFT UK Co-ordinator. He included a passage on the security of back-up international lines: 'Their [USA] reason for dissenting was ... that they do not agree with the whole idea of crypto', said Robinson.[46] Little other opposition was expressed. The minutes of the meeting support this and note Mr Wadman of the USA's opinion that there was "no need for crypto protection."[47]

Wadman, representing the United States, had expressed his ideological objection with the idea of cryptographic scrambling of messages and resultant privacy. This is just one example of the difficulties brought about by attempted international co-operation, between countries with different experiences of automation and new technology, accompanied by different feelings about its successes, its dangers and its impact.

Unsurprisingly it was Wadman who was first to enquire about the testing of the authenticator algorithm that SWIFT had commissioned Gretag, the manufacturer of cryptographic equipment, to supply them with.[48] He was told that two companies would perform this check, but it was the UK banks who requested more precise information about the authenticator and it was decided that David Robinson, the UK representative, would send a list of questions on security prepared by the UK banks to the General Manager of SWIFT.[49] When the algorithm had been tested, it was to be the General Manager's responsibility to distribute a 'lay-man's specification' of the algorithm and also to disclose and discuss the reports from the checking companies with representatives of the inspection and audit sides of member banks.[50] At around this time the Board decided that the Swift Interface Device would be adapted to include the authenticator routine rather than using a specific bank-to-SWIFT encryption key and the associated routine for handling the authenticator key.[51] It was also deemed necessary, during discussions around cryptographic security measures, for back-up lines to be protected against 'professional criminal action'.[52] If

[46] BoE, File 7A383/1, 'Letter from David Robinson to Derek Balmforth', 16 June 1975.

[47] BoE, File 7A383/1, 'Minutes of 12th Meeting of the Board of Directors of SWIFT', 12 June 1975, p. 5.

[48] Ibid., p. 6.

[49] Ibid., p. 6.

[50] BoE, File 7A383/1, 'SWIFT – Notes on Board Meeting', 17 October 1975, p. 2.

[51] BoE, File 7A383/1, 'General Manager's Report to the Thirteenth Board Meeting', 14 October 1975, p. 9.

[52] BoE, File 7A383/1, 'Minutes of 12th Meeting of the Board of Directors of SWIFT', 12 June 1975, p. 5.

the contingency lines had to be used, the banks felt it important to ensure that these did not make their users' messages vulnerable to monitoring.

Approaching Launch

Around this time in 1975 SWIFT decided that the possibility of an external security audit function should be investigated.[53] Nevertheless, by October of that year, having explored this option, SWIFT decided not to exercise it. Seemingly as a result of cost, the Society deemed that a more appropriate approach would be to hire a 'very high level Security Officer' to be assisted by 'low level technical staff as required.'[54] Two companies had previously offered 'suitable proposals, one focusing more on the 'technical design and physical security aspect' than the other, with prices for their initial analyses and recommendation phases ranging from \$30,000 to \$54,000 with annual audits costing between \$4000 and \$9000.[55] General Manager Charles Reuterskiold also implied that an external audit at this stage, in October 1975, could have adverse effects on system development.[56]

It was therefore agreed by the Board that a security officer should be appointed on the condition than an annual external audit, estimated to cost \$10,000, would take place each year from Spring 1977.[57] The new security officer was to report directly to the General Manager, but also to the Board of Directors.[58] Recognition that such a line of communication was required highlights the level of importance that was being placed upon this role, and on managing security more broadly.

As the launch of SWIFT approached, the banks recognised that they needed to identify and protect the system's core assets, including its own proprietary software. For example, discussion took place about how to manage the security of the algorithm used in the SWIFT authenticator. In early 1976 at a SWIFT Board Meeting Mr Wadman, representing the United States of America, stated that he did not see the necessity for bank users of the authenticator to sign a non-disclosure agreement as 'even if the algorithm was public knowledge nobody would be able to break the authenticator.'[59] Mr Robinson, representing the UK, expressed similar feelings and said specifically that the 'non-disclosure agreement' had only a 'psychological and

---

[53] BoE, File 7A383/1, 'General Manager's Report to the Thirteenth Board Meeting', 14 October 1975, p. 5.

[54] BoE, File 7A383/1, 'General Manager's Report to the Thirteenth Board Meeting', 14 October 1975, p. 9.

[55] Ibid., p. 9.

[56] BoE, File 7A383/1, 'Minutes of 13th Meeting of the Board of Directors of SWIFT', 16 October 1975, p. 8.

[57] Ibid., p. 8.

[58] Ibid., p. 8.

[59] BoE, File 7A383/1, 'Minutes of the 15th Meeting of the Board of Directors of SWIFT', 11 and 12 February 1976, p. 15.

legal effect' but did not 'add anything to improve security.'[60] However, the rest of the Board was more cautious and favoured continuing to request the non-disclosure agreement from banks.[61]

A comprehensive security plan had been developed by the Society in time for the first message to be sent across the SWIFT network in 1977. Clear delineation of responsibilities had been established. SWIFT would be responsible for the maintenance of security across the parts of the system it controlled: national concentrator rooms; processing centres; and communication facilities and transmission lines between the national concentrators and the processing centres, as well as between the processing centres themselves.[62] Users would be responsible for the security of any communication facilities and transmission lines between the national concentrators and the users terminal facilities and for security of their own premises and terminal facilities.[63] Such delineation brought with it accountability. SWIFT recognised that such granular detail could be beneficial if, for example, a dispute arose or if messages were intercepted and used for fraudulent financial gain.

External Audit

Having employed the services of Logica to scope the MSP project when it was first mooted, SWIFT continued the trend of seeking expert guidance for advice on securing the service. The Society selected the Stanford Research Institute (SRI), the 'independent research center serving government and industry' that became SRI International in 1977, to undertake the annual external audit of the service from Spring of that year.[64]

Tasked with studying the 'security, liability and reliability' of the SWIFT system, SRI first undertook a system review between 19 and 26 November 1976 that analysed: 'telecommunications aspects; system development and programming standards; Burroughs system software; and S.W.I.F.T applications software.'[65] The main recommendations from this first phase focused on the responsibilities of the banks. SRI concluded that 'the security of the S.W.I.F.T system is only as strong as the enforcement and use of the security mechanisms by the member banks themselves.'[66] If users did not ensure the correct implementation of methods for minimising risk, then this weakened SWIFT. While created with security in mind,

[60] Ibid., p. 16.

[61] Ibid., p. 16.

[62] BoE, File 7A386/4, 'SWIFT User Handbook: Chapter 7, SWIFT Responsibility and Liability', 1 March 1977.

[63] Ibid.

[64] SRI International, 'About Us', https://www.sri.com/about [Accessed 21 December 2015].

[65] BoE, File 7A383/2, 'Minutes of 23rd Meeting of Board of Directors of SWIFT: General Manager's Report to the 23rd Board Meeting', 10 February 1977, p. 1.

[66] Ibid., p. 1.

a chain of dependence existed between the banks, meaning that a lax attitude towards security on the part of one institution could have knock-on repercussions for others.

SWIFT felt that collaboration between individuals with requisite access to the system was a potentially dangerous threat. Even though SRI were satisfied that the level of collusion necessary for unauthorised persons to access the system was sufficiently high to act as a disincentive, it was also suggested that SWIFT, 'at its convenience, should develop a better randomising algorithm for the log-in table random numbers' and 'should establish a reporting procedure so that member banks can receive information about all unsuccessful log-in attempts from each member bank's terminals.'[67] However, collusion would have required substantial collaboration: 'various elements of the log-in process are sufficiently spread throughout the system so that a significant amount of collusion would be necessary for any one person to gain unauthorised access to the system', SRI assessed.[68] Measures such as those mentioned here added reassurance that only operators with permission to do so were actually able to transmit payment instructions across SWIFT.

Recommendations from SRI's *Status of the Security of SWIFT's Operations* provide a relatively positive assessment of the steps already taken by the Society: 'criticisms made of the security at SWIFT should be taken in the context that SWIFT does have substantially higher levels of security than might be considered normal commercial practice', the report stated.[69] Whilst also highlighting that management priorities had been more focused on operational availability than on security, SRI made clear that SWIFT should view security within a wider 'changing business/political/economical environment.'[70] 'No major problems were detected' during security inspections of SWIFT Concentrators in Canada, Denmark, Finland, Sweden, the United Kingdom or the United States of America.[71] At SWIFT Headquarters at the World Trade Centre in Brussels, physical security was bolstered by making the 20th floor a 'protected area' and on that same floor an access control system was implemented for entry to the Swift Interface Device area.[72] Physical security of the computer hardware involved in powering the system was still a core part of computer security in this period, despite the range of technological measures available similar in SWIFT to the development of BACS at around the same time. Technical security measures would be irrelevant should anybody be able to sufficiently damage SWIFT's hardware to render it inoperable.

---

[67] Ibid., p. 1.

[68] Ibid., p. 1.

[69] BoE, File 7A383/4, 'SRI Recommendations Contained in the Report "Status of the Security of SWIFT's Operations- September 1977, progress as at May 1978"', 30 May 1978, p. 1.

[70] Ibid.

[71] BoE, File 7A383/3, 'General Manager's Report to the Twenty-Ninth Board Meeting of SWIFT', 7 April 1978, p. 9.

[72] Ibid., p. 10.

Progress?

In 1978 SRI were mainly concerned that SWIFT had not made sufficient progress on computer security since their last report. Headway had been made on the easiest recommendations to implement, with 'low level-of-effort' assessments by SRI, but in many other cases progress meant the creation of discussion drafts and concept papers rather than tangible implementation plans.[73] The level of operational advancement, in SRI's opinion, was therefore 'limited'.[74] SWIFT no longer simply had to discuss security but also had to practically enact it.

Several specific issues were detailed. For example, SRI pointed to: the 'absence of operational documentation' as no operations manual existed after more than a year of live operation; 'training', in which 'lack of training and subsequent lower level of operation knowledge are serious causes for concern'; 'Chief Inspector's Office', in which the 'most important position' of an additional Security and Audit Officer remained vacant; 'contingency planning', under which plans were yet to be 'exercised to ensure their practicality, comprehensiveness and effectiveness'; and 'software development', namely on 'the control exercised by software over operator actions ... and the control exercised by management over software development and maintenance'.[75] A number of issues are evident here. Firstly, SRI recognised the importance of security personnel for undertaking many of the practical aspects of computers operations and their security. Secondly, they stressed the need to monitor and control the actions of personnel when using computer terminals suggesting they felt SWIFT staff were a potential threat to security. Thirdly, SRI placed focus on contingency planning, thinking about security through the prism of resilience. Overall, SRI was offering some support to SWIFT in their need to transform their thinking on computer security into reality.

SRI stressed the vital role played by staff. They accentuated the need to employ the requisite quantity and quality of staff but also implied that these very employees could be a potential vulnerability, explicitly referring to managing physical 'access control' to the computer facilities.[76] At the SWIFT concentrator site in the Netherlands, for example, access control features were not followed.[77] Also, at the Belgium site the measures for controlling the cleaning staff were deemed insufficient, as the outside contract cleaning staff were allowed 'all-zone/any-time unregistered access' around the building.[78] 'The operational performance of the SWIFT network is manifestly dependent upon the quality, knowledge and experience of the

---

[73] BoE, File 7A383/4, 'SRI Recommendations Contained in the Report "Status of the Security of SWIFT's Operations- September 1977, progress as at May 1978"', 30/5/1978, p. 1.

[74] Ibid., p. 1.

[75] BoE, File 7A383/4, 'SRI Recommendations Contained in the Report "Status of the Security of SWIFT's Operations- September 1977, progress as at May 1978"', 30 May 1978, pp. 2–3.

[76] Ibid., p. 4.

[77] Ibid., p. 4.

[78] Ibid., p. 4.

computer operations staff', the report read. With considerations such as 'increasing traffic volumes' and 'the increasing rigidity which comes with "established practice", SRI felt 'concerned' that SWIFT was 'losing time in establishing security at a level in line with its long term requirements.'[79] Nevertheless, awareness of the issue, exemplified even by hiring an external auditor, showed that SWIFT was acutely aware of the need for awareness of computer security amongst its workforce.

The 1978 report offered a relatively blunt and detached assessment of SWIFT's progress on security but all in the context of SWIFT already operating at a level of security that surpassed the commercial norm. Interestingly, a month later, the SWIFT board decided to opt for a different auditor for their 1979 security audit.[80]

A thorough and collaborative approach had been taken towards security throughout the entirety of SWIFT's development from its inception through to its launch. This, however, did not prevent it from occasional failures.

SWIFT in Operation: Breakdowns

Despite computer security measures being at the core of its creation and development, SWIFT's inauguration was not entirely faultless. This was not always due to security, but sometimes caused by operational issues such as a fault in the system hardware or software or the service becoming overwhelmed by the volume of traffic being transmitted across it. Despite being accidental rather than deliberately malicious, they had the same potential impact as security failures: they brought the reliability of the system into question, ultimately allowing user trust in SWIFT the chance to falter.

For example, Lloyds Bank International Limited experienced the consequences of a lack of availability of the SWIFT network. In April 1978, 16 payment instructions from the New York branch of Lloyds to Deutsche Bank in Hamburg, totalling 68 million Deutsche Marks, were delayed as a result of undelivered messages, resulting in 'substantial operational loss'.[81] Lloyds in New York and the UK were 'quite concerned' noting that 'confidence in the SWIFT system has been shaken at a time when our New York branch were gaining confidence.'[82] Warning that a number of banks still did not have full confidence in SWIFT and suggesting that losses like this would 'inevitably make them doubt the system' was part of Deutsche Bank's attempts to persuade SWIFT to reimburse them.[83] However, the problem faced was a very real one for the banks: reliance on the system meant just that.

---

[79] Ibid, p. 5.

[80] BoE, File 7A383/3, 'Minutes of the 31st Meeting of the Board of Directors of SWIFT – 15th June 1978', 15 June 1978, p. 2.

[81] BoE File 7A386/4, 'Letter from Lloyds Bank to The Manager of SWIFT (U.K.) Ltd.,' 3 May 1978.

[82] Ibid.

[83] Ibid.

Should it not be available, or not be operating as planned, it would impact upon the banks' core operations and therefore their profitability and success.

The SWIFT system also experienced issues in Belgium on the morning of 13 December 1978, when the queue of back-dated messages between switching centres reached over 10,000.[84] By April 1979, no explanation had been uncovered and the General Manager's Report said there was 'almost no chance' of finding one.[85] The same was also thought of the 'interlock between programs' that occurred on 14 December 1978 in the Netherlands, although all other problems had been 'corrected by patches or new program versions' by April 1979.[86] One patch had been deemed so urgent that it was prepared by the software team overnight.[87] Later on in December two further disturbances occurred, on 21 December 1978 when a 'huge queue of log-in and retrieval requests affected the access to the system for users' and on 22 December in Holland when a 'simultaneous failure on both Central Processing Units (CPUs) costed one hour of system availability'.[88]

SWIFT's rapid growth was causing it some problems. While the General Manager maintained that new areas of software appeared which were 'at the origin of the disturbances' but that traffic would no longer play 'any role in relation with those incidents', backlogged traffic of 10,000 messages was a clear indication of the growing global usage of and dependence upon the availability of the service.[89] The primary impact of the growing volume of messages, SWIFT maintained, was the 'time needed to put the system back into service', for example after it had become unavailable and then reloaded, and the resultant wait before messages could be processed.[90]

Another nervy moment occurred in March 1979 when SWIFT experienced some down time that was 'initially caused by problems with the electricity supply'.[91] This briefly highlighted the interconnectedness of the infrastructure underpinning the sector's operations, which would later be labelled critical national infrastructure (CNI), and further alerted users to the vulnerabilities that they were exposed to by becoming dependent upon the system. Nevertheless, these issues were primarily operational and impacted the availability of the system as opposed to either malicious attempts at sabotaging operations or even the manipulation or altering of messages within SWIFT.

---

[84] BoE, File 71383/3, 'General Manager's Report to the Thirty-Fourth Board Meeting', 9 April 1979.

[85] Ibid.

[86] Ibid.

[87] BoE, File 71383/3, 'General Manager's Report to the Thirty-Fourth Board Meeting', 9 April 1979.

[88] Ibid.

[89] Ibid.

[90] Ibid.

[91] BoE, File 71383/3, 'Notes re 34th SWIFT Board Meeting', 10 April 1979.

Ongoing Security

SWIFT sustained the pre-eminence of security as an aim as it continued to operate and grow in the next decade. In early 1981 it stated just this in an information book-let for prospective users: 'The objective is to handle every transaction safely, accu-rately, privately, reliably and timely. S.W.I.F.T. takes security responsibility through its network until the point of connection with members' circuits.' All transmissions over international lines were encrypted, and an authenticator was included in every money-transfer message for which members held unique bilateral keys.[92]

Such features not only maintained the confidence of current users but aimed to attract new ones. SWIFT was still stressing the importance of confidentiality of communication across its network: 'S.W.I.F.T. encrypts financial transaction details to assure the security of the operation. Aside from data concerning the identity and of the sender and receiver, and the general type of transaction involved, the actual content of the transaction instructions cannot be read, even by S.W.I.F.T. personnel except by written authorisation and subsequent security procedures.[93] Specific per-mission had to be given for even SWIFT to see the content of messages passed across its system. Security measures were thorough and procedures were in place should exceptional circumstances require emergency access. Having been con-cerned with security from the time that SWIFT was only in conceptual form the Society was confident that its security was robust: 'Security is inherent throughout S.W.I.F.T. from its physical aspects to its software features.'[94] Security, in its view, was at the very core of the service.

Physical security was also still a priority. For example, SWIFT premises used the principle of dual responsibility on access, occupancy and authorisation. Operating Centres and regional processors maintained limited access areas where strict entry and occupancy procedures were in force.[95] Even within these areas, employees were restricted to their own work zones and contingency measures could be put into immediate operations to cover such emergencies as forced entry, fire, flooding, bomb threats, cooling or power failure.[96] At each of the regional processor centres an 'automatic watch and warning system' that could detect illegal entry or an envi-ronmental fault and if this did occur, the operating centre was informed immediately so that they could take necessary action, which could escalate as far as completely isolating the regional processor.[97]

Securing the premises holding computer systems, protecting these rooms and buildings from criminal acts, was also discussed internationally. The Bank of

---

[92] Lloyds, File 10133, S.W.I.F.T. Information Booklet, 1981, p. 4.

[93] Lloyds, File 10133, 'Society for Worldwide Interbank Financial Telecommunications: Facts about S.W.I.F.T.', 15 April 1982, p. 2.

[94] Lloyds, File 10133, S.W.I.F.T. Information Booklet, 1981, p. 5.

[95] Ibid., p. 5.

[96] Ibid., p. 5.

[97] Ibid., p. 5.

England raised the issue of physical security at a 'Meeting of Experts' on central bank computer usage facilitated by the Bank of International Settlements (BIS). 'In the United States, computer rooms, where damage is easily done, seem to have become a target for unruly elements', a summary of the third BIS meeting of computer experts read, 'and ways and means of protecting this very expensive and highly complicated equipment are being sought.'[98] One European central bank was noted to be investigating the 'vulnerability of computer archives' and was considering the duplication of essential data to be stored 'in a separate building, perhaps in a different town.'[99] The banks clearly had to react to these issues as they arose and sought collaboration globally to learn about the best ways of securing their operations.

Technological measures were also still a core part of SWIFT's security arsenal. For example, log-in authorisation codes were supplied by the society to the banks in a table format, each table being tied to a particular terminal identity.[100] Each authorisation code was made up of a sequence number, random key and response key, and the tables were sent to banks in two parts and via different routes so that the loss of one, or both, did not jeopardise security.[101]

Once logged on to the system, means were included to monitor the correct usage of user terminals. Each message input to the system from a bank was given an input sequence number, and each output message from the system to a bank an output sequence number, the order of both being checked.[102] Were the input numbers out of sequence, the system rejected the message, logged the user out of the terminal and required re-identification, and should the output number be out of sequence, the receiving bank was to trigger an on-line retrieval request for the intervening messages.[103]

SWIFT utilised encryption in its service, firstly, in its relatively straightforward application, to scramble message traffic. All transmissions over international lines were encrypted and banks could, if they so wished, use cryptographic equipment on national lines.[104] Encryption keys at the ends of each international line were changed at random intervals and if no live traffic was on the lines, pseudo traffic was generated to prevent anybody establishing traffic patterns.[105]

Encryption was also still used as a means for authenticating the messages sent across the system in the early 1980s. Its usage at this point was explained to

---

[98] BoE, File 7A386/1, 'Summary Report on the Third Meeting of Experts to Study Problems Concerning the Use of Computers in Central Banks', 26 June 1970.
[99] BoE, File 7A386/1, 'Summary Report on the Third Meeting of Experts to Study Problems Concerning the Use of Computers in Central Banks', 26 June 1970.
[100] Ibid., p. 5.
[101] Ibid., p. 5.
[102] Ibid., p. 5.
[103] Ibid., p. 5.
[104] Ibid., p. 5.
[105] Ibid., p. 5.

potential users to persuade them of SWIFT's high level of security on message integrity: 'An authenticator is included in each money-transfer message to guarantee that no change has occurred in the text during transmission.' Authentication was based on an algorithm provided by S.W.I.F.T. and bilateral keys used by the sending and receiving banks. The algorithm was common to all banks but the bilateral keys are known only by the sending and receiving pair.

The sending bank then used the algorithm and the key to compute both the value and position of each character in the text and thus derive a unique coded authenticator for that text. When the message had been transmitted, the receiving bank used the same method to derive the coded authenticator. If both authenticators did not agree – the change in value or position of a single character in the text would cause this to happen – the receiver would contact the sender to resolved the matter.

Authentication was carried out automatically on computer based terminals (CBTs) by an algorithm supplied by S.W.I.F.T. It was also carried out automatically on telex terminals by special equipment supplied via S.W.I.F.T. Since the principle of authentication was the same for CBTs and telex, there were no restrictions imposed by the fact that sender and receiver have different types of terminals.[106]

Ensuring that messages were not altered in transit was still deemed crucial. Little had changed in this area since SWIFT was first conceptualised. Employing the technological means of doing so offered reassurance to users of the new system who could prove that no change had taken place. SWIFT was doing all that it could to ensure confidence in the system and to minimise the risk of fraudulent transactions going unnoticed by user banks.

Other technical measures included auditing checks built into the release procedures for any new or modified software programs, with SWIFT describing software accuracy as 'probably the most important area as far as security is concerned.'[107] The execution of sensitive programs such as data base changes were under the direct control of SWIFT's Chief Inspector.[108] Internal and external auditing checks were carried out at random intervals to make sure that the safety of sensitive data, functions and operations were maintained.[109]

Many of the measures that had first been described by Logica for the so-called Message Switching Project almost a decade earlier were being deployed in SWIFT's running. SWIFT had been thoughtful and taken a long-term view of how to protect their service as it grew. Its principles had broadly remained constant, and the measures employed to bolster security had become reality rather than imagined.

---

[106] Lloyds, File 10133, S.W.I.F.T. Information Booklet, 1981, p. 5.

[107] Ibid., p. 5.

[108] Ibid., pp. 5–6.

[109] Ibid., 1981, p. 6.

Fraud

An example of how the SWIFT system could potentially be manipulated occurred in early 1983. Slavenburg's Bank in Holland were reported in *The Economist* to be missing 'tens of millions' in a fraud related to \$65m of international transfers.[110] The bank had 'acted fast' to inform police and public and the main suspect had been arrested on his return from a trip to London.[111] Although lacking specific detail, the article said that at Slavenburg's it was thought 'possible to acquire information that enabled banking codes to be abused in Rotterdam without arousing suspicion elsewhere in the network.'[112] SWIFT agreed that this could have taken place but insisted that the fault lay with the internal security system at Slavenburg's.[113] A printed version of this article in the Barclays archive shows the paragraph containing these last two quotations circled with black pen and 'Who are the losers?' scrawled alongside by a Barclays employee.[114]

This question evoked a response from a General Managers' Assistant within Barclays, who bluntly responded that it seemed the only losers at that point in time were Slavenburg's.[115] The same note outlined how investigations were still proceeding but it seemed that the fraud took place 'solely within the Slavenburg Bank systems and procedures' and that if this was the case, then all messages received by correspondent banks from Slavenburg's via SWIFT had been acted upon 'in good faith' as all such messages would have been fully authenticated and tested.[116] Similarly, messages from correspondent banks to Slavenburg's would also have been fully authenticated and so any fraud perpetrated after receipt would be the responsibility of the Dutch bank.[117] Also detailed was how SWIFT insurance only covered losses incurred because of transmission errors or loss of messages within the SWIFT system, and this had only been known to occur on two or three occasions since the inception of SWIFT, never involving Barclays.[118]

A more ominous tone was present in this note's conclusion. It referred to a potential situation in which the remitting bank may not be able to meet its liabilities for the losses in a fraud like this. The note warned, 'If Slavenburgs went to the wall as a result of their recent losses, then the answer to your original question "who loses" could be very different.'[119] Such were the risks inherent in new and evolving

---

[110] 'Slavenburg's Bank: Accident Prone', *The Economist,* 26 March 1983, p. 88.

[111] Ibid., p. 88.

[112] 'Slavenburg's Bank: Accident prone', *The Economist,* 26 March 1983, p. 88.

[113] Ibid, p. 88.

[114] Ibid., p. 88.

[115] Barclays, File 0328-0026, 'Slavenburgs Bank – Fraud', 30 March 1983, p. 1.

[116] Ibid., p. 1.

[117] Ibid., p. 1.

[118] Ibid., p. 1.

[119] Ibid., p. 1.

technology increasingly depended upon for the process of international transfers of significant sums of money.

Integrity Problem

In 1984 SWIFT detected a potential issue with the software used in ST 200 terminals, the name for those used as SWIFT Interface Devices (SID) to access the network. An 'exposure risk' was detected, arising from the fact that Users' program passwords could be bypassed by entering into the Burroughs operating system through a 'command word routine' which was available and was displayed during the normal disk copying housekeeping routines.[120] Once into the SWIFT software it was also possible to display other banks' authentication keys for the system.[121] Further, it was discovered that the ST 200 authenticator software did not cover the whole message construction owing to a software issue in the authenticator program, meaning only part of the message was being encrypted.[122]

Such an issue caused great concern for SWIFT's users. 'If we have a felon in our midst then our other correspondents are at risk', Barclays assessed, and also if an 'unauthorised "person"' at the office of a correspondent bank could gain illegal access if they could obtain free usage of a SWIFT Interface Device.[123] It was noted that the relevant programs had been 'debugged' and a new release of the software had been sent out to ten 're-release' sites for testing for a month, thereafter being released to all users if there were no issues.[124] While this delay could have caused more consternation, Barclays – who had discovered this weakness – said that the issue had already 'pertained for some 2/3 years already since the software was initially issued'.[125] Very few banks knew of the discovery, Barclays said, and unless there was someone who was specifically trying to obtain details of other banks' keys and had free access to a correspondent bank's computers then there was 'little risk' involved.[126]

Demonstrated above is that computer security in SWIFT was very much an ongoing, risk management process.

---

[120] Barclays, File 0328-0026, 'SWIFT – Possible Integrity Problem with ST 200 Software', 12 December 1984, p. 1.

[121] Barclays, File 0328-0026, 'SWIFT – Possible Integrity Problem with ST 200 Software', 12 December 1984, p. 1.

[122] Ibid., p. 1.

[123] Barclays File 0328-0026, 'SWIFT – Problem RE. ST 200 Software', 12 December 1984, p. 1.

[124] Ibid., p. 1.

[125] Ibid., p. 1.

[126] Ibid., p. 1.

Continuous Threats

SWIFT had taken computer security extremely seriously since the very origins of its service. Preparations had been thorough, implementation scrupulous, and its continued management seen as vital. One member bank, the Royal Bank of Scotland, said of security in SWIFT: 'Security, as would be expected with an international banking system, has been of paramount importance in the implementation.'[127]

Security played a pivotal role in developing trust and confidence in SWIFT, and this had been noted by its developers from the outset. This perception was seemingly a successful one, given SWIFT's growth in membership over the period studied above and its current existence as a core piece of financial market infrastructure.

Through a combination of the physical and technical, sufficient disincentives were developed to make it difficult for the system to be manipulated and users unwittingly deceived. Whilst a limited number of instances did occur which caused some panic for SWIFT's overseers, the service was seen to offer a dependable and reliable function, and thrived as a result. Its security measures were developed in direct response to the threats it felt it faced, helping mitigate risk in the areas it deemed most crucial to its success.

Such international collaboration drew upon the experience of individual banks in financial sectors from various countries who had already pushed ahead with automation. Security discussions were relatively specific, developing mitigations in relation to specific potential risks and with an understanding of potential actors. Having likely thought about these scenarios previously, SWIFT was able to benefit from a level of understanding that it may not have if it had been developed a decade earlier. The organisation was also humble in its approach to security, seeking the expert advice of external companies when required and drawing upon the advice of services in other countries who were ahead of them in terms of development.

Computer and network technology created new dependencies which required the financial institutions involved to quantify the new risks they faced. SWIFT is an explicit example of institutions' need to adapt. Alongside managing people and processes, the service's overseers also had to deal with new issues of a technical manner which could have far-reaching impacts on the confidence of users in relatively new technology.

By blending the old and new, the physical and the technical, SWIFT's Board managed to steer their new system through its crucial years of development, implementation and launch with a clear understanding of what security meant, what the main threats to it were and how it could mitigate against them. This discernment, and prioritisation, advanced the capability of the financial sector towards becoming a far more modern and innovative marketplace.

---

[127] Royal Bank of Scotland, File RB/1453/1, J. Nicholson – Assistant manager, International Division of Royal Bank of Scotland Ltd., 'Society for Worldwide Interbank Financial Telecommunication', 1977, p. 279.

Chapter 5
Consolidating Growth: 1978–1985

The Governor of the Bank of England, Gordon Richardson, spoke at the opening of National Westminster Bank's new Management Services Centre at Goodmans Fields in London in 1979. Both reflective and upbeat in tone, the Governor was proud of the contribution that British banks in particular had made to the employment of new technology in the financial sector in the preceding years, acknowledging their role in establishing SWIFT and BACS, before turning to the facility he was opening:

> Goodmans Fields itself is also a notable example of the investment that British banking is making in the future. In thinking of the massive battery of computers and automated equipment that I understand we are about to inspect upstairs, I am irresistibly reminded of Dr. Johnson's remark at the sale of Mr. Thrale's brewery. "We are not here", he said, "to sell a parcel of boilers and vats, but the potentiality of growing rich beyond the dreams of avarice." If I could catch something of that spirit I might say that what we have here at Goodmans Fields is not just a collection of silicon chips and transistors, but the means of keeping British banking in the forefront of a very competitive league. Goodmans Fields is a building and complex admirable in many respects and I am both honoured and delighted to perform this opening ceremony.[1]

Richardson recognised that enhanced connectivity between these institutions, exploiting the power of electronic communication, would be key to the UK financial sector remaining competitive against other global financial centres.

By the late 1970s the major London clearing banks were in a period of consolidation. They had contributed to significant, co-ordinated progress in the implementation of new technology in the sector in major projects such as BACS and SWIFT, and were continuing to bolster their internal operations through investment in new hardware and software. These institutions' dependency on such technology was still growing deeper, and so efforts to develop contingency plans were maintained,

---

[1] Bank of England (hereafter BoE), File G13/5, 'Speech Given by the Rt. Hon. Gordon Richardson MBE, Governor of the Bank of England, at the opening of the new Management Services Centre, Goodmans Fields, of the National Westminster Bank Limited', 25 April 1979, p. 2.

© Springer Nature Switzerland AG 2022
A. Sweetman, *Cyber and the City*, History of Computing,
https://doi.org/10.1007/978-3-031-07933-7_5

alongside the consideration being given to the overall security of these operations. Banks had far bigger and more powerful technological installations to manage and protect against damage and fraud. Government at this time began to offer encouragement to the financial sector for technological uptake whilst also beginning to think about the wider implications of this to employment and business operations. This chapter considers these developments between 1978 and 1985, also taking a detailed look at what exactly bank computer networks were comprised of at this time, how they had grown, and how their security was understood and protected.

The Potential for Fraud

International co-operation between financial institutions by the late 1970s involved attempts to understand the challenges arising from greater connectivity. The United Nations Commission on International Trade Law (UNCITRAL) created a Study Group on International Payments, and in May 1978, the Bank of England was amongst attendees, alongside central banks of the Group of Ten countries, plus Switzerland, of a discussion run by the Bank of International Settlements on electronic funds transfers (EFT).[2]

Submitted to The Study Group was a 59-page dossier from Bradley Crawford, a Canadian consultant, which offered extensive advice on the legal issues of EFT systems. Of particular interest is his discussion of security and privacy of such systems. Crawford felt that both the system of Electronic Funds Transfer itself and its operating personnel posed a problem. 'It should be appreciated that there are risks present in every facet of the operation,' Crawford said. 'That must be appreciated as including not only the electronic links between members, but also selection of personnel and such matters as the methods of distributing access cards attributing Pin numbers and notifying Customers of them.'[3] Computer security in Crawford's description here involved both technical security but also the physical, specifically the management of people and their access.

A report by UNCITRAL in 1978 outlined what it described as some established facts which echoed the themes present in Crawford's concerns. Firstly, it noted that s computer-based systems were extremely vulnerable to manipulation by 'anyone with the necessary expertise and access', and that 'many apprehended embezzlers, especially employees, have often indicated that they have been tempted to try by the seeming simplicity of the process and the large reward that could be reaped in a computer-aided fraud.'[4] New computer networks enabled individuals to commit

[2] BoE, File 7A386/4, 'Problems of Liability Arising From Electronic Funds Transfer', 27 September 1978.

[3] BoE, File 7A386/4, Bradley Crawford, 'Elements of Electronic Debit and Credit Funds Transfer Systems', 15 November 1978.

[4] BoE, File7A386/4, 'Report of the Secretary-General, Annex 3: Some Legal Aspects of International Electronic Funds Transfer', 28 April 1978.

fraud on an unprecedented scale at unprecedented speed. These qualities, key motivating factors for financial sector institutions to invest in new technology, were to be enjoyed by them but could also potentially be exploited by criminals. Often this was achieved by individuals using their permitted access for unpermitted purposes.

Fraud of this type was thought to be difficult to defend against: 'It seems very doubtful that a system could be devised that is completely fraud-proof, although the level of sophistication required of the thief could be made very high indeed,' according to Crawford.[5] In this description, the report recognises that perfect security is likely unachievable, but that measures could be put in place which created the requisite disincentive affect to prevent those with malicious intent opting to commit crime. Controlling access to computers and certain files or stores of information was a means of mitigating such risk. Once exploited, new technology could be commanded to help cover up the perpetrator's actions. Though computer fraud was seen as relatively easy to commit, its detection was described as 'very difficult and costly' because not only was there no physical paper to examine for alterations, but also because the computer could be 'commanded to "forget" (i.e. erase) any traces of the fraudulent transactions, leaving, as it said, no "audit trail"'.[6] Fraud could now be committed by manipulating computer commands. Large amounts of money could theoretically be misdirected, transferred to other accounts controlled by the user, and the traces of these actions obfuscated or deleted. Ultimately the banks involved were concerned with their profitability. The banks recognised the potential losses that could occur as a result of fraud and just how challenging it would be to eliminate this risk entirely.

Furthermore, international linkages enhanced the risk of such occurrences for electronic funds transfer. Not only did this increase the number of potential access points for those wishing to monitor communications across new systems, as the United Nations' advice noted, but also meant that levels of effective security at various points could be uneven, especially should lines have to be leased from public carriers in the respective countries, resulting in breaches becoming harder to track down.[7] Accompanying the benefits of efficient global operations were the burdens of an increasingly large base of infrastructure underpinning the work, providing greater opportunity across larger geographies for physical attempts to monitor or damage the machinery.

However, such criminal activity was not only limited to financial transactions. Theft of intellectual property also began to occur. The same UNCITRAL report referred to one case from the United States in which a 'company's highly valuable trade secret' was gained by a competitor, the latter 'tapping' the line of the company's central computer's communications with 'equipment at an outside location'.[8]

---

[5] Ibid.

[6] Ibid.

[7] BoE File7A386/4, 'Report of the Secretary-General, Annex 3: Some Legal Aspects of International Electronic Funds Transfer', 28 April 1978.

[8] Ibid.

Access to valuable information proved an irresistible prospect for the perpetrating organisation.

Security therefore maintained its importance to the banks, and physical security still played a key role in this. For example, in the late 1970s Midland Bank in the United Kingdom was developing a new computer centre and one of its principal requirements was 'maximum security ... a large site so that the centre would be physically separate from adjacent buildings and public areas.'[9] Even as the technology involved became more advanced, there was no escaping the need to protect the buildings housing computer equipment and the perimeter of their sites.

Despite such actions and international collaboration to discuss the implications of new financial sector communications infrastructure, some questioned whether the financial sector had done enough to secure their systems again fraud and misuse by the end of the 1970s. Ray Ellison, of the National Computer Centre, still believed they were lagging behind, saying 'it is like having a jet with a Mach3 engine without fitting ejection seats. It can be very dangerous.'[10] Ellison felt that lack of security had the potential to undermine this powerful new technology.

There was perhaps some good reason for Ellison's concern. On 11 February 1979 *The Sunday Telegraph* reported a story about Roswell Steffen, a junior manager with a New York savings bank, who had 'systematically set about instructing the bank's computer', which he was an authorised user of, to 'remove quantities of money from customers' accounts.'[11] By concentrating on accounts that had been dormant for some time in order to avoid exposure, he acquired over 1.5 million dollars over 18 months and was only caught when the police raided his bookmakers and investigated how he could afford such prodigious gambling.[12] Examples such as this had the potential to evoke concern. Uptake of information technology was still relentless for the banks, and such experiences reinforced the reality of the risks involved.

Government Takes Notice

In the early 1980s the United Kingdom Government acknowledged the increasing up-take of information technology by businesses throughout the country and sought to understand its own role in stimulating this investment.

The Central Policy Review Staff (CPRS), the Cabinet Office-based advisory body colloquially know as government's "Think Tank", offered some detailed thoughts on this which Sir Robert Armstrong, Secretary to the Cabinet, sent to Sir

---

[9] HSBC, 'Computer Operations Division News: New Computer Centre', March 1978.

[10] Quoted in Jonathan Davis, 'Wide open to the computer rip-off', *Sunday Telegraph*, 11 February 1979.

[11] Ibid.

[12] Ibid.

Douglass Wass, Permanent Secretary to HM Treasury, on 11 February 1980. It began with some definitions: 'From information we acquire knowledge. The raw material of information is data. Information processing assembles and structures data to convey knowledge.'[13] This cerebral description illuminates how the CPRS viewed computers: as a potential tool, for government, businesses and citizens, to help improve knowledge and understanding. Beginning from first principles, government was attempting to assess how new technological methods, in this case information processing, could impact commercial entities and the nation.

Government's analysis, in the case of the financial sector, was that rapidly developing technology had the potential to fundamentally alter or even destroy the basis of the existing industry. The CPRS paper detailed some of the implications of what it called the 'Communications Revolution.'[14] Under the title 'Immediacy/Delay – financial', the paper warned that 'many businesses exist on the leads and lags which are now an integral and unavoidable part of commercial life (the clearing banks and money markets, for example). Instantaneous fund transfer may eliminate the concept of credit and the services which depend on it.'[15]

Whitehall's "Think Tank" seemed relatively concerned that the development of technology, in this case electronic funds transfer, could potentially change the financial industry by offering efficiencies so significant that they could render certain forms of business redundant. Government recognised that advancing technology offered commercial opportunity to the United Kingdom. It was at this point unclear, however, as to where this opportunity would appear and what its costs would be.

Whitehall was initially relatively reluctant to adapt its own structures to the speed of change in technology. Sir Robert Armstrong described his and Prime Minister Margaret Thatcher's lack of enthusiasm for a 'Ministry of Information Technology'.[16] Sir Robert recommended the creation of a Steering Group, under Cabinet Office chairmanship, and with all concerned departments represented, including the Central Policy Review Staff.[17]

Armstrong suggested that the Steering Group decide what was to be done on nine areas outlined by the CPRS in which, they recommended, government should 'maintain an active interest': 'manpower'; 'the telecommunications system'; 'transmission frequencies'; 'technical standards'; 'public sector purchasing policy'; 'public sector usage'; 'R & D'; 'reducing the vulnerability of information flows to strikes, sabotage or fraud'; and 'privacy'.[18] This diverse range of issues provided significant opportunity for government to support the adoption of new technology in the UK's commercial sector. Moreover, developments in information

---

[13] The National Archives (TNA hereafter), File T390/698, 'CPRS note attached to Armstrong to Wass' 11 February 1980.

[14] TNA File T390/698, 'CPRS note attached to Armstrong to Wass' 11 February 1980.

[15] Ibid.

[16] TNA, File T390/698, 'Armstrong to Wass', 11 February 1980.

[17] Ibid.

[18] TNA, File T390/698, 'Information Technology: A note by the Central Policy Review Staff', February 1980, pp. 2–4.

technology were attracting the attention of those at the highest levels in Whitehall who were tasked with thinking about how best government should manage its involvement.

The Central Policy Review Staff outlined two themes particularly pertinent to the London banks which were impacts of recent investment in information technology by those institutions.

Firstly, the CPRS noted a 'convergence of communications and computing.'[19] The interconnection between the two fields would be the basis upon which the financial sector could revolutionise its operations.

Secondly, the CPRS predicted that the UK would 'need to re-consider [Britain's] distinctions between civil matters and military defence' given rapid developments in technology.[20] Implied here was the need to understand just how vital computer systems were going to become to industry in the United Kingdom and how any potential manipulation, sabotage or espionage using the new technology involved would be treated from a national security perspective. Government's "think-tank" was using its detachment from the banks to consider the strategic impacts the uptake of information technology could have in the long-term. A sense of the revolutionary potential of technology was now palpable in both the financial sector and Whitehall.

Government and Industry

Government placed increasing focus upon information technology later in 1980. By June of that year a *National Strategy for Information Technology* was proposed by Conservative Member of Parliament Kenneth Baker, calling for, amongst other suggestions, a Minister for Information Technology in the Department of Industry.[21] Information technology was debated for approximately four and a half hours in the House of Commons on 11 July 1980.[22] As well as this, a United Kingdom Information Technology Organisation (UKITO) was created by a group of wholly-UK owned computer companies – such as International Computers Limited (ICL), Ferranti Computer Systems and Digico - to act as a pressure group to ensure that Britain would 'retain control over research, development, manufacture and marketing' in its own computer industry.[23]

---

[19] TNA, File T390/698, 'Information Technology: a brief description, February 1980, p. 2.

[20] Ibid., p. 10.

[21] TNA, File T390/698, 'A National Strategy for Information Technology: Business Telecommunications Conference, London Press Centre', 18/19 June 1980.

[22] TNA, File T390/698, 'Information Technology: House of Commons', 11 July 1980, pp. 916–1015.

[23] TNA, File T390/698, 'United Kingdom Information Technology Organisation (UKITO)', 25 July 1980.

By the end of summer 1980 increasingly detailed work was published by the government on information technology, highlighting more focused thinking on specific implications for various sectors of the UK economy. For example, on 15 August 1980, the Advisory Council for Applied Research and Development (ACARD), the advisory committee serviced by the Cabinet Office, released a report that reiterated some of the specific implications for financial services that the Central Policy Review Staff had outlined in February 1980: 'Financial services may be considerably affected by IT. The time taken for information transmission, at present accepted and sometimes used to advantage in some business operations, can be effectively eliminated.' Specifically, it was thought possible to arrange instantaneous transfer of funds, which would have implications for credit services that depended on payments taking time to be completed, and also the stock and commodity markets.[24]

While a certain amount of optimism is visible in the above extract, specific concern persisted around new information technology potentially eliminating pre-existing strands of business.

The above description also suggests that government's thinking lagged slightly behind that of the banks given the development, beginning in the previous decade, of large-scale projects such as the Society for Worldwide Interbank Funds Transfer (SWIFT) and Bankers Automated Clearing Service (BACS). Nevertheless, later in the report there seems to be some awareness of how insurance, banking and finance had already been affected: 'Rapid communications and computers have already markedly influenced financial transactions. Terminals in branches are already linked with central computers; these terminals will have steadily more powerful data handling capabilities.' The report also set out what it thought the future held in store. 'More services, including self service, will be accessible through plastic card with magnetic or microprocessor memories or through closer integration of the IT systems of the financial institutions with those of corporate and private customers.' The report also recognised that international already provided financial and commercial information around the world and that further developments in rapid international data communications would have important implications for London and the world's other major financial centres.[25]

In the above extract the report emphasised just how reliant upon technology the financial sector had already become. Yet it also acknowledged the future potential that "rapid international data communications" could have for the financial sector globally.

---

[24] TNA, File T390/698, 'Advisory Council for Applied Research and Development: Information Technology', August 1980, p. 21.

[25] TNA, File T390/698, 'Advisory Council for Applied Research and Development: Information Technology', August 1980, pp. 27–28.

Data

Interwoven with thinking around information technology was the issue of data protection and its implications for the financial sector. An extract of a report by the interdepartmental Industrial Policy Group saw the United Kingdom's lack of any data protection legislation as a problem, potentially meaning that other countries 'may act to prevent or restrict the flow of data into the UK.'[26] The paper cited an example of how the Swedish equivalent to the UK Department of Health and Social Security (DHSS) had refused to sign a contract with an unnamed UK company to process computerised personal data onto plastic cards with a magnetic stripe, due to a lack of legal safeguards over the misuse of data.[27] It was also noted that American Express, the American financial services company, was reportedly considering moving their operations out of the United Kingdom for the same reason.[28]

At this time, a report submitted in December 1978 by the Data Protection Committee was under consideration by the Home Office who were attempting to distinguish a balance between enacting privacy legislation and the increasing the costs of computing which this would bring.[29] Just as information technology offered the potential for significant advantage to the UK economy, and specifically to its financial sector, there was also the need for government to keep pace by providing the necessary safeguards for financial services firms to take full advantage of new technology.

Context: Wider Impacts of Technology

Wider societal impacts resulting from new technology also concerned politicians in the early 1980s. Come September 1982 and Kenneth Baker MP was now Minister for Information Technology. At a speech at Liverpool University on 7 September 1982, Baker discussed the UK's 'Move Towards an Information Economy', but he started off in rather peculiar fashion:

> 1982 is not just Information Technology Year, it is also the 50th anniversary of the publication by Aldous Huxley of "Brave New World". In that great novel, Huxley forecast a society that could be manipulated by technology and much of it may seem to be true today. In the Brave New World, citizens began life as an egg, fertilised on a dish; subsequently they were to become slaves to television which in 1932 barely existed and whenever they were bored they would sniff a drug. This anti-Utopian nightmare seems almost to have been realised. But Huxley was an optimist; he believed that man did have free will and could exercise it as

---

[26] TNA, File T390/698, 'Attached to R B Butt to Mr Gulvin', 10 September 1980.
[27] Ibid.
[28] Ibid.
[29] Ibid.

he wished. Men do not have to become the slaves of technology – a choice exists and we all have to decide what we want.[30]

While the extract may seem that Baker was worried by the negative impacts of information technology, he was an optimist too, and believed in the long-term benefits of new machines and their industrial applications. Speaking as he was in the month immediately following the UK's successful military campaign in the Falklands, with optimism and patriotism in the United Kingdom and its prime minister at a high watermark, Baker went on to offer a receptive audience a utopian image of the future of Britain including more flexible working practices and less centralised employment as a result of this revolution in computing technology.[31] Baker was an enthusiastic cheerleader for ongoing technological investment, particularly in the major London clearing banks.

Government had begun thinking about the general implications of information technology alongside the specific impacts on certain industries. While the integration of technology into financial services and the industry's dependence upon this technology was referred to by central government, there was a notable absence: discussion around security of these networks and systems. Driving this strand of thinking were the banks themselves.

Dependency and Contingency

Enjoying the benefits of new technology for banks meant that they had to find a balance: between efficiency and cost savings on the one hand and security, in the form of confidentiality, integrity and availability of data and systems, on the other.

Banks had begun to utilise advances in networking technology by the early 1980s in order to increase the efficiency and scale of their internal operations. For example, two of Midland Bank's computer centres were involved in providing an 'online service' to branches in the early 1980s: the London Computer Centre at Brent in North West London and the North Western Computer Centre near Sheffield, serving branches in the south and north of the UK respectively.[32] These centres held customer account information, including balances, personal addresses and information on loan limits for each of the approximately seven million accounts held with Midland.[33] Post Office telephone lines linked at least one computer terminal in each branch to the relevant computer centre and allowed the branches to share real-time information with the central repository.[34] Traditional constraints created by

---

[30] TNA, File T471/45, 'Kenneth Baker MP: Towards an Information Economy', 7 September 1982, p. 1.

[31] Ibid., pp. 6–7.

[32] Midland Bank, *Banking on Computers*, October 1981, p. 4.

[33] Midland Bank, *Banking on Computers*, October 1981, p. 4.

[34] Ibid., p. 4.

geography and time were beginning to be dismantled to the advantage of businesses and consumers.

For a retail bank like Midland, the ability to share information was vital to their operations. Networking technology substantially increased the speed with which they could do this. Morning Reports, for example, were sent from the computer centres to branches with information on the processing that had occurred overnight, detailing stopped cheques, overdrawn accounts or any loan limits that had been exceeded.[35] These could be queried by sending a message to the computer centre, and in a few seconds a printed balance for a certain account could be available.[36] Amendments could also be made, and as of 1981, Midland's London Computer Centre received on average approximately 550,000 transactions and 73,000 amendments per day.[37] The 'Real Time' service operated from 0800 to 1900 each day, after which overnight processing would begin, during which two 'very powerful Burroughs computers' operated, capable of processing up to 480,000 accounts per hour.[38] The benefits of speed and efficiency that computer networks offered became more explicit, these machines became increasingly integral to the operations of banks such as Midland. Alongside this came reliance on the machines and new expectations from customers around available services. Plans had to be made in case this hardware and software became unavailable.

Midland: Contingency

Increasing dependence on new networking software and hardware for core functions meant that banks began to investigate how they could replicate these processes in the event of technological failure or deliberate disruption. Midland Bank showed an awareness of the need for these computer operations to work as reliably and predictably as possible and implemented contingencies to mitigate the potential disruption from breakdown or malfunction. At both computer centres, in London and the North-West, Midland installed: a back-up power supply via standby diesel generators; air-conditioning to maintain a cool operating environment; and a non-fluctuating power supply, as they believed a 'power surge or dip of just eight volts' could cause the computers to shut down.[39] Such measures aimed to supply certainty and reassurance. Although these measures offered a level of defence against deliberate physical damage, they were not developed to specifically prevent malicious threats. They were to ensure continuity of normal operations in order not to alarm customers and effect their confidence. Security here concerned failure and loss of

---

[35] Ibid., p. 4.

[36] Ibid., p. 4.

[37] Ibid., p. 4.

[38] Ibid., p. 4.

[39] Ibid., p. 5.

service at least as much as, perhaps even more so, than it did manipulation or intentional disruption.

Midland also took steps to ensure that back-ups of their information were available should any loss occur. In a description of how branches at Midland Bank updated balance and account information in preparation for the following day, the company said, 'For security reasons, the information is also copied onto magnetic tape in duplicate.'[40] One is stored for a 'period of time' at either the London Computer Centre or North Western Computer Centre, dependent on geography, and one is sent for storage at an external site 'in case some catastrophe, such as fire, destroys the Centre'.[41] This means of physical data storage required the banks to consider computer security as both a physical and technological issue. Duplicates and back-ups provided reassurance that processing could begin again with minimal disruption should the system become unexpectedly unavailable. The bank's posture was to develop its resilience: assuming the inevitability of such an event and establishing plans for rapid recovery.

The technology employed at the banks had to be managed and overseen by operators with the requisite skill. 'Vital services' to branches were provided by the work of 'well trained and highly skilled staff', for example those who worked in the Network Control Department at Midland who were 'highly trained technicians' considered to be 'using very sophisticated equipment to diagnose faults in the system'.[42] Burroughs, the manufacturer of Midland's computers, had engineers and programmers on hand 24 hours a day to ensure that equipment ran as predicted and that any programming errors could be corrected.[43] Availability of the system was key to evoking a sense of reliance and reassurance for those becoming increasingly dependent upon these machines and this required technically skilled individuals to monitor and repair the system.

Contingency planning was therefore a core tenet of security thinking in the early 1980s. Midland, by offering vivid imagery of the scale of their operations, provided justification for their focus on resilience in the form of contingency. In the early 1980s, the number of cheques processed in a year by Midland would, by their count, exceed the height of Mount Everest, should they be piled into a single column.[44] Considering Everest reaches a height of 8848m above sea level, this striking example helps explain the bank's focus on predictable operations that served their customers with consistency. The hardware and software that Midland invested in therefore needed to be extremely reliable to constantly cope with such demand.

Even though efficiency was often the primary driver of technological adaptation in the financial sector, security thinking routinely permeated considerations. In 1984 Midland Bank produced a report evaluating a Xionics Office Automation

---

[40] Midland Bank, *Banking on Computers*, October 1981, p. 4.

[41] Ibid., p. 4.

[42] Ibid., p. 4

[43] Ibid., p. 5

[44] Ibid., p. 7.

system which had been installed in selected areas of their Corporate Finance Division based at Watling Court in London. Amidst a generally positive assessment of the system lay specific reference to security. A recommendation was made to evaluate the usefulness of a magnetic tape drive as a 'secure and efficient means' for archiving the system 'as soon as possible', as currently the Xionics system was incapable of doing this.[45] Alongside this was a recommendation to change from their current communications protocol, IBM's Binary Synchronous Communications, to IBM's newer Systems Network Architecture communications protocol, in order to find a 'permanent solution to a major Xionics "IBM 3270 emulation" security limitation' and comply with existing Bank communications policy standards.[46] Xionics' software was seen to offer the flexibility necessary to meet the security requirements of a large and varied number of users, operating a 'Record access right rating' and 'User group membership' system which was defined and controlled by the dedicated system administrator.[47] Midland was further concerned with computer and communications security as it began utilising technology for larger-scale applications in the early-mid 1980s.

Speed of Change

Coping with the pace and scale of technological change was relatively difficult for some financial institutions. In 1985 the Bank of England tasked its auditors, Deloitte Haskins & Sells, with publishing a guide following a conference of central bankers and supervisory authorities held in May 1983.[48] The Bank said that the timing of publication was for three reasons: the increasing complexity of computer systems; the development of 'on line and real time systems'; and the linking of processing procedures into continuous systems, specifically the linking of 'telecommunications funds transfer systems direct to banks computers', seemingly in reference to the recent launch of Clearing House Automated Payments System (CHAPS) in 1984.[49]

Although an archival record of the guide does not appear have survived, it was described as a 'self-help' aid for banks on security and control procedures in the use of computer and telecommunications systems. It offered broad coverage: it covered fraud; the risks that could emanate from establishing new systems or amending current ones; mistakes due to errors; the consequences of computer and

---

[45] Midland Bank, Corporate Customer Systems Department, Xionics Office Automation Study: Final Evaluation Report, 22 June 1984, p. 46

[46] Ibid., p. 46.

[47] Ibid., p. 21.

[48] BoE File 7A371/5, 'Press Notice', 22 February 1985.

[49] Ibid.

telecommunication failure; and unauthorised access to confidential information.[50] Pace of change of these systems was cited as having the potential to reveal a weak link in chain of control procedures.

Real time systems replacing batch processing, as well as telecommunications funds transfer systems being linked direct to bank systems were identified in the guide as potential pitfalls for banks. It was stressed, however, that no incident affecting individual banks had necessitated the preparation of the guide.[51]

Instructive here are outlines of the typical computer infrastructure of a major bank in the early-mid 1980s. Three examples are explored here.

Midland Bank: Midnet

Midnet, approved in 1983, was Midland Bank's data and voice network, a system comprised of computerised exchanges and circuit links that united the communications services of the business.[52] For data, routes between branch users and central computers were 'combined into one data transport system' through packet switching exchanges.[53] Packet switching is the technology which divides messages into segments, labels them and sends them to their required destination, where they are placed back together once more to recreate the entire message.[54] For voice, local telephone networks were linked together by digital Private Automatic Branch Exchanges (PABXs).[55] Midnet used digital circuits as the 'main connecting highways in the network' and could transmit voice and data services simultaneously.[56] Such a network allowed customers using branches to enter what Midland described as a 'private telephone and data complex' with the information resources of any Midland Group member company available to them.[57] It would also allow the Midland Group to develop telecommunications into a common resource and cost centre for the entire organisation.[58]

Midland truly believed that efficient use of technology to enhance communication ability would have a transformative impact on the company. The organisation's Midnet advertising brochure opened on a philosophical note, asking 'What is Communication?' Following this was a comprehensive answer: 'The ability to

---

[50] Ibid.

[51] BoE File 7A371/5, 'Press Notice', 22 February 1985.

[52] Midland Bank, File UK 0649, 'Midnet', undated, p. 1. Given information within the booklet, it must date from at least 1983, and is likely to have been produced in the years immediately following that date.

[53] Ibid., p. 5.

[54] Ibid., p. 5.

[55] Ibid., p. 5.

[56] Ibid., p. 5.

[57] Ibid., p. 5.

[58] Ibid., p. 5.

deliver information; the ability to explain your needs and understand the needs of others; the ability to bring together separate entities; the ability to always remain open to the familiar and the unfamiliar, the commonplace and the unexpected.' Midland believed that an organisation became more unified, more powerful' as its parts communicated more effectively. That was Midland's idea behind Midnet.[59]

Midland also described communication as a hybrid of both creativity and technicality: 'Communication is both an art and a science. The art is clarity of thought and economy of expression. The science is telecommunications: the ability to send and receive any type of communication – voice, picture, or the printed word – over distances and time spans never before attainable.'[60] Clearly the investment in this technology was justified by the potential increase in business performance. Being able to transmit information across the United Kingdom far quicker than ever before meant that Midland, or any bank with a similar infrastructure, could operate at a previously unachievable pace and scale.

Sending large amounts of sensitive data in such a fashion made it imperative that the system was secure. Midland described three 'salient' security features that were built into Midnet: building security; system design; and encryption and passwords.[61]

Firstly, a 'high level of access security' was applied to the computer centre which housed the Network Management Centre (NMC).[62] Midland's South Yorkshire Computer Centre hosted this NMC, where two computers were assigned to specifically monitor and control the operation of the packet switching centres, concentrators and telephone exchanges and to 'display status information' for the whole network.[63] 'Service', 'security' and 'statistics' were the principle functions of the Network Management Centre.[64] Premises housing all of the packet switching exchanges and digital telephone units had 'excellent environmental controls' and were equipped with 'stand-by' generators to maintain operations in the event of a power failure.[65]

Secondly, packet switching made the network 'inherently less convenient for the eavesdropper' according to Midland since the exchanges' job was to open and close lines or re-route data as required, meaning there was no identifiable path for tapping information.[66] It was also deemed difficult to read the flow of data on any given line, as they contained mixtures of packets from various sources.[67]

---

[59] Midland Bank, File UK 0649, 'Midnet', undated, p. 2.

[60] Ibid., p. 5.

[61] Ibid., p. 21.

[62] Ibid., p. 21.

[63] Ibid., p. 21.

[64] Ibid., p. 21.

[65] Ibid., p. 21.

[66] Ibid., p. 21.

[67] Ibid., p. 1.

Thirdly, Midland described Midnet as 'one of the most secure networks in the country' in terms of encryption and passwords.[68] It could support the transmission of encrypted information from the terminal or central computers for particularly sensitive material and each user had passwords for dial-in access to the data network.[69] Midland's understanding of security revolved around confidentiality of information and protecting its vital infrastructure from interference.

Bank of Scotland: Computer Network

Another example that can be described in some detail, due to available archival material, is that of the Bank of Scotland (BoS), a retail bank in the UK. As of 1984, BoS operated a network of 559 branches in the UK, of which 500 were in Scotland, and as of February that year the bank held £4,450 million in deposits and employed 8,600 people.[70] A snapshot of the hardware used in BoS' computer network from 1984 outlines a centralised system, the majority of which was manufactured by IBM. Branch computers were linked to the central mainframe computer at its Edinburgh Computer Centre through an IBM 3601 minicomputer which had only limited storage facilities. Communications generally took place via leased lines, though backup links via the ordinary telephone system were available. Branch terminals were mainly used for data entry.[71]

In this case, all branch computers linked back to the mainframe at a central computer centre. Alongside the network, a new system using Philips equipment was being installed to replace 'some paper and microfiche information sent physically to branches' which would provide 'much more local processing power and storage.'[72]

The main Bank of Scotland Computer Centre in Edinburgh also had several interfaces with outside bodies.

Four of these involved transmitting data to other institutions. For example, information was sent to and from the Nottingham Building Society for the HOMELINK banking venture, running in batch mode and utilising International Computers Limited (ICL) computers; information was transmitted between BoS and Alliance Building Society for the Alliance BankSave venture, again in batch mode and over a leased line, but this time effected directly between mainframe computers; a similar batch mode system and leased line was used to transfer information from the Bank of Scotland's mainframe to its subsidiary's (North West Securities) mainframe; and information was also sent directly from the Bank of Scotland's mainframe computer

---

[68] Ibid., p. 21.

[69] Midland Bank, File UK 0649, 'Midnet', undated, p. 21.

[70] London Metropolitan Archive, File MS32456/2, 'Existing Draft of Chapter for EEC Survey', 24 July 1984, p. 33.

[71] LMA, File MS32456/2, 'Existing Draft of Chapter for EEC Survey', 24 July 1984, p. 33.

[72] Ibid., p. 33.

to GEISCO's mainframe over a leased line in order to update information held there for the bank's cash management system SCOTLINK.[73]

The Bank of Scotland also had links into three sector-wide systems of banking infrastructure: it transmitted information to Bankers' Automated Clearing Services (BACS) using a batch system over leased lines and using ICL computers at each end; it had a terminal in London that could link into CHAPS using Barclays' Clearing House Automated Payments Service (CHAPS) gateway; and it also operated a link to the Society for Worldwide Interbank Financial Telecommunication (SWIFT).[74]

On the Bank of Scotland's consumer side there were also computer interfaces that operated. Magnetic tapes were physically sent to corporate customers which contained 'details of credit and debits on their accounts'.[75] Bank of Scotland operated a network of 203 Automatic Teller Machines (ATMs) across Scotland. These ATMs were manufactured by IBM and were linked into the computer network at branch level, providing customers with withdrawal facilities, as well as balance inquiries and facilities for statement and cheque book requests.[76] Bank of Scotland noted that in 1983 some 412,000 cardholders used ATMs to make some 11 million transactions with an average value of about £30.[77] PIN numbers for accessing these services with an accompanying card were 'authorised on-line'.[78]

Trustee Savings Bank: Computer Network

The Trustee Savings Banks (TSB) was a retail bank that, as of 1984, operated 1,622 branches covering all regions of the United Kingdom, comprising approximately 11% of the total bank branches in the country.[79] TSB was structured as four regional banks in a group structure which included the Central TSB, a credit card company called Trustcard and a finance house known as the United Dominions Trust.[80]

TSB operated a centralised, on-line and real time system serving its savings account and cheque book account customers which had been in operation since the early 1970s.[81] In TSB's branches, 'intelligent' counter terminals, which included badge card readers to identify the tellers, screens and keyboards, were linked to the central mainframe computer which held details of all accounts through a network of leased lines and concentrators. The choice of line speed was related to the amount

---

[73] LMA, File MS32456/2, 'Existing Draft of Chapter for EEC Survey', 24 July 1984, p. 34.

[74] Ibid. p. 34.

[75] Ibid., p. 34.

[76] Ibid., p. 34.

[77] Ibid., p. 34.

[78] Ibid., p. 34.

[79] Ibid., p. 35.

[80] Ibid., p. 35.

[81] Ibid., p. 35.

of traffic expected along it. All of TSB's equipment across the network were manufactured by Burroughs, except for one mainframe in its Manchester computer centre.[82]

Similar TSB networks also existed in parts of the UK which were not covered by this system, and the details varied slightly, for example the Scottish network being based on Burroughs mainframes and Philips terminals.[83]

London was not at this point included in the network but it was planned to be included once a second computer centre was built in Milton Keynes, which would share the workload of the networks between two centres and 'in the event of a catastrophe at one site' the other centre could run the entire system.[84] Central TSB operated an IBM mainframe that handled cheque clearing operations for the four regional TSBs.[85]

In terms of its interfaces with other organisations, TSB operated no computer links to the bank's customers and relatively few links to other organisations, but the TSB's link to CHAPS and BACS were through the Central TSB, where tapes were physically handed to BACS and CHAPS payments were made through a Tandem computer and 'gateway' software.[86]

The Trustee Savings Banks did operate a national ATM network that, as of November 1983, linked some 400 ATMs of which 270 were in England and Wales.[87] The machines linked in to the bank's computer network as branch level and Burroughs manufactured the machines in England and Wales while Philips manufactured the Scottish machines.[88] These ATMs formed part of the 'on-line system' as withdrawals were immediately debited from current accounts, and the machines also offered balance inquiries, statement and cheque book requests and bank information requests.[89] In Scotland the machines also offered deposit facilities and the ability to transfer money between accounts.[90]

Primed for Innovation

By the mid-1980s banks had developed relatively complex computer systems and networks that were increasingly customer-facing. The two decades leading up to this point had seen significant investment in new technology and banks becoming increasingly reliant upon it for their operations.

---

[82] LMA File MS32456/2, 'Existing Draft of Chapter for EEC Survey', 24 July 1984, p. 36.

[83] Ibid., p. 36.

[84] Ibid., p. 36.

[85] Ibid., p. 36.

[86] Ibid., p. 36.

[87] Ibid., p. 36.

[88] Ibid., p. 36.

[89] Ibid., p. 36.

[90] Ibid., p. 36.

Central government had allowed, until the early 1980s, the banks to pursue this rapid modernisation of their operations with minimal comment. However, government began to think more deeply about the wider impacts of such change on the financial industry and offered some encouragement to the banks involved that they were following an appropriate path.

Security for banks at this time was focused around contingency planning. For these institutions, resilience was the goal for which they for, meaning the ability to cope with a disruptive situation, manage it in the short-term and return to normal working as soon as possible and with the minimum impact on customers. At this stage, much was made of the potential threat to banks but little concrete evidence existed that truly tested the banks' plans which had been created in isolation.

Despite wholesale change over the decades leading up to the 1980s, the banks still focused on maintaining trust from their customers. There were now signs that government supported their endeavours, and that the banks were now prepared to cope with the security requirements of much greater numbers of computers which were increasingly linked together. Consolidation in this period served to enhance the confidence and ambition of these institutions for future modernisation.

Chapter 6
CHAPS: 1972–1984

Banks in the United Kingdom continued to embrace technological advances in computers and telecommunications in the 1980s. The ability for terminals in individual bank headquarters and branches to communicate with each other via networks meant quicker and more fluid internal operations. Linking individual bank networks to one another offered the potential to revolutionise the operations of the entire sector. Adapting new pieces of hardware and software into operations in order to realise these benefits, however, also brought with it some risk.

Still leading the adaptation of new networking technologies were the major London clearing banks, of which there were six in 1970: Barclays Bank, Coutts & Co., Lloyds Bank, Midland Bank, National Westminster Bank and Williams & Glyn's Bank.[1] This group of large banks operated the clearing systems in the UK and held special clearing accounts with the Bank of England, using this account according to agreed procedures at the end of each day to make the payments due to or from each other which were the net of that day's transactions.[2]

Manual completion of tasks – such as paper-based payment instructions, or phone calls between branches – were common ways of undertaking tasks which offered a level of certainty and reassurance having been the primary methods of communication previously. These attributes had to be replicated when implementing new methods in order to instil and maintain confidence in these new hardware and software that was now being relied upon. Banks therefore had to evaluate both the opportunities and vulnerabilities presented by technological development.

---

[1] Cheque Credit & Clearing Company, 'Emergence of Technology', https://www.chequeandcredit.co.uk/information-hub/history-cheque/emergence-technology [Accessed 16 February 2016].

[2] London Metropolitan Archive, File MS32452X/2, Inter-Bank Research Organisation (IBRO), 'CHAPS- A New Approach to Payment Systems', October 1982, p. 4.

© Springer Nature Switzerland AG 2022
A. Sweetman, *Cyber and the City*, History of Computing,
https://doi.org/10.1007/978-3-031-07933-7_6

CHAPS

Modernisation of communication methods was a key driver of security thinking for banks from the early-mid 1970s throughout the period until the mid-1980s, culminating in the launch of the Clearing House Automated Payments System (CHAPS) in 1984.

This thinking primarily focused on three key concerns for usage of new networking technology: the confidentiality of any information sent across networks; the authentication of those messages, or ensuring that electronic messages were sent by legitimate operators; and reliability of the system, including significant attention given to contingency planning should these new methods fail.

Individually, these three factors garnered significant attention from the clearing banks, highlighted in this chapter through the case study of the development of CHAPS between 1972 and 1984. Methods were discussed in detail in order to mitigate each of these potential vulnerabilities: encryption to ensure confidentiality of communications; the requirement for more than one operator to sign-off payments into the system to ensure their authenticity and integrity; and plans for paper-based fallback operations in the event of system unavailability. From the project's outset, banks offered specific scenarios in which each of these vulnerabilities could be capitalised on and offered increasingly specific approaches to mitigating them as the project progressed. This was a collaborative project that illustrates both the collective standards held by the banks on security as well as their views on potential threats they faced.

Collectively, the concerns amounted to a strategic worry that persisted throughout the project's development: that users of the system should remain confident enough about its security to use the system and pay for that privilege. Mitigating these potential weaknesses was ultimately an exercise by the leading UK banks to embrace computer and communications technology into the operations of the financial sector and show that they could be relied upon for business that instructed the transfer of vast amounts of money between financial institutions. Alongside the concerns specific to these type of financial transactions, the project represented a case study in discussing the wider implications of placing technology at the heart of commercial operations.

Structure

CHAPS provides an insightful example of the thinking around computer security in this era due to its structure: decisions on its technology, and therefore its security, were a collaborative effort between the foremost institutions in the financial sector, the clearing banks, who owned and developed the system. At first the group of banks involved in the discussion were the aforementioned clearing banks alongside the Bank of England.[3] By the time of CHAPS' launch this group of settlement banks also included Central Trustee Savings Bank, Clydesdale Bank, Co-operative Bank, Coutts & Company, National Giro Bank and the Royal Bank of Scotland.[4] This allows for a detailed examination of not only what was considered to be best practice at this time, and the standards that individual banks set regarding security, but also about how the banks interacted with each other, and the Bank of England, as well as their willingness to contribute to the discussion over the security of the system.

Therefore, the development of CHAPS between 1972 and 1984 warrants detailed exploration here.

This chapter is presented as three sub-chapters owing to the substantial amount of previously unused archival material available. The first of these outlines the substantial development period of the system over the first half of the 1970s. It shows how from the preliminary planning of the project onwards, even before it was officially sanctioned, the London clearing banks, the developers of the system, were aware that the security of the system would be integral to its success. The second sub-chapter covers the period between 1976 and 1980. It examines the detailed planning for the implementation of the system, including potential means via which criminals could manipulate CHAPS, such as fraud. Presented here is an exploration of the detailed security mitigations included in the system as well as comments from the banks on the level of security being offered. The third sub-chapter takes the period from 1980 to 1984 and outlines the security measures employed in a new iteration of CHAPS and the discussions between banks around prioritising certain features. It also, for example, details one instance of alarm over the issuance of the system's source code and object code together to individual institutions. It also assesses some of the early failures of the CHAPS system.

Together, these sub-chapters provide an in-depth example of how computer and network security perceptions and planning evolved over the course of the 1970s and first half of the 1980s. It includes detailed study of discussions by the key banks in the United Kingdom around issues such as confidentiality and integrity of data, methods to ensure these qualities including encryption and authentication measures, as well as system resilience and contingency planning.

---

[3] Bank of England (BoE hereafter), File 1A18/1, 'New York Clearing House: Inter-Bank Payments System (CHIPS)', 7 March 1972.

[4] United States Federal Reserve, 'International Finance Discussion Papers, *An Appraisal of the CHAPS Payments Mechanism,* Number 217, February 1983', https://www.federalreserve.gov/pubs/ifdp/1983/217/ifdp217.pdf [Accessed 8 February 2017].

Sub-Chapter One: 1972–1975

CHAPS

The Clearing House Automated Payment System (CHAPS) is a real-time gross settlement (RTGS) system, still in use, that facilitates electronic payments in sterling between banks, building societies and other payment service providers.[5] Its primary uses include business-to-business money transfers, domestic and international wholesale payments, such as foreign exchange transactions, and facilitating house purchases.[6] Every six working days, CHAPS turns over the equivalent of the annual UK Gross Domestic Product (GDP), and in January 2017 the system processed on average £313 billion per day, or £6.6 trillion over the 21 settlement days in the month.[7]

CHAPS was launched nearly a quarter of a century ago on 9 February 1984. It was developed over a period of 12 years with the aim of providing the United Kingdom's financial services industry with an advanced, reliable and secure means of communication which would allow it to maintain its competitiveness with other global financial centres. It was to replace the current means of Town Clearing – the process by which cheques drawn against the Bank of England and the London clearing banks were exchanged – as the 'core clearing mechanism' for sterling-denominated transactions.[8] By the end of 1984 the system was processing 7000 payments and an aggregate value of £5 billion per day.[9]

The Town Clearing system was a paper settlement system for high value transactions, with a lower limit of £10,000 in 1982, meaning a far lower volume of transactions passing through daily than normal cheque clearing, but a total value being approximately 20 times greater.[10] The values of payments involved, according to the Inter-Bank Research Organisation, were enough to cause 'even the most hardened banker to look twice and count the zeroes', payments of several million pounds being commonplace.[11] If for example, a bankers payment – a particular cheque used between banks – was presented on a given day, then funds would normally be made available to the beneficiary in the afternoon following the 3:00 PM Town Clearing deadline and the beginning of reconciliation and settlement.[12] Payments via this

---

[5] CHAPS Co, 'About CHAPS', http://www.chapsco.co.uk/about-chaps [Accessed 8 February 2017].

[6] CHAPS Co, 'Who uses the CHAPS system' http://www.chapsco.co.uk/about-chaps/who-uses-chaps-system [Accessed 8 February 2017].

[7] Ibid.

[8] United States Federal Reserve, 'International Finance Discussion Papers, *An Appraisal of the CHAPS Payments Mechanism,* Number 217, February 1983', https://www.federalreserve.gov/pubs/ifdp/1983/217/ifdp217.pdf [Accessed 8 February 2017].

[9] CHAPS Co, 'History of CHAPS', http://www.chapsco.co.uk/about_chaps/timeline/ [Accessed 14 December 2015].

[10] LMA, File MS32452X/2, Inter-Bank Research Organisation (IBRO), 'CHAPS- A New Approach to Payment Systems', October 1982, p. 1.

[11] Ibid., p. 1.

[12] Ibid., p. 1.

method were not guaranteed, and even though it was a rarity, bankers payments could potentially "bounce".[13]

Developing a system that would become an extremely valuable technological advance forced its creators – the London clearing banks, and the Bank of England – to think deeply about the measures they needed to take to ensure its reliability. For example, hardware and software choices for the system were scrutinised and debated at great length; methods of encrypting the data passed across the system were evaluated; procedures to manage access and privileges to enter instructions into the system were discussed in minute detail; and contingency planning in case of system failure was also thought about from the outset. The institutions involved seemed to believe that CHAPS offered advantages over the paper-and human-based Town Clearing that already existed. Specifically, they saw two key benefits of the new system as being a 'high degree of security' and a 'high level of reliability.'[14] Nevertheless, they do not give any examples of the Town Clearing system's failures on security, and little direct evidence exists in the archives of the banks that suggests a specific security weakness in Town Clearing, though evidence of the prioritisation of security in CHAPS is abundant.

Origins of CHAPS: Competition

Banks in the City of London initially began thinking about modern payment systems and money transmission services in the early 1970s. This was prompted, at least in part, by potential competition from international financial centres who had already embraced technological advancements.

On 7 March 1972 representatives of the UK's clearing banks met in London with John Lee of the New York Clearing House. The meeting was in response to a letter from Lee on 15 December 1971 about the possibility of establishing in the United Kingdom a 'satellite facility of CHIPS', the acronym used to denote the clearing mechanism operated in New York City, known as the Clearing House Inter-Bank Payments System.[15] The New York banks stressed that they would not wish to establish a satellite against the wishes of UK banks, but also took care to inform the UK clearing banks that such a satellite could be operational within four to six months.[16] They also warned that 'at least some' of the New York banks were anxious to proceed 'as soon as possible' given the significant potential for cost savings accompanying such a system.[17] Such preparedness on the part of the New York banks to

---

[13] Ibid., p. 1.

[14] Lloyds Bank (Lloyds hereafter), File 10599, 'CHAPS – Interim Guide', December 1982, p. 6.

[15] BoE, File 1A18/1, 'New York Clearing House: Inter-Bank Payments System (CHIPS)', 7 March 1972.

[16] Ibid.

[17] Ibid.

embrace new technology served to impress upon the British representatives around the table that competition from across that Atlantic was fierce. A warning had been disseminated, prompting the UK banks to react.

CHAPS: European Competition

Potential competition not only emanated from financial services in the United States; there also existed a competitive threat from financial centres within member countries of the European Economic Community (EEC) which Britain was to join on 1 January 1973.

A month after the meeting between John Lee of the New York Clearing House and the UK clearing banks, on 11 April 1972, Deputy Governor of the Bank of England Jasper Hollom made a speech at a conference of the British Computer Society. Hollom was aware of the need to utilise technology to be competitive in Britain's new international political circumstances as a full member of the European Economic Community, which was already home to many major financial centres: 'London will take its place as one of several financial centres in the community.; To meet this challenge, Hollom declared that London needed to make 'full and imaginative use' of an extensive and growing range of advanced technological resources, amongst which computers would continue to play a dominant role.[18]

Not only was Hollom taking care to stress the need for innovation and creativity in financial services' use of technological resources, but he was also, due to his role, allowing it to appear that the Bank of England also held such a view. Such language and vision used by the UK's central bank were a clue to its own perception of its role in encouraging this technological adaptation.

SOVEREIGN

A first attempt to outline a transfer and settlement system to replace the current manual process of Town Clearing was authored by the Inter-Bank Research Organisation (IBRO) the research arm of the Association for Payment Clearing Services (APACS), the trade association 'for those institutions delivering payment services to end customers'.[19] The project and system that were proposed – and the original concept that eventually morphed into CHAPS – was first known by the

---

[18] BoE, File 1A18/1, Quoted in 'Sovereign Report', July 1972.

[19] European Commission, 'APACS Response to the European Commission Interim Report on Payment Cards', http://ec.europa.eu/competition/sectors/financial_services/inquiries/replies_report_1/05.pdf [Accessed 20 February 2017].

acronym SOVEREIGN (System of Value Exchange Relayed Electronically by Intergroup Network).[20]

This rather cumbersomely-titled project was envisaged as having two primary functions: communication between banks and the ability to act upon the messages that were delivered within this transmission system. Its communication requirement was to take 'any string of bits of any length, any input speed, at any time and for any destination at any output speed ... and deliver it intact.'[21] It was crucial that banks could trust the system to transmit its messages with certainty that they could not be altered. For acting on the delivered messages, it was envisaged that the range of possible actions was so wide that no single system 'could possibly handle them all.'[22] New technology allowed these previously manual processes to be far more efficiently completed, a prospect that would aid the banks in their time-sensitive marketplace.

This inventive thinking seemingly stemmed from London's banks worrying that the pre-eminence of the United Kingdom's financial sector may be in doubt. In a document outlining SOVEREIGN it was noted that as opposed to 'any specific fears', it was a 'general uneasiness about the future' which prompted London's banks to consider an improved payment and settlement system.[23] This uneasiness seemed to stem, the report said, from known present competition in the form of mainly American banks operating in London and the threat of future competition from European financial centres – such as Amsterdam, Brussels or Frankfurt – when Britain joined the EEC.[24] UK banks felt increasingly compelled to explore the opportunities afforded by technology in order to remain competitive.

Anxiety about competition had not subsided some nine months after the initial meeting between John Lee and the UK clearing banks. The Inter-Bank Research Organisation (IBRO) issued a warning that London needed to keep up with other financial centres, and included in this was the need to embrace technological advancement. The report entitled *International Money Transmission and Cash Management Services* noted that there was a 'danger ... that London may fail to compete effectively with other centres as an international money transmission centre ... for a variety of reasons, perhaps in combination.'[25] These warnings were a reminder to British banks that London in particular had to embrace technological change in order to remain comparatively advanced in its financial expertise.

British banks concluded that innovation was necessary. It was suggested that there was a 'widespread' feeling in the City, that 'there must be a better way' for Town Clearing to occur, given that newly-launched Society for Worldwide Interbank Financial Telecommunication (SWIFT) meant British non-clearing banks were

---

[20] BoE, File 1A18/1, 'Sovereign Report', July 1972.

[21] Ibid.

[22] Ibid.

[23] Ibid.

[24] Ibid.

[25] BoE, File 1A18/1, Quoted in 'Sovereign Report', July 1972.

likely to have a quicker and easier communication channel with foreign clearing banks than with London clearing banks, due to the lack of a technological link.[26] A rather rousing paragraph ended the introduction to the 1972 report on the SOVEREIGN project: 'This project begins from the assumption that the unease is justified, and that the technology exists now to provide London with the world's most effective payment and settlement system for City, national and international business.' Following this opening, the report continued by stressing the need for any such system to be designed to make the undertaking of financial business in London so simple for both British and foreign customers that they would choose to do their business there rather than elsewhere. 'We believe that we have an edge over our foreign competitors in financial expertise; our payment and settlement system "infra-structure" should support rather than negate it,' the paragraph continued.[27] British banks were now braced to compete with their international rivals by utilising technological advancement to bolster and enhance their pre-existing financial expertise.

At the core of this innovation was to be a revolution in the way that City institutions were able to interact with each other. SOVEREIGN – which some felt was 'rather pretentiously named'[28] – was envisaged as a 'standardised City-wide communication system', its prime function being to transfer messages between financial institutions.[29] Bolted on to this could be a number of secondary functions, or 'active subsystems',[30] such as settlement systems that could act upon the transmitted instructions.[31]

Whilst primarily driven by the desire to remain competitive, SOVEREIGN, in the eyes of the City, could ease the pressure on the current Town Clearing system in the event of an emergency such as a security-related incident by acting as a complementary system. In a discussion on the project at the Bank of England in 1972, an Inter-Bank Research Organisation representative noted that there did not currently seem to be 'any adequate overall disaster contingency plans' for the present Town Clearing system, and that, for example, in the event of a 'major strike' the 'City could be crippled to the extent that it might not be possible to maintain even a small residual service for foreigners'.[32] Automation of the process, or at least an automated complement to the existing system, was seen as a way of avoiding any unforeseen circumstances and offering a more secure and reliable service even if such an event occurred.

---

[26] BoE, File 1A18/1, 'Sovereign Report', July 1972.

[27] Ibid.

[28] BoE, File 2A89/1, 'CHAPS- whither next?', 21/1/1980.

[29] BoE, File 1A18/1, 'Sovereign Report', July 1972.

[30] Ibid.

[31] BoE, File 1A18/1, 'Sovereign', 27 September 1972.

[32] BoE, File 1A18/1, 'Discussion on the Sovereign Project at the Bank on 18th September 1972, 21 September 1972.

Not everybody in the City of London was keen for such change. Some concern existed within the Advanced Developments section of the Bank of England (BoE) that an argument able to convince bankers of the need for the project was still missing.[33] However, some in the Bank cavilled at the new system. For example, the Chief Cashier's Office at the Bank of England objected to the acronym SOVEREIGN because the name was 'already well known in City circles as representing the Bank of England Hockey Club touring and Sunday side whose tie and name have received approval from Buckingham Palace, no less.'[34] Not everybody in the City was galvanised for technological revolution. Nevertheless, the benefits of this change were becoming increasingly explicit to many of the major City banks.

CHAPS: Early Development

The renamed project began to take shape in 1973 and hypothetical specifications were outlined and passed to the banks. At its core was to be a central computer installation at the Clearing House – the organisation providing clearing and settlement services for London banks – owned and operated by the London clearing banks; terminals linked in to the system would be housed in a number of bank branches and in the Chief Accountant's office in each of the clearing banks.[35] By the end of December 1973 an alternative feasible option was seen to be housing the computer installation at Bankers Automated Clearing Services (BACS) in Edgware.[36] The central computer installation would record and store all messages passing through the system and retain them for 'a limited period only'.[37] Passing through the system would be instructions to transfer significant sums of money between London's clearing banks.

Requirements for reliability and security affected the design of the system from its outset. Even in its earliest manifestations CHAPS offered measures to counteract the possibility of failure or improper usage given the values of money involved in the interactions between banks.

Firstly, to lower the potential impact of component failure, early plans envisaged several hardware mitigations. The central installation was to be comprised of a 'central complex of interlinked computers', configured for contingency in that it would continue to function even if some parts of it were not working.[38] The system was to have 'a number of redundant components' in order to provide a 'very high level of reliability', and consideration was to be given to whether a separate paper based

---

[33] Ibid.

[34] BoE File 1A18/1, 'Sovereign', 27 September 1972.

[35] BoE File 1A18/1, 'CHAPS: A hypothetical outline Specification', 24 April 1973.

[36] BoE File 1A18/1, 'Clearing House Automated Payments Systems', 30 November 1973, p. 2.

[37] Ibid., p. 2.

[38] BoE, File 1A18/1, 'Clearing House Automated Payments Systems, 30 November 1973, p. 2.

system was required in case of a 'total systems shut-down' occurring.[39] Smooth transition to redundant components or a paper fall-back would minimise the impact on users and help stem any loss of confidence.

Secondly, to prevent and spot unauthorised usage, several software-based solutions were proposed. There were to be 'strict in-system' and 'in-house' control procedures, as well as 'security safeguards'.[40] Such safeguards would include a number of features: 'error detection'; 'message sequence controls'; 'load scheduling'; and 'Identity codes'.[41] Controls would also exist in an attempt to manage 'terminal access' and 'Clearing Centre access' in order to lower the chances of fraud.[42] The banks seemed aware of the ways in which the system could potentially be manipulated and from a very early point in CHAPS' history were considering the potential risks involved and specific methods to mitigate them.

Reassurance for Banks

The CHAPS system had the potential to streamline and modernise the way that London banks undertook their clearing, but its success would depend upon banks being confident that the technology offered them a secure and reliable service.

Before signing up for participation the banks needed a few reassurances, a significant component of which was around security. In a summary of meetings between both the clearing and non-clearing banks up to November 1973, the positivity of 'most banks' towards the system was tempered by the consensus from the banks that three principal points needed to be considered before joining CHAPS: 'cost', 'security' and 'systems' failure'.[43] For example, one point in the memo cited as a negative for CHAPS was 'Security – need for proper authentication of messages and terminal control.'[44] The banks also enquired about 'back-up facilities for breakdowns.'[45] The banks knew that relying on technology to undertake actions for their customers – in this case non-clearing banks, for whom the clearing banks would act as a gateway into the system – could potentially result in a negative impact on that relationship if the technology failed.

The meeting summary contained several points that reflected the banks' wishes for security in the new system to at least be of the same standard as their current practices. Some further outline of their current security provisions was also included.

---

[39] Ibid., p. 8.

[40] Ibid., p. 8.

[41] Ibid., p. 8.

[42] Ibid., p. 8.

[43] BoE, File 1A18/1, 'Summary of meetings between members of the 'CHAPS' working group and representatives of non-clearing banks', 13 November 1973.

[44] Ibid.

[45] Ibid.

For example, the banks' Overseas Treasurers who were interviewed for the memo stated that they used 'proper authorisation', which was a 'signature check', and a check that funds were available.[46] Banks' City office representatives noted that 'test codes/keys' were used, as well as 'voice recognition', presumably via telephone.[47] Despite having such measures in place, signature checks or voice recognition were certainly open to both innocent error or deliberate manipulation, and new technology in fact offered a greater level of certainty than in the measures outlined by the Overseas Treasurers.

Compounding this was the need to actively implement the checks and their dependence on human effort. Bank employees interviewed for the report acknowledged that their current checking was 'slack'.[48] The Overseas Treasurers said that their checks were only carried out for 'small' or 'risk accounts', that Bankers Payments were 'taken at face value' and that signatures were 'accepted on trust'; a note of optimism was added, however, as the Treasurers stated that 'automated systems should help overcome some security problems'.[49] The Overseas Treasurers also noted the need for back up facilities in order to keep the system operational if there was a crisis.[50] The system not only needed to be considered in terms of its potential reliability and security; it actually had the potential to enhance bank security through efficiency and easing the workload of employees.

As the project progressed in 1974, a further issue in the security sphere was highlighted: that of confidentiality. Specifically, the working group involved in the design of CHAPS considered a system of automatic approval of payment instructions within the payer's bank. However, there was some concern from the banks that this could 'pose security problems' as it might 'reveal information about a settlement bank's assessment of a customer', for example if it had to individually design criteria for automatic approval, such as a monetary limit, and this differed between certain banks depending on clearing banks' opinion of their reputability.[51] Some in the Bank of England were more sceptical, suggesting that there was little likelihood of a 'leakage of information' when the information would only be passing through the 'CHAPS central installation' itself which was actually controlled by the settlement banks themselves.[52] However, this example is typical of the considerations that banks had to make during this time of technological advancement. Information was being transferred through different means, at a much faster speed than its older physical equivalent, and so such issues needed to be considered if full advantage was to be taken of the benefits offered by the new CHAPS system.

---

[46] Ibid.

[47] Ibid.

[48] Ibid.

[49] Ibid.

[50] Ibid.

[51] BoE File 1A18/2, 'CHAPS', 5 August 1974.

[52] BoE, File 1A18/2, 'CHAPS', 19 August 1974.

The onset of CHAPS meant that investigations occurred into other parts of the financial sector to see if they too could benefit from the transmittance of payment messages through telecommunications system.

One example is an Inter-Bank Research Organisation (IBRO) study from 1974 which looked at how securities could be transmitted, which noted that there were 'very real dangers inherent in the existing system' given that over 3000 parcels were carried through the City each day containing securities with a total face value of £800 m.[53] There were doubts over motivations to steal these securities because in practice, IBRO said, nobody would buy them than from a known dealer.[54] It was also believed that 'the close City community' offered 'adequate protection'.[55] However, it was noted that that there was the potential for Certificates of Deposit and Treasury to be 'quickly sold abroad to an unscrupulous bank with British correspondents' even though they would be 'difficult to dispose of in the UK'.[56] The report concluded that the only justification for change would be to guarantee the safety of securities and personnel against loss or theft.[57] Nevertheless, the fact that CHAPS opened up the potential for change and development acts as an example of the interaction between technology and security in that there were some, albeit difficult to justify, security benefits to be enjoyed provided significant investment was made.

Security & Control in CHAPS

Approximately 10 years before its launch, the Inter-Bank Research Organisation (IBRO), the research arm of the Association for Payment Clearing Services (APACS), had commissioned a study of the security and control aspects of CHAPS by Logica, the IT management consultancy firm. Copied in to the letter and asked for their detailed views were representatives from the leading UK clearing banks including Barclays, Coutts, Lloyds Bank, Midland Bank, National Westminster Bank, Williams and Glyn's and the Bank of England.[58] Channels for dialogue existed between the public and private sector that meant that both could be closely involved in security discussions from the outset.

---

[53] BoE, File 1A18/3, Inter-Bank Research Organisation, 'Securities Handling in the City', December 1974, p. 15.

[54] Ibid., p. 15.

[55] Ibid., p. 15.

[56] Ibid., p. 15.

[57] Ibid., p. 15.

[58] BoE, File 1A18/3, Stephen Dennis to Corp et al, 'Security and control in CHAPS', 25 November 1974.

Logica defined three types of potential risk: equipment failure, malicious damage and criminal subversion. They also defined three locations at risk: the CHAPS central installation in Edgware in North London, the terminal sites and the interconnecting Post Office line network.[59]

The report by Logica opened with a statement that noted a widely-held awareness of the risks of computers in banking. 'The need to ensure a high level of security and control for computerised banking systems is well recognised', they proclaimed.[60] This continued: 'the advent of real-time systems such as CHAPS, designed to facilitate the inter-bank transfer of large sums of money, very considerably increases the problems which may arise in this area.' Accordingly, Logica noted that it was of the utmost importance that the security and control aspects of the system should be built in from the outset rather than added on later.[61] Logica's report, in their own words, proposed methods to protect the 'integrity of the system and ensure its continued availability'.[62] Now that instructions to transfer large amounts of money were to be sent electronically it was important that banks felt they could fully rely on the new procedures for doing so.

Authentication would also be key to CHAPS' successes. To act based upon an electronic instruction meant having to believe that this came from a legitimate source. Logica were particularly aware of this threat from insiders: 'malintent by any individual having access to CHAPS' or the 'ability to extract unauthorised information from the system...[which] may well be as valuable as the possibility of more direct abuses of the system.'[63]

The latter point was particularly pressing for the banks. Logica identified that this point carried 'special importance bearing in mind the traditional privacy associated with banking' and the wider context of uncertainty from the general public over the security of computer systems.[64]

Logica's thinking was not simply that the most stringent measures possible should be employed. The report said that 'the level of protection provided must be appropriate to the risks involved and the magnitude of the potential gain from criminal activity.'[65] The responsibility was upon individual banks to understand the individual risks they faced and to consider the precautions needed in proportion to the relative threat.

---

[59] BoE, File 1A18/3, Logica, 'Security and Control in CHAPS', 25 November 1974.

[60] Ibid.

[61] Ibid.

[62] Ibid.

[63] Ibid.

[64] Ibid.

[65] BoE File 1A18/3, Logica, 'Security and Control in CHAPS', 25 November 1974.

Logica: Physical Security

Despite the need to safeguard information and transfers of money, the physical threat was still also in the forefront of Logica's thinking. They identified the 'IRA, anarchist and extreme student groups etc.' as those who may well be inclined to inflict malicious damage upon the central CHAPS computer installation, which particularly worried Logica should CHAPS and the Bankers' Automated Clearing Services' (BACS) central installations not only be located at the same site but also within the same computer room.[66] Equal weight was placed upon limiting access within the building and establishing perimeter security; it was suggested that consideration be given to the installation of 'electronic protection against access to the CHAPS area of the main computer hall' and to 'physical isolation of the communications equipment and its associated switchgear.'[67] Monitoring physical spaces to prevent unauthorised personnel entering could greatly minimise the threat of fraudulent or improper transactions being made.

Not only was attention given to insiders physically accessing machines. What an individual could do once they had access to a machine also had to be managed. 'Criminal or potentially criminal activity within the CHAPS organisation must also be recognised as a significant risk', the report read.[68] It continued in some detail, describing how possible security exposures could occur as a result of unauthorised program changes or file copying. In the case of the former, Logica believed that effective protection may be gained by control of access to program libraries and periodic audits to check that no changes had been made. Additionally, subdividing each part of the system would deny any individual the knowledge and opportunity to make clandestine changes. Unauthorised file copying could be prevented by a combination of physical security of the library and passwords associated with the files and checked by routines incorporated into the computer's operating system.[69] The threat at CHAPS terminal sites, the user banks, from unauthorised persons using the machines, was explicit: a breach of confidentiality, manipulation of valuable information, or even manipulation of software or in extreme cases the potential directing or misdirecting funds, could have had significant adverse effects.[70] CHAPS needed to replicate the qualities of authentication and trust that were previously offered by the paper-based systems.

A third area of concern was the communications network itself. Two interconnected problems were identified in this area: that the network was beyond the direct control of CHAPS; and that the Post Office Corporation, through whose Switching Centre at Colindale and the Post Office Tower in central London the telecommunications would be routed, could not provide 'any guarantees concerning the security

---

[66] Ibid.
[67] Ibid.
[68] Ibid.
[69] Ibid.
[70] Ibid.

of its facilities.'[71] Logica's major concern here was that of criminal intent, particularly breaches of confidentiality through line tapping techniques that could result in the leakage of information.[72] It was feared that such information, combined with a knowledge of financial affairs, could be used to make deals and so it was 'felt necessary' to 'incorporate encryption techniques into the system' to prevent the extraction of useful data.[73]

Preliminary investigations had suggested the use of the Vernam method of using a one-time pad of encryption keys.[74] Yet they faced the problem suffered by many before the introduction of public key encryption: the need to generate and distribute confidentially the storage medium holding the pad. They speculated that in the banking environment transit security would be less difficult than elsewhere, but also that other techniques, such as hardware encryption, may prove possible and offer 'similar levels of security without the problems and expense of one-time pad storage devices and generation and distribution.'[75]

Availability and reliability of the system were also placed at the forefront of Logica's thinking. The reasons for this were threefold: user confidence; the fact that CHAPS was handling a critical banking activity in Town Clearing, and so having to regularly return to manual procedures would diminish the status of the City in the eyes of the international banking community; and also that each failure would represent a loss of control.[76] Equipment suppliers were required to meet exacting availability criteria: 99.9% for the central installation, 99.5% for the terminal connection and 99.95% for the network connection.[77]

While Logica felt that after a 'settling down period' it was unlikely that the computer system would ever experience a 'failure sufficiently serious to result in its prolonged unavailability' they still stressed the need for a back-up paper system 'capable of being rapidly activated in the event of such an occurrence.'[78] This system would also act as a back-up in case of 'catastrophic damage' to the system.[79]

Consideration was also given to how the system would be brought back to full operation if there was an issue which rendered it disabled. It was seen as necessary to equip it with 'diagnostic aids' to permit the 'rapid identification of the cause of failure' in order to take the requisite steps towards restart as quickly as possible.[80] It was also seen as necessary to design the system so as 'to require the

---

[71] BoE, File 1A18/3, Logica, 'Security and Control in CHAPS', 25 November 1974.
[72] Ibid.
[73] Ibid.
[74] Ibid.
[75] Ibid.
[76] Ibid.
[77] Ibid.
[78] Ibid.
[79] Ibid.
[80] BoE, File 1A18/3, Logica, 'Security and Control in CHAPS', 25 November 1974.

minimum operator intervention following a failure'.[81] A number of specific measures were also outlined to reduce the recovery time: all files being duplicated on separate physical devices, updated for every transaction; core tables were to be periodically 'dumped' to disk or drum and each change to a core resident file or table should be logged; and this logging would occur both on receipt and transmission from the central installation for each message, with all dumps and log records including a time stamp and each transaction being allocated a unique system number.[82]

Even at this stage in CHAPS' history, security considerations were given serious thought because of the need to maintain confidence in the system. Logica recognised that security meant both the prevention or detection of any breaches of confidentiality or integrity of messages, but also the reliability of the system components. A significant part of security was ensuring the predictability of the system through reliability of its software and hardware.

Security Versus Cost

Throughout CHAPS' development its designers, representatives of the clearing banks, had to carefully balance the benefits of efficiency with a sufficiently robust plan for securing the new means of doing business. No more is this apparent than in consideration of how banks would access the CHAPS system.

It had been assumed until early 1975 that the settlement banks would all link to CHAPS using network access, but it quickly became apparent that the banks may not have this capability in time for CHAPS' launch and may instead begin by having terminal access, moving towards network access later on.[83] It was planned that participants – those using CHAPS as customers – would all access via terminals in designated branches connected directly to the central CHAPS installation, as opposed to network access which would mean any terminal in a bank's branch network could connected indirectly to the central installation, with the correct software, via its main computer sites.[84] Part of the debate here evolved around the respective costs of each method, but also around the development of suitable software for accessing CHAPS.

Security was a key consideration alongside the relative merits of either network or terminal access. One advantage of network access, outlined in a document jointly authored by the Inter-Bank Research Organisation and Logica, was that 'existing

---

[81] Ibid.

[82] Ibid.

[83] BoE, File 1A18/4, Inter-Bank Research Organisation, 'User software for network access to CHAPS', 14 January 1975, p. 1.

[84] Ibid., p. 1.

management control facilities' such as financial monitoring and security checks could be 'applied to all payments entering or leaving CHAPS' rather than relying on the CHAPS system; 'attempted breaches of security', for example, could be 'detected by the bank itself'.[85] One proposed function of any potential CHAPS software applications was 'message text encryption' because it had been decided that 'all CHAPS messages should be encrypted due to the potential insecurity of Post Office lines.'[86] However, it was the encryption itself, to maintain confidentiality, that took precedent over the actual method. The report noted that while it was likely that software would undertake this encryption, the 'availability of hardware on-line encryption devices (at reasonable prices)' was being 'investigated'.[87] Visible as the plans for CHAPS became more developed and detailed was awareness from its creators that maintaining the confidentiality of its paper-based systems would be key for its operations which were now utilising potentially interceptable electronic means.

The CHAPS steering committee was aware of the need for contingencies and again explicit in their discussions was the trade-off, or balance, between security and cost. 'At present it was proposed not to use the public switched network but rather to provide duplicate leased lines from the CHAPS central installation to the Post Office branching panels in the City' the minutes of a CHAPS steering committee meeting from 23 January 1975 read, 'with users being given the option to have duplicate leased lines from the branching panels to their terminals.'[88] The advantages of this were outlined: 'This arrangement would be operationally simpler, would allow private modems to be used (which are superior in several respects to the Post Office No 7 modems currently available) and would ensure that the system was always 'closed', which would result in better security.'[89]

Nevertheless, these advantages had to be balanced with the cost and necessity of doing so: 'it would be £40–50 per annum per terminal cheaper to use the public switched network and, if message encryption were adopted (as at present proposed), there would not be so much need for a closed system. In addition, the Post Office have recently announced new 2400 bits/sec modems which will be greatly superior to the currently available No 7 modems.'[90] Security was to come at a cost, and decisions had to be taken as to just how important this was to the success of the system.

---

[85] BoE, File 1A18/4, Inter-Bank Research Organisation, 'User software for network access to CHAPS', 14 January 1975, p. 3.

[86] Ibid., p. 5.

[87] Ibid., p. 5.

[88] BoE, File 1A18/4, 'Minutes of the meeting of the CHAPS steering committee held at CLCB, 10 Lombard Street on Thursday 23 January 1975', 10 February 1975.

[89] Ibid.

[90] Ibid.

Rising Costs vs. Security

Objections to rising potential costs of CHAPS became vehement in 1975. Barclays Bank in particular were unconvinced based on three factors: the costs of the system, the complexity of the proposed system and user reluctance to accept the notion of automatically approved payments.[91] At this point, five companies were selected to tender for the mainframe computer equipment that would be installed: Burroughs, Honeywell, IBM, ICL and Univac.[92] A relatively thorough outline of the proposed system had also been written which, after a brief introduction and elucidation of the benefits of a computer-based system compared to the pre-existing Town Clearing system, placed 'Security and Availability' as a key heading.[93] The document described how 'much attention' was being given to this particular section of the system's design, and offered some detail on the proposed plans: 'The central installation (to be located at Bankers Automated Clearing Services at Edgware) will be subject to stringent security arrangements and all information passed between the central installation and bank terminals will be coded [encrypted]'. Each terminal would also be protected by at least two systems to prevent unauthorised use and if appropriate, to restrict usage to certain individuals. Terminals would be provided by CHAPS and their use would be restricted to CHAPS business only.[94]

Confidentiality of the information passed across the network was seen by the developers as vital, but so too was the availability of CHAPS. The design of the system, the CHAPS steering committee said, would 'try to ensure almost 100% availability of the central installation' and 'most failures should not be detected by the users', as well as a 'fast replacement service' which would operate in the event of severe failures of CHAPS terminals.[95] The concepts of confidentiality and availability were at the forefront of thinking in the minds of the creators of CHAPS as these were far more manageable and easier to guarantee in a traditional, paper-based system.

Considerations of confidentiality dominated the security thinking around CHAPS as its development continued throughout 1975. For example, as the functional specification developed, it was decided that 'encryption should remain in the specification'[96] despite the opinion of the Bank of England's Management Services Department that they were 'not convinced that the greatest risk to security necessarily lies in the transmission of payments over Post Office lines'.[97] However, the

---

[91] BoE, File 1A18/4, 'CHAPS', 26 March 1975.

[92] BoE, File 1A18/4, 'Report to clearing committee from clearing house automated payments system steering committee', 7 April 1975.

[93] BoE File 1A18/4, 'CHAPS – Clearing House Automated Payments System', 7 April 1975.

[94] Ibid.

[95] Ibid.

[96] BoE, File 1A18/4, 'Summary of CHAPS Liaison Officers' Meeting 1 May 1975', 2 May 1975.

[97] BoE, File 1A18/4, 'Comments on the Draft Functional Specification for the CHAPS System', 15 April 1975, p. 5.

CHAPS Liaison Officers were as far as discussing the means of implementation of encryption of the lines stating that 'hardwired encryption devices were not favoured, especially if they were separate from the terminal controller' and that specifically 'software algorithms were preferred, the one-time-pad method giving rise to too many logistic problems.'[98] It was also decided that each terminal's keyboard should either possess a 'security keylock' or 'a badge reader' in order to ensure that access to the system was limited.[99] As the system developed, increasing focus was given to the very specific details of how security, and therefore successful operation, could be ensured.

Cost still remained high on the agenda and as the system neared the finalisation of its full specification this seemed to focus the minds of CHAPS' developers as to what was absolutely necessary when it came to contingency planning and security. For example, the 'target "meantime to recover" from major failures' of the system, the time for restart and recovery, was to be extended from five to fifteen minutes in the specification because of the 'significant benefits in relation to cost'.[100] On encryption, prospective suppliers were to be asked to quote separately for the cost of encrypting messages between terminals and the central installation.[101] It was stated that at the time, encryption was 'little used in the banks own branch networks and, while they recognise it as a desirable feature for CHAPS, there is likely to be a limit to what they are prepared to pay for it.'[102] Again the banks were looking for proportionality in terms of the balance between security methods they invested in and their cost.

Detailed discussion of fallback arrangements here considered those non-settlement banks who would access CHAPS by using one of the clearing banks as its settlement agent. It was proposed that there would be two options for them in the event of fallback arrangements being required: one was to ask their chosen settlement bank to make and receive CHAPS payments on their behalf; the other was to revert to the manual Town Clearing process.[103]

Decision Time

By April 1975 a final decision to proceed with the CHAPS project had not yet been taken. A clear image of how the system would look had, however, been formed.

---

[98] BoE, File 1A18/4, 'Summary of CHAPS Liaison Officers' Meeting 1 May 1975', 2 May 1975.
[99] Ibid.
[100] BoE, File 1A18/4, 'CHAPS', 12 May 1975, p. 4.
[101] Ibid., p. 4.
[102] Ibid., p. 4.
[103] BoE, File 1A18/4, 'Exhibit 2: Other Agreed Revisions to CHAPS Functional Specification', 15 May 1975.

Of its list of seven main features, two directly concerned security. Firstly, CHAPS would offer 'secure initiation and release procedures so that only authorised staff could permit payments to go forward.[104] Secondly, and slightly duplicating the first point, a 'high level of security at each stage of the system' to prevent unauthorised access was also listed.[105] Two of the core features also indirectly linked to security for users: the immediate notification of payments to recipients at the time of transmission and the overnight reporting to users of all payment to which they were a party.[106] Offering a significant level reassurance to potential users of the security of the system was seemingly a crucial part of persuading the banks to back the project.

Also outlined were expectations for the hardware that users would need in order to access the system. A simple terminal would consist of a keyboard, a Visual Display Unit (VDU) and a single-platen printer, although this could be expanded up to a maximum configuration of four keyboards, four VDUs and either two split-platen printers or four single-platen printers.[107] Each terminal would have the option of an auxiliary storage device in the form of either floppy disc or cassette.[108]

Decisions had also been made over security and availability features of the system. For confidentiality, all information passed between the central installation and bank terminals would be encrypted; for authentication, each terminal would be 'protected' to prevent unauthorised use or restrict usage to certain nominated individuals; and for reliability and availability, a fast terminal repair and replacement service would operate, the principal data communication lines would be duplicated and the Public Switched Network (PSN) would be available as a back-up.[109] Allaying any fears about the system's security or reliability was fundamental in order to persuade banks to fully back the development of the system. Seemingly persuaded, the banks pressed ahead with the project.

Sub-Chapter Two: 1976–1979

Plans for Implementation
For the settlement banks in charge of developing CHAPS much of 1976 and 1977 was concerned with plans for its implementation. The need for security impacted heavily upon the decisions made. One of the most significant choices in this period was over who should supply the main computer installation for CHAPS, and eventually this was narrowed down to two computer manufacturers,

---

[104] BoE, File 1A18/5, 'An Outline Description of CHAPS', 15 April 1975, p. 2.

[105] BoE, File 1A18/5, 'An Outline Description of CHAPS', 15 April 1975, p. 2.

[106] Ibid., p. 4.

[107] Ibid., p. 4.

[108] Ibid., p. 4.

[109] Ibid., p. 5.

Honeywell, who were preliminarily favoured by the CEOs of the settlement banks, and International Computers Limited (ICL), who already operated the BACS computer terminal.[110]

Consideration turned to cost and reliability of both company's software and hardware. The primary sticking point was over ICL's VME/K operating system, which was a 'cause for concern' according to the Inter-Bank Research Organisation (IBRO), who had heard through 'two unofficial sources', was in a 'state of chaos' where it was operational for the European Space Agency (ESA) in Darmstadt.[111] Following a visit to the ESA, the only comparable system to CHAPS which was utilising the potential operating system software proposed by ICL, there was 'unanimous' agreement that Honeywell should be recommended as the supplier.[112]

Following this decision, ICL made an attempt to reverse the thinking of the CHAPS steering committee by offering a relatively drastic reduction in price – from £2,092,391 for the central computer installation to £1,500,000 – with an additional £150,000 in cost if ICL hardware encryption equipment was required.[113] Moreover, ICL used their position as the current equipment supplier to BACS to put forward an argument on the grounds of security: 'the extra security in having further standby equipment immediately available', referring to equipment currently on site.[114] ICL explained that were a contingency centre or centres required off-site, either on a dedicated or shared premises, this was much more feasible given a single supplier with whom to deal; resilience of BACS and CHAPS work would be increased, ICL argued, and any contingency sites which had to be developed via two separate suppliers would incur significantly higher cost.[115]

Encryption also became a factor affecting Honeywell's tender: given that the CHAPS developers had not decided whether to utilise hardware or software encryption, the IBRO noted that performance of Honeywell's NT1, and upgraded NT2 communications software, could be 'significantly affected' by software encryption whereas hardware encryption to the US National Bureau of Standards requirements was likely to be 'possible at comparatively little expense.'[116]

The argument seemed to work – and on 14 March 1977 it was noted that the Chairmen of the clearing banks had ratified a proposal of the CEOs in favour of ICL – conditional upon ICL accepting 'severe penalty clauses … covering both the delivery and performance of the system.'[117]

---

[110] BoE, File 2A183/1, 'CHAPS', 24 November 1976.

[111] BoE, File 2A183/1, 'ICL and the CHAPS Project', 27 October 1976.

[112] BoE, File 2A183/1, 'CHAPS', 17 December 1976.

[113] BoE, File 2A183/1, 'P.V. Ellis to C.J. Montgomery', 18 January 1977.

[114] Ibid.

[115] BoE, File 11A70/1, International Computers Limited, 'CHAPS: The case for a combined BACS/CHAPS installation', October 1976.

[116] BoE, File 11A70/1, 'CHAPS: The Current Position of ICL and Honeywell', 12 November 1976, p. 1.

[117] BoE, File 2A183/1, 'CHAPS', 14 March 1977.

Payment Notification

As the proposed implementation of CHAPS got closer banks were forced to evaluate operational matters and the practicalities of banks using the system. This was particularly the case in attempting to understand the release procedure for payments. Once payments were released, and upon 'receipt of the notification' via their terminal, the recipient bank could regard it as 'a payment for which he is assured of credit in the CHAPS settlement that day', so the notification of a payment was the equivalent of a 'cash or guaranteed payment over his counter'.[118] The debate around definition that this statement referred to was a problem directly resulting from the translation of a manual process into one that was still completed by individuals but communicated via a computer and telecommunications network.

This clarification meant that some banks were prompted to consider the security implications of releasing CHAPS payments across the network, and therefore began to think in detail about the procedure involved. As of October 1977, the proposed system for releasing a CHAPS payment provided dual control: one group of operators using individual passwords could only input payment data while another group using different passwords could only release payments. Until both of these processes were complete, no payment information was available to the recipient.[119] It was noted that within individual banks, the aforementioned facilities may be 'reinforced by the security of the terminal itself, 'including a key lock', or various 'administrative controls', such as the acceptance docket produced after the initial input requiring one or two signatures before the release procedure could be enacted.[120] There had previously been suggestions that the release procedure could be strengthened, to require two signatures before it could be operated, 'equating the release to requiring two signatures on a bankers payment or cheque.'[121] It is clear that banks had been thinking from relatively early on about just how they could replicate the security of their paper-based systems in their new technological implementation.

Physical & Technological Security

The need to combine both physical security measures and technology-specific security measures in CHAPS was clear in the late 1970s. Some such measures were included as recommendations in a note from the Bank of England which tried to find solutions to three requirements: having positive actions from at least two people

---

[118] BoE, File 2A183/1, 'CHAPS', 31 October 1977, p. 1.

[119] Ibid., p. 2.

[120] Ibid., p. 2.

[121] Ibid., p. 2.

for a CHAPS payment to be made; requiring a higher level of authorisation for larger sums of money; and some users wishing to dedicate terminals to functions.[122]

Firstly, technological methods were suggested to ensure that there were limits on who could enact CHAPS payments. For example, the 'signing-on procedure should restrict the use of the terminal to certain functions according to the password used'; 'each user will have a valid set of authorization codes each valid for the release of payments up to a certain limit'; and each user bank 'will specify a "two-stage" limit"', a value above which payments would require two release operations.[123] Each bank that became a user would also be given a master password that would enable them to change any of the signing on passwords.[124]

Secondly, physical security was also recommended in the form of 'what[ever] steps' each user 'wishes'; recommendations included locating Visual Display Units (VDUs) or printers in restricted areas within the user's premises, and fitting VDUs with key locks so that they could not be used without the correct key.[125]

Further, it was recommended that users did not opt to dedicate terminals to specific functions, a suggestion that was partially based on security grounds. For example, in terms of availability, 'sensitivity to terminal failure' would be increased given the separation of functions to different computer terminals.[126] Additionally, dedicated terminals would be less secure than the software method of being able to access multiple functions, or at least those afforded to the member of staff by their password privileges.[127] This was because the terminal dedication could be 'circumvented by modifying the software in the [ICL] 7502 [the planned computer model for user terminals] while the software method can only be circumvented by modifying software in the mainframe.'[128] Given that this would be held at BACS' Edgware central installation, this would have meant potentially having to surpass far greater security than at user organisations.

To this point, banks had seemingly been happy that they had managed to replicate or even enhance the security from their previous paper-based system, but concerns were raised by two banks – Lloyds and Barclays – who questioned whether the proposed release procedure for CHAPS offered adequate security. A document outlining a discussion on the subject from a CHAPS Steering Group committee in October 1977 details some of the key issues, including the main objections which had come from Lloyds Bank, whose representative stated at the meeting that after considerable internal discussion they remained satisfied that the two-level procedure proposed was 'adequate to prevent mistakes' but, in their opinion, was 'unsatisfactory for the prevention of fraud'. Lloyds argued forcibly that a 'determined

---

[122] BoE, File 11A270/1, 'CHAPS Security and Release Procedures', 31 October 1977.
[123] Ibid.
[124] Ibid.
[125] Ibid.
[126] Ibid.
[127] Ibid.
[128] Ibid.

person with legitimate access' to a release password could acquire knowledge of an input procedure password, with or without the collusion of an operator. If a CHAPS payment was regarded as having the settlement bank's guarantee, then the recipient could immediately use the funds, possibly using SWIFT to give instructions for transfers abroad, and it would be difficult to recover the position. Barclays' representative also argued that when looking at the security of the system one should discount the input by the lowest level of operator. Therefore, they felt that there should be the opportunity to have dual release.[129]

Thos exchange of views is significant for three reasons. Firstly, one of the key settlement banks who would be vital to CHAPS' operation, both as owners, and as providers of the gateway to the service for non-settlement banks, was pointing to a specific crime type which could be undertaken with use of the system and therefore a significant potential weakness. The benefits of speed of communication that the system brought highlighted how quickly a fraud at significant scale could occur. Secondly, Lloyds had also "red-teamed" the system and even proposed a specific scenario – that of a person determined enough to acquire two passwords – who could then also manipulate the system, so they were able to envisage certain scenarios in which the system may be exploited. Thirdly, they highlighted the interconnection of two of these new, technologically advanced systems – CHAPS and, in this case, SWIFT – which could also use the benefits of fast communications allowed by both systems to make instructions for transfers of money so quick that it would be difficult to recover any of the money fraudulently transferred.

The Bank of England, in the person of L.W. Corp, its Assistant Chief of Administration, felt that if any banks 'had any doubts about the security aspects of the system' then it would be 'quite wrong for the Bank of England to attempt to persuade them to accept a lower level'.[130] Consideration had to be given to the real concerns and examples given by these two major banks.

Having been invited to comment on the issues raised by Barclays and Lloyds, the Audit Division of the Bank of England supported their case. Citing that they preferred 'machine controls rather than physical/administrative constraints, the Audit Division also said that 'much must depend upon the level at which password protection is operated, in the sense of assessing whether the input procedure can legitimately be regarded as an authorisation control or is merely a preparation process'.[131] They were also quite sure of their opinion on the release process: 'the process of authorisation (release) must, with certainty, be controlled by more than one party, given the "guaranteed" nature of the output', and also supported the idea of the system allowing for two separate release procedures.[132] Security of the system, its operators and procedures would be fundamental to its success and so

---

[129] BoE, File 2A183/1, 'CHAPS', 31 October 1977, p. 2.

[130] Ibid., p. 2.

[131] BoE, File 2A183/1, 'CHAPS', 4 November 1977.

[132] BoE, File 2A183/1, 'CHAPS', 31 October 1977, p. 2.

having thought a lot about the efficiency benefits of the system, the potential implementation drawing close focused minds on security the system.

A Security Assessment

In April 1978, a paper authored by the CHAPS Manager outlined the current status of CHAPS security. The analysis provided a detailed look at very specific threats in relation to specific crime types, looking at authentication, integrity of data sent across the system, availability of the system, confidentiality of the data sent across it and contingency should the software or hardware fail.

The paper argued that interpretations of security in the system depended on the perspective from which it was viewed. 'System security', it said, was a 'broad topic and it tends to mean different things to different people'.[133] For example: 'protection against fraud' to the inspectors; 'confidentiality of data' to the bankers; and 'guarantee of data integrity' to the technicians.[134] Subsequently, the document was split into four key areas – system security, data integrity, system resilience and fallback – each with their own specific definition.

System Security

System security referred to 'all of the aspects of CHAPS that pertain to general security', such as physical security, systems features and procedures.[135] Much of the physical security here referred to features provided as a result of CHAPS' location and running: the dedicated central system meant even though in the case of an emergency it was possible to switch the CHAPS application from one computer to another, the central computer would be exclusive to CHAPS, guarding against 'accidental or deliberate access to CHAPS from external agents'; the central site, at BACS premises, offered 'extensive' internal security arrangements; the location of terminals at CHAPS user sites could be 'physically undertaken in the most…secure location' and before any activity could take place on a CHAPS Visual Display Unit, a keylock must be turned, as well as a further keylock exclusively for releasing payments, with such locks being limited to named staff members only.[136] Unusually, also listed under physical security was data encryption: 'to guard against eavesdropping or active interference' with CHAPS messages, all data was to be encrypted during transmission. In the case of terminal links to the central installation, this was

---

[133] Ibid., p. 2.

[134] BoE, File 11A70/2, 'CHAPS Security', 25 April 1978, p. 1.

[135] Ibid., p. 1–13.

[136] Ibid., p. 3–4.

to be done by software, but for Network Access links, the plan was to encrypt using hardware.[137]

Systems features included outlining the use of passwords. It was the responsibility of individual users to establish and maintain their set of sign-on passwords under the control of their master sign-on password, with each password being linked to certain CHAPS functions meaning that it would 'not be possible to use the system' without knowing the specific credentials.[138] A similar process of users establishing their own set of authorisation codes under a master authorisation code was also to be set in place, with codes being linked to individuals; it was also recommended that 'separation of responsibility' could be established in the user's organisation by issuing the master authorisation code to somebody who did not have access to a regular authorisation code.[139]

It was stated, given the types of measures outlined in the above paragraphs regarding CHAPS security, that 'illegal CHAPS payments could only be created in a disastrously lax environment or by collaboration between individuals.'[140] Furthermore, 'passive detection features' would augment the more active preventative measures previously outlined, for example, in the ability to display on a VDU, using the appropriate authorisation code, all payments made by a user, allowing for the presence of any unauthorised payments to be revealed.[141]

Several other measures would also be in place to enable a detailed assessment of activity from the CHAPS hardware. For example, payment documentation would result in an 'Accept docket' and a 'Release docket' being printed from the terminal printer, highlighting full details of any payment in question, which could be corroborated with an on-screen tally of released payments.[142] Also, to 'guard against the possibility of interference with the terminal software' or the 'introduction of illegal programs or routines' all terminal software was to be loaded into the local controllers direct from the CHAPS system, with no local access being permitted.[143] In addition, security notifications would inform central CHAPS operators of possible breaches, for example due to 'illegal' log-ons, sign-ons, 'attempted use of an unauthorised facility' and the 'use of an illegal account or user name'.[144] A central broadcast facility also existed which allowed the central installation to send and then display messages on all Visual Display Units, potentially useful in 'extreme' circumstances for warnings or directives to CHAPS users.[145] At this stage, there

---

[137] BoE, File 11A70/2, 'CHAPS Security', 25 April 1978, p. 4.

[138] Ibid., p. 4.

[139] Ibid., p. 5.

[140] Ibid., p. 5.

[141] Ibid., p. 6.

[142] Ibid., p. 6.

[143] Ibid., p. 7.

[144] Ibid., p. 7.

[145] Ibid., p. 7.

were also plans to provide a 'comprehensive audit trail and archive' facility, although specific plans had not yet been established.[146]

Procedures outlined here, as discussed above, included requirements for one or two-stage release; the ability of settlement banks to suspend CHAPS facilities from any participants; to make enquiries within the system around, for example, full details of specific payments; and exclusive operations, for example separating the roles of initiating and releasing a payment.[147] Also, master passwords and authorisation codes could only be changed using the Master Terminal at the central computer installation.[148]

Data Integrity

Data integrity was defined as being concerned with 'data corruption and protection'[149] and the document suggested that protection against either of these eventualities was offered 'in part by precautions built into the CHAPS applications programs.'[150] Alongside a number of protections against data corruption provided by the ICL 2900, such as the operation of virtual machines and segmentations of programs and data, CHAPS also planned to undertake precautions: allowing the ability to encrypt certain data at rest, such as the 'more sensitive' items like approved limit, passwords and authorisation codes; a new payment file would be created each day providing the 'complete record' of the day's activity on the system; data within transactions was to be, 'wherever possible', validated, for example the checking of passwords and CHAPS account numbers with the reference file, a standing file in CHAPS containing data about individual users.[151]

System Resilience & Fall-Back

System resilience was defined as 'the ability of the system to maintain an acceptable level of service to users in the event of component failures.'[152] Primarily, attempts to maintain this level of reliability were done through duplication of components, including duplication of devices at the central site, duplication of

---

[146] BoE, File 11A70/2, 'CHAPS Security', 25 April 1978, p. 8.

[147] Ibid., p. 9.

[148] Ibid., p. 9.

[149] Ibid., p. 1.

[150] Ibid., p. 14.

[151] Ibid., p. 15–16.

[152] Ibid., p. 2.

significant master files and working files and the duplication of transmission lines.[153] Some significant detail was offered on the latter. 'Trunk transmission lines for Terminal Access users will be duplicated and separately routed from the centre to the Post Office branching panel. All Network Access Links will be duplicated, with the two lines being used together in load-sharing mode, but each line will be able to take the full busy period load.' Building in resilience was clearly pivotal to the success of the system. 'Circuits will be separately routed in their entirety, leaving the centre at different points and following different geographical routes to the exchange serving the particular user's computer installation.' If possible, lines would be routed via different local exchanges at the user's installation and enter their building at different points to provide further resilience to physical attack. If a spur line, branching panel or the second trunk line failed, users will be able to reconnect with CHAPS using the public switched network, providing an extra level of resilience for users.[154]

Using the language of resilience helped manage expectations. The system would be set up in a way that gave it the best possible chance of maintaining availability even if there were component failure or deliberate damage done. While CHAPS may not be entirely secure or completely infallible, measures were taken to ensure that should unforeseen circumstances interrupt its operation, there were alternative means through which it could still run and ensure that the banks still had access to it. Maintaining confidence in the system through reliability and resilience were key features.

Contingency

As planning progressed, security still formed a major part of the Committee of London Clearing Bankers' thinking. At a meeting on 5 May 1978, for example, the CHAPS Steering Committee considered a paper on security and it was concluded that extra thought needed to be given to contingency planning should there be a 'breakdown' of CHAPS.[155] A note to all member banks in 14 June 1978 – at this stage the 12 'Settlement Banks' who would be the only members of CHAPS on its launch – outlined some of the key security features that the system would operate. 'CHAPS will be protected by a variety of security features which are intended to counter the risk of failure, error and fraud,' the note explained. Those features included message encryption and duplicated equipment at the centre, keylocks, passwords and a release system for the user, whereby a senior official could

---

[153] Ibid., p. 17.

[154] BoE, File 11A70/2, 'CHAPS Security', 25 April 1978, p. 17.

[155] HSBC, File UK 0200-1014A, 'Meeting of the CHAPS Steering Committee on 5th May 1978', 23 May 1978, p. 2.

independently authorise a payment once it had been entered into CHAPS, but before notification to the payee.[156]

The minutes of this meeting also noted that a further meeting, subsequently held on 21 July 1978,[157] had been arranged with 'the representatives of certain Banks' to discuss security and that their views were to be sought on whether 'there was a need for arranging for storage of sensitive data in encrypted form'.[158] A CHAPS Security Working Party was subsequently created and its terms of reference were accepted at a CHAPS Steering Committee meeting on 3 November 1978.[159]

Security was becoming a defining feature of the system. Such specific detail on procedures highlights the seriousness with which banks took security, and how it became one of the advantages provided by the new technology for CHAPS.

Encryption

Encryption was a prominent subject of discussion throughout the development of CHAPS but it became particularly pertinent in 1979 as the system's proposed launch date approached. The developers inquired into the detail of the encryption algorithm that International Computers Limited (ICL) would use – ICL's Software Encryption Algorithm Mark 3 – and in return ICL supplied CHAPS with a note from the National Physical Laboratory (NPL), the United Kingdom's National Measurement Institute, outlining the strength of their cipher.[160]

The detailed report was authored by Donald Davies – the renowned Welsh computer scientist famed for developing the concept of packet-switching – who was Head of Computing in the Technology Unit of the National Physical Laboratory at this time.[161] Davies offered, firstly, wisdom on ciphers more generally: 'There is no cipher (except the one time tape) which is in any sense provably secure. It is impossible to examine, exhaustively, all the possible methods of attack since these are obtained by a mixture of experience, intuition, ingenuity and good luck.'[162] Despite Davies' caveats, the National Physical Laboratory undertook a thorough evaluation of the ICL cipher in question. Around 35 man-hours of examination were given to

---

[156] HSBC, File UK 0200-1014A, 'Clearing House Automated Payment System (CHAPS)', 14 June 1978.

[157] HSBC, File UK 0200-1014A, 'Meeting of the CHAPS Steering Committee on 4th August 1978', 14 August 1978, p. 2.

[158] HSBC, File UK 0200-1014A, 'Meeting of the CHAPS Steering Committee on 5th May 1978', 23 May 1978, p. 2.

[159] HSBC, File UK 0200-1014A, 'Meeting of the CHAPS Steering Committee on 3rd November 1978', 17th November 1978, p. 2.

[160] National Physical Laboratory, 'What is NPL?', http://www.npl.co.uk/about/what-is-npl/ [Accessed 20 February 2017].

[161] BoE File 11A70/4, 'Assessment of the strength of the ICL Mark 3 cipher', 15 May 1979, p. 1.

[162] Ibid., p. 1.

the Mark 3 cipher, by individuals who had previously worked full-time on data security and had done 'occasional investigations for many years.'[163]

The National Physical Laboratory's assessment was relatively positive. It described two potential methods that it regarded as '"weaknesses" of a sort' but concluded that neither method led to a 'very serious threat by an attacker'.[164]

The first scenario was one that used a source of matching plaintext – the text before it is encrypted – and ciphertext – the text after it is encrypted, although the relative amount of information required by an attacker to successfully work out the encryption key was relatively high. The NPL was able to describe a computing scheme which, they believed, would '"identify" the cipher (enable it to be reproduced [sic], together with decipherment, with the aid of 1 million characters.' This material had to consist of a 'number of runs of text', not necessarily all consecutive but with the runs not too short and all with the same key.[165]

NPL also assessed with 'confidence' that 0.5 million characters may be a sufficient number to find out the key, although they hadn't demonstrated this themselves.[166] They described how the 'heaviest computational task involved' would be the sorting of 1 million items of approximately 40 bits each, and how it would be difficult to programme some of the subsequent computation, as well as noting that it would likely require 'development work' in order to 'get the numerical methods correct and "tuned" to the task.'[167] However, NPL noted that this could be done 'off-line', without the need for real transmissions across the system on which to work.[168]

The second scenario outlined by NPL offered a more pessimistic view, but was very specific in its required conditions. They suggested that using 'chosen plaintext' – a string of identical characters – could reduce the quantity of ciphertext required, although this was not followed up, and it was noted that even in this scenario the method still required a minimum of 50,000 characters.[169] Davies also suggested that the 'unusual event' of chosen ciphertext and known plaintext' could perhaps shorten the process further, offering a rough estimate of 16,000 characters of ciphertext which was 'carefully chosen' and applied to the algorithm to yield the corresponding plaintext, though he could not see how this was relevant to 'any likely method of attack'.[170]

Davies, while noting that the potential threat was not that serious, did offer one method that could, theoretically, work for manipulating the system:

> Perhaps the only method suggested is that the attacker wishes to insert false messages by an active line-tap. He is able to bug the sending terminal and read the plaintext almost

---

[163] Ibid., p. 1.

[164] BoE, File 11A70/4, 'Assessment of the strength of the ICL Mark 3 cipher', 15 May 1979, p. 3.

[165] Ibid., p. 2.

[166] Ibid., p. 2.

[167] Ibid., p. 2.

[168] Ibid., p. 3.

[169] Ibid., p. 2.

[170] Ibid., p. 2.

faultlessly (errors would greatly complicate the calculations). On a given day he would record the first 1 million characters of plain and ciphertext, make the calculation and be ready to insert the false messages later that same day. An alternative would be to bug the receiving terminal and send out the 16,000 characters of chosen ciphertext (estimated). This would fail because the receipt of 16,000 bytes of rubbish would not be allowed to continue. This is worth remembering as a potential attack. If there is any evidence of strange character patterns coming from the line the current key should be abandoned.[171]

It was recommended by Davies that his clients think about firstly, whether the scenarios he outlined were plausible, and secondly, whether there may be people available to criminal organisations who are able to devise better cryptanalytic approaches that could work with less material or with a practicable amount of ciphertext only.[172] CHAPS were also warned that using software programmable devices for encipherment and decipherment carried dangers, since the software could be altered, and that these dangers were potentially more serious than crypt-analysis itself.[173]

The CHAPS developers took this analysis seriously but concluded that because each user's encryption key was changed daily, the intruder would need to collect the required characters so early in the day to perform the computations and insert his fraudulent transactions into the system that the two outlined methods were unfeasi-ble.[174] It was concluded that whilst CHAPS could not 'categorically' claim that the system could not be violated through a weakness in encryption, it would be 'virtu-ally impossible' because the cost and resources would be 'colossal' and a 'high degree' of collusion would be required.[175] A CHAPS document noted that should such collusion be arranged on the required scale, then there were 'far easier ways to defraud the system', which was not 'particularly comforting' for the banks involved but did suggest that the proposed encryption algorithm would 'serve its purpose'.[176]

Fraud

An internal analysis by CHAPS following the National Physical Laboratory's test-ing of the ICL cipher provided a detailed evaluation of the means through which CHAPS could be defrauded.

The analysis is illustrative of a core tenet of CHAPS' security that had been implicit throughout: that while the system may not theoretically be completely secure, the amount of effort involved in manipulating it would act as a barrier and disincentive to anybody attempting to commit a fraud. Significant detail is offered

---

[171] BoE, File 11A70/4, 'Assessment of the strength of the ICL Mark 3 cipher', 15 May 1979, p. 3.

[172] Ibid., p. 4.

[173] Ibid., p. 4.

[174] BoE, File 11A70/4, 'Data Encryption', 5 June 1979, p. 3.

[175] Ibid., p. 3

[176] Ibid., p. 3

into how CHAPS envisaged this being attempted and their assessment of the requirements and likelihood for it being successful.

The document outlined four non-time critical activities that could be carried out prior to the fraud taking place. First was the need for the fraudsters to obtain details of the CHAPS software encryption algorithm which was assessed as being difficult in practice, although it was noted that 'no reliance should be placed' on a software encryption algorithm remaining secret.[177] Secondly, they would need to design and produce analysis software that required knowledge of CHAPS message formats.[178] Thirdly, any would be attacker needed to identify the Post Office lines that would be used for a large CHAPS terminal access user and place line taps on them, connected to one or more minicomputers.[179] An assessment of the likelihood of successfully employing lines taps was provided: 'one could presumably assume that physical access to the lines would be no more difficult than tunnelling into bank vaults.' The insinuation here was of just how difficult this would be. If access could be achieved close to the user's premises, as opposed to the CHAPS computer centre at Edgware, identification of the lines would probably be relatively straightforward.[180]

Fourthly, those committing the fraud would have to design and produce software for the minicomputers to record all traffic passing across the lines, requiring technical knowledge of International Computers Limited's XBM communications protocol, although this was already in 'fairly wide' circulation.[181]

The document also outlined six time-critical activities that would have to be carried out on the day that the fraud would take place.

Firstly, all encrypted data passing down the line or lines would need to be recorded and secondly, the corresponding plaintext would have to be acquired.[182]

The later point was described as 'the really difficult step', and once acquired the text would have to be input into the analysis computer.[183] This plaintext occurred in CHAPS on three types of media: in notifications and other unsolicited outputs which appeared on the receive platens of terminal printers, as well as payment accept and payment release dockets which were printed on the send platens of the printers; on Visual Display Unit screens in the form of VDU input and output messages; and as payment release and notification data that were potentially stored on floppy discs.[184]

The methods of obtaining a 'one-for-one' match between ciphertext messages recorded on the lines using the wire taps and the corresponding plaintext messages obtained for the media above were also evaluated.

---

[177] BoE File 11A70/4, 'Data Encryption', 5 June 1979, p. 1.

[178] Ibid., p. 1.

[179] Ibid., p. 1.

[180] Ibid., p. 1.

[181] Ibid., p. 1.

[182] Ibid., p. 1.

[183] Ibid., p. 1.

[184] BoE, File 11A70/4, 'Data Encryption', 5 June 1979, p. 2.

One possible method would be obtaining a copy of all unsolicited dockets, such as notifications, which could be matched relatively easily with the printer messages on the line, in the opinion of CHAPS, because of the address in the unencrypted header of the message and the fact that all messages directed to the printer were printed.[185] It was thought that a means of acquiring these dockets could be collusion with a member of the user's organisation, although it was suggested that the need to photocopy such document would result in management controls detecting this occurrence.[186] A second possibility was the 'long distance photography of the printers through office windows' although it was said this could easily be countered by 'proper siting of equipment'.[187] It was calculated that an average notification was 341 characters long, and given the requirement for 500,000 characters of plaintext, this would mean the fraudsters would need 1466 documents; however, even the largest terminal access users with five printers would only receive 900 notifications in a whole working day with the printers 'going flat out'.[188] This means was deemed 'not feasible' on its own.[189]

A method of obtaining a 'one-to-one' match between ciphertext and plaintext messages using the VDU media was also outlined although it was ultimately deemed to require collusion of many people and therefore infeasible.[190] The possible method here was to obtain copies of all messages to and from one or more VDU screens and recording them to match with the ciphertext acquired from line taps.[191] Again the potential means was through collusion with an insider who could do screen prints of every VDU screen, but with an average VDU message size of 235 characters, on the basis of requiring 500,000 characters to possibly break the encryption algorithm, 2128 messages would be required.[192] CHAPS estimated that each VDU could process approximately 360 messages per working day, so six VDUs would have to be involved in this process, making it extremely unlikely given the level of collusion needed.[193]

The third time-critical activity was seen to be converting the plaintext data into machine readable format, for example using 'extremely expensive' Optical Character Recognition (OCR) equipment or the punching of 500,000 characters.[194] This was seen as 'extremely time critical' and would require 'about 100 punch operators' working for an hour, and would be 'particularly difficult' if the long

---

[185] Ibid., p. 2.

[186] Ibid., p. 2.

[187] Ibid., p. 1.

[188] Ibid., p. 2.

[189] Ibid., p. 2.

[190] Ibid., p. 2.

[191] Ibid., p. 2.

[192] Ibid., p. 2.

[193] Ibid., p. 3.

[194] BoE, File 11A70/4, 'Data Encryption', 5 June 1979, p. 3.

distance photography method had been used.[195] The fourth time-critical activity was the need to analyse the plaintext and ciphertext using a 'powerful computer' to obtain the encryption key which would then lead to the fifth activity, which was decrypting sufficient messages to obtain password and authorising codes to use in inserting bogus payments.[196] Sixthly, using the minicomputer, the bogus messages would have to be inserted into CHAPS and, moreover, these bogus payments would still have to pass any scrutiny which the CHAPS payee might make on money received for its customers.[197]

This highly logical security assessment is useful for understanding how CHAPS perceived its own vulnerabilities and how it thought these could be protected against. Although hypothetical, critical evaluation of all the means through which the encryption algorithm could be broken were assessed based on the National Physical Laboratory's feedback. Confidentiality of messages passed across the system was clearly a vital tenet of security in CHAPS for its users. It had developed a specification that made the steps required to undertake fraud so significant as to almost be insurmountable. A level of risk still existed, but it was one acceptable to each of the parties involved. This was a remarkable achievement and offered suitable reassurance to the banks about preventing fraud.

Sub-Chapter Three: 1980–1985

CHAPS is Dead, Long Live CHAPS

Despite significant progress over the past nine years, in January 1980 it was decided to put the CHAPS project on hold. It was announced on 14 January 1980 that the clearing banks and the Bank of England were 'reappraising their objectives for automated payment systems against a background of technological advancement'.[198] In particular, it was the system's setup that caused the banks to reappraise the situation, as technological progress had led them to conclude that the system based on a central computer was unlikely to be the best for their needs in the 1980s.[199]

Technological development had outpaced the bureaucracy and indecision involved in this collaborative effort. A project designed in the early 1970s did not offer, in the eyes of the banks, the best possible option by the beginning of the 1980s; it was seen as too complex, increasingly costly, too inflexible and potentially insecure.[200] IBRO described the difficulties involved in CHAPS I 'trying to obtain the level of security necessary in a system which would deal with such enormous

---

[195] Ibid., p. 3.

[196] Ibid., p. 3.

[197] Ibid., p. 3.

[198] BoE, File 11A70/4, 'Draft Press Release', 14 February 1980.

[199] Ibid.

[200] BoE File 2A89/2, 'The CHAPS Project', 31 March 1983', p. 1.

sums of money' while retaining flexibility, and also outlined how the introduction of an automated system 'not only raised new security worries' but also 'tended to call into question the adequacy of existing procedures which had grown up over the years.'[201]

For example, Midland Bank held the preference for the system to offer network access and therefore did not want to continue with a system based solely on terminal access, and Barclays and Lloyds did not wish to continue with the current ICL System given its cost for this particular format.[202] Costs had risen, at least in part, due to 'over-cautiousness regarding security measures' according to Charles Read, the Director of the Inter-Bank Research Organisation.[203] Also, while trying to solve such problems, it seemed impossible to maintain security of the level considered necessary without imposing unacceptable constraints on some users.[204] It could be argued that such thoroughness on security, as detailed in this chapter so far, had actually jeopardised the entire project.

Despite the termination of the project at this stage, all the banks involved, National Westminster, Barclays, Lloyds, Midland and Williams & Glyn's, were still in consensus that they desired an automated same-day settlement system.[205] A note to the CHAPS Steering Committee, outlining the ceasing of its operation, was sent on 27 August 1980. Scrawled on this note by an unknown recipient was the phrase: 'CHAPS I is finally dead. Long live CHAPS II!'[206] A project that had once promised technological revolution was obsolete before it could be implemented.

CHAPS II

As of 1980, the project in its initial format came to an end. 'CHAPS-whither next?' was the title of one letter from 21 January 1980 from a member of its Steering Committee, noting how CHAPS' demise was 'undoubtedly a merciful release' given that it would have been a 'continuing source of anguish' to its 'parents' had it survived.[207] The list of CHAPS settlement banks by this point had expanded to 13: Bank of England; Bank of Scotland; Barclays Bank; Central Trustee Savings Bank; Clydesdale Bank; Co-operative Bank; Coutts & co; Lloyds bank; Midland Bank;

---

[201] London Metropolitan Archive, File MS32452X/2, Inter-Bank Research Organisation (IBRO), 'CHAPS- A New Approach to Payment Systems', October 1982, p. 3.

[202] Lloyds Bank, File 10599, 'Informal Note of discussion by Chief Executive Officers following their meeting on 20 December 1979', 20 December 1979, p. 1.

[203] Lloyds Bank, File 10599, 'CHAPS Presentation- IBRO', 13 November 1979, p. 6.

[204] LMA, File MS32452X/2, Inter-Bank Research Organisation (IBRO), 'CHAPS- A New Approach to Payment Systems', October 1982, p. 3.

[205] Lloyds, File 10599, 'Informal Note of discussion by Chief Executive Officers following their meeting on 20 December 1979', 20 December 1979, p. 1.

[206] BoE, File 11A70/4, 'Note for the CHAPS Steering Committee', 27 August 1980.

[207] BoE, File 2A89/1, 'CHAPS- whither next?', 2 January 1980.

National Girobank; National Westminster Bank; The Royal Bank of Scotland; and Williams & Glyn's Bank.[208] Each of these would operate a CHAPS Gateway, standard software across the banks, which would then exchange payment messages over British Telecom's Packet Switching Service (PSS), providing a standard interface to each bank's payment system, and in turn supporting connections to bank customers.[209] Key to success would be maintaining consensus amongst these many institutions.

At the beginning of 1980 it was decided that 'technology more suited to the banks' future needs was becoming available'.[210] Networking and packet switching technology had advanced to the point where machines were now able to communicate directly with each other, offering substantial benefits over the previous iteration of CHAPS in which a central mainframe computer would be connected, by leased Post Office lines, to manually operated terminal units at banks and later to banks' existing computer networks.[211] The mainframe configuration no longer offered the long-term technological solution but many aspects of CHAPS' planning and thinking, especially around security, retained their importance.

By the latter part of 1980 a CHAPS II was in the pipeline and meetings were beginning to be held to discuss the potential for a renewed project. As of November 1980 CHAPS II had been outlined and offered a very similar service to its first iteration: 'providing a secure pathway by which guaranteed credit payments … can be transferred from one settlement bank to another with end-of-day settlement being effected at the Bank of England'.[212] It was envisaged that the project would become operational in early 1983.[213] The need for new methods of financial transaction had now been waiting for a solution for nearly a decade.

The demise of CHAPS and its reincarnation into CHAPS II was primarily due to the rapid development of technology; the bureaucracy and decision-making apparatus amongst the banks had simply not been able to keep pace with technological advancements. This was reflected in the initial 1980 CHAPS II proposal for the structure of the new system. The settlement banks, as opposed to CHAPS I with its central mainframe installation, had decided upon a 'distributed system structure, centred on the Post Office's new Packet Switched Service.'[214] Each settlement bank was to operate through an interface device which would be separate from the bank's main data processing systems. All interface devices were going to be supplied from a compatible range of equipment provided by a single supplier, each containing

---

[208] LMA, File MS32452X/2, Inter-Bank Research Organisation (IBRO), 'CHAPS- A New Approach to Payment Systems', October 1982, p. 5.

[209] Ibid., p. 4.

[210] BoE, File 2A89/1, Banking Information Service, 'Clearing House Automate Payment System (CHAPS), 2 February 1981.

[211] Ibid.

[212] BoE, File 2A89/1, 'Note on the CHAPS 2 Concept', November 1980.

[213] BoE, File 2A89/1, Banking Information Service, 'Clearing House Automate Payment System (CHAPS), 2 February 1981.

[214] BoE, File 2A89/1, 'Note on the CHAPS 2 Concept', November 1980.

standard software jointly developed for the settlement banks in order to facilitate correct routing of payments, the provision of secure audit trails, the logging of message total during the day and end-of-day settlements.[215] The concept aimed to utilise the latest technology and provide a system which would maintain its usefulness into the future.

Despite the clear indication that the new system would be passed on the Packet Switching Service (PSS) the banks were also considering a dedicated network based on leased lines in early 1981.[216] The PSS was a service provided by British Telecom – the new name for the communications arm of the Post Office – which used a communications procedure known as X25 which had been adapted as an international standard for the packet switching developments that were proceeding in numerous countries at this time.[217] The PSS, which began initial operation in September 1980, was based on a national network of nine switching centres, each of which was designed, as far as possible, to offer 'non-stop operation'.[218] A CHAPS brochure from 1982 described how the PSS, one of the newer data communication facilities offered by British Telecom, provided a nationwide public switched data service, with its name derived from the fact that transmitted messages would be broken down into 'discrete quantities' and 'wrapped' separately in control information, as they were sent through the network as distinct entities known as 'packets'. As in modern Internet communications, these packets would be reassembled at their destination into their correct order, the control information would be discarded, and the message would re-appear in its original form. Notably, BT described how the PSS provided full duplex working so that any device with a similar capacity which was connected to the system could both transmit and receive messages simultaneously.[219] Connection to the PSS was by 'leased "Dataline"' to the nearest PSS exchange, which were situated in most large towns and cities throughout the United Kingdom.[220] CHAPS could utilise this new technology in its service to offer a resilient and reliable settlement system.

Continuity

The banks were keen to build upon and maintain the previous security arrangements involved in CHAPS I in the project's new iteration. It was noted in an outline of the project from 1 January 1981 that the system 'must be extremely reliable, provide a

---

[215] Ibid.

[216] BoE, File 2A89/1, 'CHAPS background working papers', 1 January 1981, p. 7.

[217] Ibid., p. 19.

[218] Ibid., p. 19.

[219] Lloyds, File 10599, 'CHAPS – Interim Guide', December 1982, p. 9.

[220] Ibid., p. 9.

high level of security, integrity and auditability'.[221] A hard line was also drawn on maintaining confidentiality of payment instructions: 'It is an absolute requirement that all CHAPS payment messages passing through the common network should be encrypted. It is also considered preferable that a different key should be used for the logical connection between each pair of settlement banks.'[222]

Aims were set out for CHAPS security as of late 1981 which sounded very similar to those in the previous project. Three key aims were listed: 'to prevent unauthorised insertion, alteration, deletion or diversion of payments between the sender and receiver'; 'to prevent unauthorised access to any confidential data'; and 'to prevent attempts to render CHAPS unusable or to create serious loss of confidence in the system.'[223] These aims reflected the need for banks to control access to the system in order to manipulate its functions by sending false messages, and also to ensure secrecy as well as maintaining its availability. As alluded to in the third aim, 'confidence' was key for the functioning of such a system and indeed the financial markets and clearing systems. For the project to launch, let alone prosper, this confidence from key financial institutions was a pre-requisite.

Vital to maintaining such confidence was authentication – or the level of certainty with which you could operate, by deciding that the messages appearing on your computer screen were legitimate instructions. CHAPS saw their method of 'end-to-end authentication codes' as the 'most powerful protective measure' specifically to guard against fraud, as an authentication code would be added to each payment prior to passing it to the gateway software, allowing network access to the system, with the receiving bank then checking it upon receiving the payment.[224] A CHAPS document outlined how this would ensure protection as the message passed through all of the physical components of the system, which might include 'telecommunication lines, modems, front-end processors, Tandem Gateways, PSS links and nodes'.[225] Any payment not including an authentication code field would be rejected automatically.[226] Protecting against fraud and reassuring member banks that sufficiently rigorous checks were in place to prevent illegitimate instructions being passed through the system maintained its importance in CHAPS II.

Significant focus was also still given to encryption, as well as its application in authentication, in order to maintain the confidentiality of messages being passed across the system. It was stated by the banks that 'there is no guarantee of the security of data transmitted through PSS [the Post Office's Packet Switching Service]' and therefore the data was 'vulnerable to both wiretapping and interference with the software in PSS nodes'.[227] All CHAPS data transmitted through the Packet Switching

---

[221] BoE File 2A89/1, 'CHAPS background working papers', 1 January 1981, p. 1.

[222] Ibid., pp. 3–4.

[223] BoE, File 2A89/1, CHAPS-GSFS', 2 November 1981.

[224] Ibid.

[225] BoE File 2A89/1, CHAPS-GSFS', 2 November 1981.

[226] Ibid.

[227] Ibid.

Service was to be encrypted, which the Committee of London Clearing Bankers had decided would be achieved by 'interfacing in-line hardware devices on the PSS links between the Gateways and their modems' using 'one global encryption key for all the settlement banks within CHAPS', which would be changed frequently.[228] Significant precautions were being taken in order to make it as difficult as possible for anybody wishing to read and intercept such messages to do so.

CHAPS in Banks

The new CHAPS system opened further requirements for security, as banks could offer access to the new system to their corporate customers, therefore allowing these institutions to utilise the benefits of CHAPS. For example, Lloyds reassured their customers that reliability and security formed a 'vital part' of their CHAPS offering given that the funds transferred via the system were for same-day value and were guaranteed and irrevocable.[229]

Indeed, Lloyds stressed, the security measures to be adopted between customers and Lloyds bank were designed to be 'as stringent' as the security that would apply between the settlement banks across the central system.[230] They also reminded potential customers that they would also need to adopt the 'strictest possible disciplines' in relation to control of staff and the release of payments.[231] Customers would connect to Lloyds via the Packet Switching System, linking to the bank via their own mainframe computer, and had to meet Lloyds' specifications, including on authentication measures.[232]

A further option for customers was to purchase from Lloyds a ready-made CHAPS terminal which it was, in 1982, developing with the American computer company NCR Limited.[233] The terminal would be a customised version of Lloyds' NCR 2950 Genera Purpose Terminal used with specific CHAPS software produced and supplied by Lloyds.[234] Lloyds took security particularly seriously in this terminal and outlined five key potential features: key locks to both the keyboard and the audit roll compartment; battery powered memory protection in the event of a power failure; protection of program tapes and stored data against unauthorised access or corruption; and, where necessary, terminal functions were subject to Personal Identification control.[235]

---

[228] Ibid.

[229] Lloyds, File 10599, 'CHAPS – Interim Guide', December 1982, p. 19.

[230] Ibid., p. 19.

[231] Ibid., p. 19.

[232] Ibid. p. 7.

[233] Lloyds, File 10599, 'CHAPS – Interim Guide', December 1982, p. 8.

[234] Ibid., Appendix 1.

[235] Ibid., p. 19.

The first of these features was expanded upon in greater detail. A printer included in the CHAPS terminal incorporated a physically lockable 'audit-roll compartment' that, any time printing was done using any keyboard application, would print a copy in duplicate, with this version remaining within the locked compartment to act as a full audit trail of all CHAPS activity or attempted activity.[236] At the end of each CHAPS day Lloyds would produce a hard-copy listing showing each user's payments and receipts for the day, and this was transmitted to the user and could be used to confirm the relative day's audit list.[237] Additionally, any CHAPS payment or receipts were marked with 'EFT' (Electronic Funds Transfer) on the users bank statement and the reference number of the originator of each transaction was also shown alongside.[238]

Also explained were Personal Identification Codes, (PIC) which had to be entered by an operator before they could use any of the functions supported by the CHAPS terminal.[239] The entered code was automatically checked against the PIC file stored in the terminal memory to confirm that the operator was properly authorised to carry out their desired function.[240] Each of the CHAPS terminal functions were to be accessed in a similar way.[241] The PIC file stored in the terminal memory was 'under the protection and control' of at least two 'master PICs', which were normally senior officials within the user organisation.[242] PIC codes were comprised of an alpha/numeric identifier of up to seven characters and an alpha/numeric password of up to six characters, and the password was 'under the sole control of', and could only be changed by, the individual operator.[243]

Lloyds also drew attention to the fact that every validated CHAPS payment message needed to incorporate a unique Authorisation Code, which would also be used to calculate an authentication word to prevent transmission error.[244] The bank also stressed that to preserve the confidentiality of payment message encryption would be introduced at two levels, both between the settlement banks, and between users' CHAPS terminals and Lloyds.[245] Authorisation would be undertaken by a peripheral module known as an NCR C9950, which also performed the packet-switching technique, while encryption would be enacted via an in-line encryption device that would be provided to the banks by Lloyds at an additional cost.[246]

---

[236] Ibid., p. 21.

[237] Ibid., p. 21.

[238] Ibid., p. 21.

[239] Ibid., p. 22.

[240] Ibid., p. 22.

[241] Ibid., p. 22.

[242] Ibid., p. 22.

[243] Ibid., p. 22.

[244] Ibid., p. 20.

[245] Lloyds, File 10599, 'CHAPS – Interim Guide', December 1982, p. 20.

[246] Ibid., Appendix 1.

To bolster reliability, Lloyds also explained that alongside the internal-back up facilities included in their own central CHAPS computer, which was also supported by a second computer that could be brought into action at any time, that users would be able to initiate payments via their account-holding branch should their terminal become inoperable.[247] British Telecom, Lloyds said, had also undertaken to provide their own comprehensive back-up for the PSS.[248]

Ultimately, users of the terminals would be responsible for every payment released into the principle and, while CHAPS could provide the means of ensuring secure operation procedures, their effectiveness was, to a large degree, in the user's hands.[249]

The CHAPS II System

By March 1983 a clear outline of CHAPS II had been developed. This more modern system allowed settlement banks to 'plug in' to the CHAPS II 'ring-main', a network using British Telecom's Packet Switching Service (PSS), which only these banks had access to.[250] As opposed to the standard terminal access requirement of CHAPS I, the settlement banks were offered greater flexibility when plugging in to the network. All others, including corporate customers of the banks and non-settlement banks, would connect via their respective settlement banks.[251]

There were three requirements for settlement banks to become members: installing Tandem non-stop computers to a minimum specification; using jointly developed common software known as Gateway; and agreeing to 'certain inter-bank rules and standards'.[252] The Gateway software provided audit, routing and communications control functions to ensure 'orderly and secure operation' of the overall service, but banks were responsible for devising their own software to interface between Gateway and their own internal services.[253]

---

[247] Lloyds, File 10599, 'CHAPS – Interim Guide', December 1982, p. 21.

[248] Ibid., p. 21.

[249] Ibid., p. 21.

[250] BoE, File 2A89/2, 'The CHAPS System', 31 March 1983, p. 2.

[251] Lloyds, File 10599, 'CHAPS – Second Phase', February 1982.

[252] BoE, File 2A89/2, 'The CHAPS System', 31 March 1983, p. 2.

[253] Ibid., p. 3.

CHAPS II: Implementation

In 1983 some of the first work began on installing the CHAPS system and security had to be considered in this phase given the potential for collusion between various parties involved in the software development of CHAPS. At the Bank of England, for example, all Logica staff who were working on the Gateway software had to have been cleared for security purposes before visiting the Bank in July 1983.[254] Logica staff were expected to follow the directions of the Bank's Computer Centre Managers at all times and there was to be 'no contact of a working nature' between the Logica Gateway team and the Logica staff working in the bank on the development of the Bank of England's own bank specific software for using CHAPS.[255] Placing rules on these relationships was an attempt to ensure that collusion could not occur in order to manipulate the system by having a detailed knowledge of how both software implementations worked.

Only days later there was agitation in the Bank about the issuance of the software both to itself and to the settlement banks. The Assistant to the Chief of Corporate Services in the Bank of England noted how he was 'alarmed to discover' that both the source code – the computer program written in human-readable language – and the object code – the computer program written in computer-readable format having gone through a compiler[256] – of the Gateway software had been delivered together.[257] This was done because the Chairman of the Security and Encryption subcommittee of CHAPS decided that the code belonged to the banks and that they would wish to audit it.[258] Producing the Gateway software and individual banks' software separately was seen as an 'inherent security feature' of the system but the issue of Gateway source code was seen as potentially nullifying this feature; the Bank took 'immediate but unfortunately tardy' action to secure their copy of the sources.[259] Having put significant thought into the theory behind the security features during the development of the system, the Bank was concerned to follow this through during the actual implementation of CHAPS.

In this instance it was an old-fashioned security method that helped allay the Bank's fears. The original tape containing the source code was locked in a safe within the Bank, although it was feared that potential copies may have existed on mirrored disks.[260] Logica ran 'a routine' to identify any sources on their equipment

[254] BoE, File 2A89/3, 'Guideline for the CHAPS Project Office staff and members of the Logica Gateway Team during their stay in the Bank of England', 8 July 1983.

[255] Ibid.

[256] Daniel Sin, Matthew Sag & Ronald Laurie, 'Source Code versus Object Code: Patent Implications for the Open Source Community', *Santa Clara High Technology Law Journal,* 18/2 (2002), p. 238.

[257] BoE, File 2A89/3, 'Security of Gateway Software', 13 July 1983.

[258] BoE, File 2A89/3, 'CHAPS: Ad Hoc Security Meeting', 20 July 1983.

[259] BoE, File 2A89/3, 'Security of Gateway Software', 13 July 1983.

[260] BoE, File 2A89/3, 'Gateway MK I – Source Code', 15 July 1983.

and the Logica Project Manager signed a statement that declared, as sure as he could be, that no copies of the source code existed.[261]

This incident was brought up at a meeting of the Security and Encryption Group, on 20 July 1983, and evoked a mixture of responses that likely reflected the mixture of technical expertise within those organisations. 'The attitude of members varied from very concerned to slightly puzzled', a note about the meeting recorded, also stating that it had been agreed that all future issues of Gateway software would be made without the source code.[262] However, copies would be available on request to members of the Security and Encryption Group should the banks require it for audit purposes.[263] While it was noted that Logica could use a checksum within the software to ensure that no alterations had been made, the Audit Division of the Bank of England was clear that the risk existed more from somebody being able to examine and understand the code: 'The main exposure…is that from the source code it is easier to establish how the system works and thereby the best way to subvert it.'[264] The risk was that 'knowledge gleaned from the Gateway source code could facilitate fraudulent manipulation of CHAPS' although the Bank felt that while it was 'regrettable', the incident did not evoke sufficient concern to justify the relatively costly exercise of altering any of the CHAPS software.[265] Again, the perennial tension in CHAPS' development of balancing cost and security was explicit, even as late as the implementation phase.

The Planning and General Studies Group within the Bank summarised the incident succinctly. The exposure had lasted for approximately two and a half months and, they said, 'undoubtedly increased the risk of fraud or malicious malpractice' and that 'for such a sensitive system, which is being acclaimed in some quarters for its attention to security' the release of the source code had 'exposed a disturbing sense of naivety by Logica and the Project Office.'[266]

Security and Reliability

This new iteration of CHAPS took security extremely seriously. Part of the reason for its existence was the desire for a combination of security and flexibility. The Inter-Bank Research Organisation explained just how the integrity of the CHAPS service was maintained against both failure and deliberate manipulation:

> Given the huge sums of money that will flow through CHAPS every day, and the expectation that it will quickly become indispensable to the City, it is clearly necessary that every

---

[261] BoE, File 2A89/3, 'Gateway MK I – Source Code', 15 July 1983.

[262] BoE, File 2A89/3, 'Gateway Source Code, 3 August 1983.

[263] Ibid.

[264] Ibid.

[265] Ibid.

[266] BoE, File 2A89/3, 'CHAPS: Gateway Source Code', 12 August 1983.

precaution be taken. The lengths to which this has been carried is perhaps best illustrated by the comment of the banker who, when the various measures were explained to him, was reminded of the man who wore both belt and braces to avoid any possibility of embarrassment. In his view, CHAPS had two pairs of braces, two belts – and probably some string and glue as well.[267]

Protection against failure was achieved firstly by the selection of Tandem computers which had every part fully duplicated, and were designed to continue operation even after multiple failures. Provision was also being made by each settlement bank to switch to an alternative site in the event of a complete Gateway failure, and alternative procedures were defined to enable service to continue even if the second Gateway fails.

Such measures, along with those employed in the Packet Switching Service, were designed to protect against system failure. IBRO were sensitive to the possibility of CHAPS becoming quickly indispensable to the banks in the City, and knew that caution had to be taken.

Additionally, CHAPS had to protect against the accidental or deliberate deletion, insertion, or modification of payment messages alongside standard procedures for detecting errors. Vital to this were cryptographic measures for ensuring the authenticity and confidentiality of payment messages sent across the system. Every payment message was authenticated by a procedure which was carried out by each settlement bank itself, rather than in the Gateway. Care had been taken to ensure the security of this process by selecting an appropriate algorithm. Steps had been taken to restrict knowledge of the details of the authentication, specifically to avoid any risk that information would be made available on this subject to those developing the overall system.

As well as encryption of each payment message passing between Gateways, security was enhanced by keeping secure audit trails at several stages in a message's progress through the system, by including a time-stamp and a total value sent to date in every payment message. An elaborate system of message numbering and "handshaking" procedures both between Gateways and between each settlement bank's own systems in its Gateway. 'When one considers that these security precautions must remain "watertight" even during all possibilities of system failure and recovery', CHAPS noted, 'some idea may be gained of the complexity of the procedures involved. The system's developers were aware of the challenge ahead: 'It is a truism that no security can claim to be completely fool-proof, but the measures taken in the CHAPS system do seem commensurate with its importance.'[268]

CHAPS, having gone through significant evaluation and change over its life cycle, was thoroughly prepared for launch. This new version of the system offered benefits of usability, resilience and of particularly deeply-thought out security measures. It was braced to stand up to scrutiny.

---

[267] LMA, File MS32452X/2, Inter-Bank Research Organisation (IBRO), 'CHAPS- A New Approach to Payment Systems', October 1982, p. 12.

[268] Ibid., p. 13.

Reception

External attention was certainly given to the security of the CHAPS system, much of it extremely complimentary. One such group bestowing acclaim on the CHAPS system for its security were the National Physical Laboratory who, in a CHAPS progress report from August 1983, were cited under the heading of 'Security Authentication' as describing the system as 'better than any other they have seen.'[269] It was also noted that the Bank of International Settlements (BIS) had praised CHAPS with regards to its security, in the context of wider comments from BIS about the general insecurity of payments systems and, it was noted, the 'deeply concerned' Federal Reserve in the United States over computer fraud.[270] Sarah Cullen from ITN had been in touch with members of the CHAPS policy committee for an interview contribution on News at Ten and potential involvement in a documentary.[271] As several settlement banks had also been approached for comment, it was agreed that the institutions would each adopt a similar line: 'the banks in the UK are very conscious of the need to maintain the highest degree of security in their systems and are active in this field ... in view of the nature of the subject, the banks are not prepared to enter into public discussion.'[272]

Despite numerous potential setbacks for CHAPS, including significant debate about the system's daily cut-off time, participation from international banks and the requirement to interface with other systems, the project was seen – at least from the UK banks involved – as a major technological advancement. In October 1983 Michael Prior, the Corporate Finance Director and Head of Corporate Cash Management for Barclays Bank, penned an article entitled 'CHAPS: An Electronic Revolution in The Treasurer' which outlined just how 'advanced' CHAPS' technology was, modernising the current system of messengers walking paper around the City.[273] Encompassed in this, according to Prior, was the security of the system, which had been 'a paramount factor in its design' given the recognition by the banks of the 'immense value' of payments set to pass through CHAPS.[274] Prior outlined the security features in as much detail as he could, including that each payment would be individually identified by time stamping and sequential numbering. Full message authentication and encryption would be applied, meaning that every payment would be scrambled as it passed between banks, making any unauthorised

---

[269] BoE, File 2A89/3, 'CHAPS Progress Report', August 1983.

[270] BoE, File 2A89/3, 'Security of Payment Systems', 2 September 1983.

[271] Ibid.

[272] Ibid.

[273] BoE, File 2A89/3, Michael A Prior, 'CHAPS: An Electronic Revolution', *The Treasurer*, October 1983, filed 9 November 1983.

[274] Ibid.

attempts to interfere 'impossible'. Full contingency procedures were also established for extreme conditions or failure at any point in the system.[275]

The thought that had been put into the security of the system was becoming one of its key selling points. Given the stark change between physical delivery, and the human acknowledgement of a transaction, trust had to be developed that an electronic system could hold itself to the same authentication and security standards. CHAPS was eventually launched in February 1984 following over a decade of discussion and implementation.

Early Failures

Despite CHAPS' much-anticipated launch, its beginnings were not without incident. One of the first major instances of failure in CHAPS occurred in August 1984 when the Royal Group – Royal Bank of Scotland and Williams & Glyn's – were unable to get their CHAPS system working by the required time of 9:30am.[276] The incident underlined not only the interconnectedness of the information technology underpinning the system, but also the requirement for all of the banks to understand the contingency procedures.

The Bank of England understood that the initial fault was due to a power failure, but following this the Royal Group tried to fall back to the inter-bank machine at the Bank of England's Computer Centre but the leased lines between there and the Royal Group – last checked only two weeks previously – failed.[277] Power was restored relatively quickly at the Royal Group's prime site, although this left 'recovery problems with the Tandem processors, although Tandem assured them that such problems would be 'quickly sorted out' in 'twenty minutes or so'.[278] The Royal Group also assumed that British Telecom would deal with the failed leased line equally as quickly, giving two possible connection methods, so they continued to prepare payments for dispatch via CHAPS.[279] However, the Bank noted that 'their faith in both Tandem and British Telecom was misplaced' and that it was clear that the Royal Group should have gone into contingency well before the close of business at 3 pm.[280]

The knock-on effect of this incident was that of CHAPS being unable to fulfil on its key criteria. For the first time since its launch, settlement figures could not be

---

[275] BoE, File 2A89/3, Michael A Prior, 'CHAPS: An Electronic Revolution', *The Treasurer*, October 1983, filed 9 November 1983.

[276] BoE, File 2A89/4, 'CHAPS Failure 20 August 1984', 23/8/1984.

[277] Ibid.

[278] Ibid.

[279] Ibid.

[280] Ibid.

reconciled automatically and had to be clerically agreed at the Clearing House.[281] In the case of Williams & Glyn's, the outward payments stuck in their system could not be processed and so the Clearing House was unable to make its normal adjustments between the clearers; this meant that Williams and Glyn's had failed payments of £79 million to Barclays, £3 million to Coutts, £43.1 million to Lloyds and £148.8 million to National Westminster, as well as a payment of £60 million from Williams and Glyn's to National Westminster that should have been made the previous evening.[282]

A further failure occurred on 15 October 1984 when a problem of the CHAPS/SWIFT interface at Williams and Glyn's left 44 of their CHAPS payments, amounting to approximately £89 million, unpaid at the end of the day.[283] A dispute arose at the time, at least in part because the Bank's CHAPS log had not showed any record of a failure[284] and therefore The Bank denied Williams & Glyn's the ability to undertake late transfers because there was no evidence at their end of a CHAPS failure.[285] The £89 million worth of transfers were being conducted by Williams & Glyn's on behalf of Hambro's bank, and the banks waiting to receive such funds from Hambro's incurred interest costs, £19,400 worth of which had been paid out by 10 December 1984.[286] The Bank refused to concede that it was at fault for this, and even 'expressed critical views on the reliability of all Clearers' CHAPS and related systems'.[287]

An update on the system's progress stated that in November 1984 the average number of payments per day was 6476, reaching a single-day peak on 30 November of 11,241.[288] Considerable dependence was placed on the system. Town Clearing volumes had fallen by 15% and the number of institutions participating in CHAPS was up to 68 from the 42 at its inauguration in February that year.[289] It was noted that when problems had occurred, they had primarily been as a result of operation of individual settlement banks' internal computer systems as opposed to the CHAPS system itself.[290]

---

[281] Ibid.

[282] BoE, File 2A89/4, 'CHAPS Failure 20 August 1984', 23 August 1984.

[283] BoE, File 2A89/4, 'Williams & Glyn's', 28 December 1984.

[284] Ibid.

[285] BoE, File 2A89/4, 'Disputes with The Bank of England concerning late transfers over Clearing Banks' accounts at The Bank of England', 10 December 1984.

[286] Ibid.

[287] Ibid.

[288] BoE, File 2A89/4, CHAPS Progress Report – December 1984', 4 January 1985.

[289] Ibid.

[290] Ibid.

CHAPS Uses

Midland Bank was one of the settlement banks who provided a link into CHAPS as a service to smaller financial institutions and organisations from other industries who required electronic same day settlement.

Lloyds Bank deemed Midland to have 'emerged as the market leader' in such services by 1987 and noted how, with 'considerable disappointment and a sense of frustration' that the CHAPS clearing business of Commerzbank and the Bank of Montreal had been lost to Midland.[291] As well as being more expensive and offering a less flexible service than Midland, Lloyds adjudged their system security to be slower and more cumbersome.[292]

In May 1988 the Qatar National Bank's London branch registered as a CHAPS participant with Midland Bank.[293] The Qatar National Bank required 'a comprehensive payment system which would allow [them] to simply input an instruction and leave "the system" to determine the most appropriate way of paying the beneficiary', which Midland was able to provide through its electronic banking utility knows as Midland Automated Products and Services (MAPS).[294]

Morgan Grenfell also opted to use Midland Bank for their gateway to CHAPS with work beginning in September 1988. A DEC MicroVax II computer, one of the bank's four computers at this time, hosted Morgan Grenfell's central message switching system which included the handling of payment messages, commonly totalling over £1 billion per day.[295] This switching system used Logica's FASTWIRE product and so one of the first steps in accessing CHAPS was for Morgan Grenfell, Logica and Midland staff to work together to 'ensure that messages generated by one party could be securely transmitted and efficiently processed by the other.'[296] The system was up and running by May 1989 and offered considerable time savings in the funds transfer process, streamlining a normally 20-minute process, with the potential for delays, down to a 4-minute process which was far more reliable.[297] This reliability, however, required there to be plans in place should the system fail. 'Contingency is important to Morgan Grenfell', Midland recognised. They continued that both the main processor and the communication links were duplicated, with the "spare set" kept in a separate building for resilience. In the event that the main system went down, or if there was a physical event such as power loss, fire or flood, the back-up site could be operational very quickly. Should the duplicate site also

---

[291] Lloyds, File 11521/2, 'CHAPS' 18 November 1987, p. 1.

[292] Ibid., p. 1.

[293] HSBC, FILE UNKNOWN, *Electronic Banking News*, Issue 5, September 1988, p. 1.

[294] HSBC, FILE UNKNOWN, *Electronic Banking News*, Issue 5, September 1988, p. 2.

[295] Ibid., p. 2.

[296] Ibid., p. 2.

[297] Ibid., p. 3.

fail, which was only a remote possibility, the plan was for cashiers to revert to issuing physical checks.[298]

News International Newspapers were another client of Midland's in the late 1980s and they utilised the TelePath service for paying contributors to their publications. As well as offering a reliable and efficient way to make payments and complete repetitive tasks, News International 'fully utilised' the security aspects of the system 'in that no one person within the organisation is able to go through all the security functions and release a payment.'[299]

Midland also offered its services to Scarborough Building Society who were impressed with the communication skills of Midland's computer specialists. An extract from Midland's *Electronic Banking News* described how Peter Turley, chief executive of Scarborough Building Society, was tactful when asked to comment on the 'infamous inability of many technical people to speak English. Turley, with a wry smile, said he had 'met some computer people who talk gobbledegook, but that Midland staff could 'talk the same language' as he and his team, and explain things in a way that 'lay people' could understand.[300]

By the end of the 1980s, almost two decades since it had first been mooted, CHAPS offered a secure, efficient and technologically-advanced system of funds transfer to the UK financial sector and associated industries.

Conclusion

Ensuring confidence in the CHAPS system was the key driver of security thinking during its creation. New means of undertaking traditional tasks brought with them uncertainty and potential vulnerability and banks required reassurance that these potential weaknesses were manageable. Being able to place trust in the new system was fundamental to its success. Without it, few of the banks would have been prepared to put their faith in it. Tangible security measures such as encryption algorithms and authentication techniques within these new technologies were helping to instil and maintain abstract feelings of security.

The major London clearing banks and the Bank of England collaborated closely at every step of the project's development. As the development went on, and as the specification for CHAPS matured, the banks' thinking evolved from simply wanting the highest means of security possible to requiring measures which acted as a sufficient disincentive to those who wanted to take advantage of the new system. This was as a result of discussion and debate by the key institutions involved. CHAPS' structure, being owned and developed by those who would be its key users, ensured that security was built in from the beginning and not simply tacked

---

[298] Ibid., p. 3.

[299] Ibid., p. 3.

[300] HSBC, FILE UNKNOWN, *Electronic Banking News*, Issue 8, January 1990, p. 3.

on when needed. Thinking about security had been proactive rather than reactive, although this meant that ultimately the decision-making bureaucracy could not keep pace with technological development.

Distinctive in the creation of CHAPS was that security for its developers encompassed both the deliberate and the non-deliberate: for the former, concern mainly around fraud and breaches of confidentiality; for the latter, concern lay around system failure, which could be through malicious actions but more often framed as a result of hardware or software breakdown. A relatively consistent focus was placed on fraud and confidentiality throughout, although this was sometimes less of a concern than placing dependence upon technology that may ultimately fail. A scarcity of technical expertise meant this eventuality was a significant worry to those non-technically minded decision-makers within the banks who ultimately had to decide to implement new networking technology. Confidence in the system came almost as much from knowing that its technology was reliable as that information passing across it could not be intercepted or manipulated.

Despite this new technology, the banks saw the key threat actors and potential security vulnerabilities through a relatively traditional lens. Committing fraud either by deliberately sending false messages across the system, or by gaining access to messages and using them to commit fraud in a secondary action, were old crimes. What had changed were the means through which these were undertaken.

It can also be assumed that those in the banks also saw those undertaking these crimes to be traditional fraudsters, either through organised crime, using collusion with insiders in the banks to aid them, or by opportunistic tampering with technology. Computer and network security in the financial sector was being defined by historical crime. Perceiving the both the types of crime and criminals as relatively narrow and specific meant that security planning could be far more targeted and based upon lessons that banks had learned previously, for example around physical access.

New technology enhanced the speed and scale of these crimes and offered the potential for anonymity of its actors if they were able to use the new systems to their advantage. CHAPS was designed so that sufficient collusion was required as to make this crime impractical at best. Also heightened was the possibility of malicious sabotage of the systems that banks were becoming increasingly reliant upon. Nevertheless, these crimes were not necessarily new or created by the technology: they were still, in the mid-1980s, old crimes able to be committed through new means. Banks had a relatively clear idea of what they needed to defend themselves against. It was not until later in the decade and early in the next decade that the number and type of actors, or new crimes dependent upon the technology, would provide them with a much broader and unpredictable security problem.

Chapter 7
Hacking It: 1985–1995

By the end of the 1980s there was broad consensus that the financial sector was one of the most aware and active sectors in relation to computer security. Henry Beker, a computer security expert who had spent time in business, primarily financial institutions, was one proponent of this opinion. Beker said that with the exception of government and the military, the financial industry was 'undoubtedly the most advanced user of security equipment ... the computer security manager of a financial organisation has, typically, already become thoroughly aware of his or her need to implement security management.'[1] The major UK banks had invested substantial resources on computer security, both within their institutions and by contributing to sector-wide collaborations, lending some credence to Beker's beliefs.

Gordon Fielding, Head of Data Processing at Barclays Bank in the late 1980s, corroborated with this opinion. He believed that the major London clearing banks were 'at the forefront in terms of computer security' as they could not 'afford to take a risk with other people's money.'[2] Fielding recognised the magnitude of the issue, aware of the potential negative impact of a breach of security within one of these institutions. For these institutions, computer security had become a cost of doing business, intensified by the specific circumstances of their work in the financial sector, namely the large financial transactions they facilitated and the confidential customer information they possessed.

---

[1] Quoted in James Essinger, *Computer Security in Financial Organizations* (Oxford: Elsevier Advanced Technology, 1990), pp. 33–34.

[2] Ibid., p. 75.

© Springer Nature Switzerland AG 2022
A. Sweetman, *Cyber and the City*, History of Computing,
https://doi.org/10.1007/978-3-031-07933-7_7

Managing the Press

Despite the opinions of such experts, the mid-1980s saw a narrative develop in the press of scepticism towards the computer security industry accompanied by fervour for reporting about security breaches. The financial sector greeted what they perceived to be 'unnecessarily alarmist' reporting of computer fraud with consternation.[3] Within Barclays, for example, the issue was deemed 'unhelpful publicity', a significant grievance being that this coverage incentivised others to exaggerate the problem. 'While the banks remain silent the computer consultants and insurance brokers have everything to gain from suggesting the banks have a sizeable problem,' one Barclays note concluded. And as the active voices, the consultants and brokers essentially began to lead the conversation on the number of incidents being faced: 'Their figures are becoming established because ones compiled by the CLCB [Committee of London Clearing Bankers] – or statements that avoid the need for figures – are not available.'[4] Barclays felt frustrated at the inability to control this phenomenon. Lacking hard evidence to support their awareness and successes, they could not rebut the stories that could alarm their potential customers.

The Committee of London Clearing Bankers' (CLCB) Public Relations Committee discussed the issue in 1985, its members hoping they would 'soon be able to mount a counter-attack.'[5] Within Barclays, greater detail on the accusations made against consultants and insurers can be found in a May 1985 document entitled 'Data Processing Security.' 'There has been increasing publicity regarding enormous losses from computer crime', the paper proclaimed, with estimates from one unnamed consultant at £2m a day, or £730m per annum alongside one unnamed insurance company who predicted that the banks alone had suffered losses amounting to £2.5bn per annum.[6] The bank refuted such claims, stating that there was 'no doubt in the minds' of their Central Management Services Department (CMSD) and Central Inspection Department (CID) that the figures were 'highly exaggerated'.[7]

Further publicity outside of newspapers also aroused frustration within the banks. At the CLCB Public Relations Committee meeting in 1985 it was felt that a recent Channel 4 report on computer fraud affecting banks 'lacked substance, evidence and contained inaccuracies', though a formal response was deemed inappropriate.[8] Acknowledging that the Channel 4 programme contained criticism from law enforcement that banks were not reporting cases of computer fraud, the committee

---

[3] Barclays Archive File 0036-0067, 'Computer Fraud, 12 August 1985, p. 1.

[4] Ibid., p. 1.

[5] Ibid., p. 1.

[6] Barclays File 0036-0078, 'Data Processing Security', May 1985, p. 1.

[7] Barclays File 0036-0078, 'Data Processing Security', May 1985, p. 1.

[8] Barclays Archive File 0036/0067, 'Extract from CLCB Public Relations Committee', 18 June 1985, p. 1.

decided that a 'suitable re-assuring letter' should be sent to the broadcasters once the CLCB Security Committee had been consulted.[9]

Within Barclays there was a push to rebut such press coverage, feeling provoked by accusations of silence regarding computer security. This occurred specifically in response to an article published in the *Daily Express* on 12 June 1985. The piece ended by taking aim directly at the banks, who continued to 'purse their collective lips and repeat that their computers cannot make mistakes.' However, the article maintained, 'Christopher Johnson of city insurance brokers Stewart Wrightson pointed out recently in 1984 four of the big banks budgeted for £85 million in respect of computer fraud.'[10] The last sentence was angrily underlined in black pen by its Barclays reader, G Miller, who said in an attached note that this was the third time that such a comment had been made in the press and that steps should be taken to refute the comment.[11] Further, Miller noted that he would be 'very concerned' were he a Barclays shareholder reading about the figure budgeted in preparation for computer fraud, despite the fact that, 'touching wood, [Barclays] have yet to experience a significant loss under this heading.'[12] Even if the bank had a strong record on computer security, this coverage had the potential to undermine customer trust in them.

Annoyance at their inability to gain traction against what they perceived to be an exaggeration of the threat they faced, the losses incurred and their preparedness to combat such threats, Barclays were prompted to think more deeply about computer security. Partly their grievances were based on feeling that computer crime was being interpreted too broadly: 'One of the problems in estimating the losses from computer crime is the loose way in which computer crime is defined. In many cases the crime has been called a computer crime merely because a computer was used somewhere in the process.' Barclays was coming to the view that a narrower definition of computer crime should be adopted, namely 'the positive use of the computer in perpetration of the crime or there is mis-use of the computer.' Under this conception, Barclays knew of only 'one minor instance' that had occurred to date, 'involving the destruction of some program tapes by a disgruntled employee (back-up copies were available and the person never seen again). However, the Bank must not be complacent – one does not allow a fire insurance policy to lapse merely because there has never been a fire.'[13] While a somewhat cynical interpretation of the above paragraphs may conclude that narrowing the definition of computer crime could allow banks, in this case Barclays, to manipulate their figures for losses resulting from such crime, the bank did offer an example of an incident they suffered to support their interpretation.

[9] Ibid., p. 1.

[10] Brian Reynolds, 'A losing card for the bank customer?', *Daily Express,* 12 June 1985, p. 25.

[11] Barclays Archive File 0036-0067, 'Computer Fraud', 13 June 1985, p. 1.

[12] Barclays Archive File 0036-0067, 'Computer Fraud', 17 June 1985, p. 1.

[13] Barclays File 0036-0078, 'Data Processing Security', May 1985, pp. 1–2.

Regardless, Barclays was finding computer security to be a more complex issue than its practical implementation. The fundamental goal was to maintain customer trust in their operations, and so negative press coverage could undermine their efforts if the opinions expressed in these articles became entrenched. Managing computer security was increasing complex and multi-faceted in the second half of the 1980s.

Impenetrable

Despite the media reporting of computer fraud, the banks were confident in their track record in defending themselves against potential dangers to their computer networks. The Bank of England in 1985 began co-ordinating the process of undertaking surveys of computer fraud amongst the 12 largest UK based banks.[14] Titled 'Misuse of Banks Computer Networks', the survey firstly described its origins, stating firmly that the banks were succeeding in their missions to be resilient in the face of threats to its computer systems. 'In September 1984 a number of major UK based banks agreed to participate in arrangements for the confidential exchange of information between Chief Inspectors of the relevant banks concerning attempts, whether or not successful, to penetrate or otherwise misuse banks' computer networks', the document noted.[15] Confidential exchange meant that banks felt able to share with each other this sensitive information relatively confident that it would not be used to enhance the competitiveness of a fellow institution. This systematic organisation of information sharing arguably foreshadowed some of the efforts which became embedded practice for financial sector organisations in the 1990s, 2000s and 2010s, and which still continue today.

A relatively concise one-page note addressed to the Chief Inspectors of the participating banks detailed its key findings: 'No such incidents [of network penetration or otherwise] having been reported under the arrangements, participating Chief Inspectors were asked by letter dated 30 July 1985 to confirm that no such incidents had occurred.'[16] Following this, the document presented its findings from the responses to the July 1985 letter. A strong and simple statement asserted the banks' successes: 'There have been no successful attempts to penetrate the networks of participating banks in the period September 1984–July 1985.'[17] The document also described how individuals avowed that they had successfully infiltrated bank networks, namely a 'small number of claims by anonymous telephone callers.' In some such cases, investigations suggested that the claims were 'wholly unsubstantiated'.

---

[14] Barclays Archive File 0036-0067, 'Computer Fraud', 12 August 1985, p. 1.

[15] Barclays Archive File 0036-0067, 'Misuse of Banks Computer Networks', 7 August 1985, p. 1.

[16] Barclays Archive File 0036-0067, 'Misuse of Banks Computer Networks', 7 August 1985, p. 1.

[17] Ibid., p. 1.

In others, callers' attempts to penetrate the computer systems were frustrated by log-on controls.[18]

The above suggest that the measures banks had put in place had enjoyed a high level of success against attackers. Attempts to penetrate bank computer networks had been thwarted by measures designed to allow access to only those with the necessary permission. Ending the document, a concluding statement offered some insight into the potential methods forming the basis of the claims: 'One bank reported evidence suggesting that these attempted penetrations are initiated by 'hackers' in the USA abusing the international telephone network.'[19] Although succinct, the findings elucidated in this document provide a significant insight into both the scale of the threats faced by the bank and their success against such threats. Though the survey findings offered no comparison to other industries, they support the idea that the UK financial sector was well appraised of the threat to their computer networks and had measures in place to mitigate risks relatively well. However, by talking about "hackers" and the penetration of networks, the report alludes to a stark fact facing the banks at this time: that the threats to them were evolving at pace as they became increasingly dependent on computer networks for their business operations.

Planning for the Inevitable

In this context of institutions operating increasingly large computer networks and technological infrastructure the feeling existed that computer security incidents, from network penetration to physical damage, were increasingly likely to occur. Planning for such an eventuality had been common throughout the preceding decade and institutions continued to focus on bolstering their resilience to such an event. The Woolwich Building Society provides an example of such contingency planning. Whilst not directly in response to the threat of criminal action, or even attempted fraud, the Building Society recognised the need for resilience in their operations. The Woolwich in the mid-1980s discussed 'computer disaster' and its consequences: 'the risks of such disaster centred upon factors such as the losses of electricity supply, telephone connections, Bexleyheath buildings/equipment and industrial action by the Society's staff.' Ramification also included the inability of branches to retrieve up to date accounting information, 'major banking problems', the loss of readily available strategic management information and difficulties in paying staff.[20]

---

[18] Ibid., p. 1.

[19] Ibid., p. 1.

[20] Barclays File 1023-1146, 'Meeting of Administration and Personnel Committee', 14 May 1984, p. 3.

This list of consequences persuaded the committee the Building Society to explore methods to minimise the risk of such events occurring. Despite noting that the 'threats that materialised to computer centres were very few each year, mainly the result of fires,' the Society felt it 'necessary to ensure that dependence on Bexleyheath computer centre was not total'.[21] Aware of the vulnerability they faced by heavily depending on a single computer installation, computer security for the Woolwich meant both attempting to prevent any major incident occurring but also being able to recover effectively if such an event did occur. The perceived risk here was not restricted to criminal activity, but the potential impact of that or some unforeseen disaster could be similar.

The Society therefore sought to minimise the disruption that could be caused by an outage in their operations in order to lessen the effect on customers and hopefully diminish their frustration. The Woolwich claimed that their 'physical security measures against a range of risks to the computer centre were comprehensive' but also that the loss of the computer centre presented the most serious single threat to continued computer operations' for them.[22] Ultimately the Society chose, subject to the approval of its auditors, to reduce the risk inherent in total dependence upon their Bexleyheath computer centre by entering a contract for access to a consortium 'warm start' back-up centre, meaning that operations could be transferred relatively rapidly, shared with up to 19 other organisations.[23] The centre could offer six to twelve weeks of operation, and would cost approximately £90k per annum, permitting the Society to use equipment comparable with the Bexleyheath computer, which was already installed at the back-up centre.[24]

It was also noted in these discussions that in June 1984 a second generator would become available, enabling computer operations to run off it for 45 hours, in the event of a failure in the primary power generator.[25] Work was also in progress towards holding all systems documentation in electronic form or on microfilm, and discussions were underway with British Telecommunications in order to 'avoid over-commitment to one telephone exchange'.[26] The Society had an understanding of the vulnerabilities they faced by utilising computer networks for an increasingly wide array of functions, and was thinking about their computer infrastructure's security through the lens of resilience.

---

[21] Barclays File 1023/1146, 'Meeting of Administration and Personnel Committee', 14 May 1984, p. 4.

[22] Ibid., p. 3.

[23] Ibid., pp. 3–4.

[24] Ibid., p. 4.

[25] Ibid., p. 3.

[26] Barclays File 1023/1146, 'Meeting of Administration and Personnel Committee', 14 May 1984, p. 3.

Technological Advancement

An increasing number of operations were utilising computer and network technology now, creating a greater demand within the banks for computing power. At Barclays, for example, the demand for mainframe computer capacity was growing at 40% per annum and disk storage space at 50% per annum, mainly because of a growth of new developments such as on-line systems.[27] These growth rates 'far exceeded advances in technology' that were 'effectively halving floor space occupied by computer and disks every 4/5 years'.[28] If this demand were sustained, even with the continuous reduction in size of hardware, Barclays estimated that the available floor space at its Gloucester computer centre would be fully utilised by mid-1989.[29]

Barclays' chosen proposal was to purchase 4.5 acres of land adjacent to the Gloucester centre for £718,000 and erect a building with 40,000 square feet of computer floor in close proximity to the present centre at the approximate overall cost of £22 million.[30] Necessarily, each building would be totally independent for power, processing and air conditioning and would be capable of absorbing a greater number of hardware and software failures than their pre-existing computer centres could.[31]

The bank also had in mind its contingency plans when evaluating their options, and in November 1985 had modified its disaster contingency guidelines on recognising that the previous system of 'one centre backing up another at distance of 100 miles or more had become ineffective' due to the 'characteristics of modern databases and the time taken to reconstruct the data to ensure integrity.' It noted how the reconstruction period would lengthen as the bank's databases increased in size, and how a unit failure within a computer centre could result in 'a significant loss of service with the consequent degradation in customer service.' Barlcays' major mainframe supplier, IBM, was 'developing products which would allow, in due course, absorption of the majority of unit failures and, if the contingency centre were within three miles, would also provide disaster contingency.' Therefore, in preparation for that facility, the bank's Central Management Services Department (CMSD) had evaluated the advantages of developing centres as twin sites: a pair of totally independent buildings under one management team capable of 'operating as a single unit or independently of each other in the event of the failure of any components.' This "Twin Centre" solution was deemed the most acceptable solution to disaster contingency.[32]

---

[27] Barclays File 0717-0161, 'Meeting of Resources Committee', 23 July 1986, p. 2.

[28] Ibid., p. 2.

[29] Ibid., p. 2.

[30] Ibid., p. 2.

[31] Ibid., p. 2.

[32] Barclays File 0717-0161, 'Meeting of Resources Committee', 23 July 1986, p. 3.

Despite making large-scale investment and seemingly being acutely aware of the potential business impacts that a computer centre disaster could have, Barclays was resigned to the fact that it may never be entirely immune to a major computer security incident. 'Although a twin site would be capable of absorbing a moderate disaster', the bank said, 'it would be susceptible to a super disaster that would cause both halves to be lost', although they also noted that the construction of their new UK Data Network could be altered to allow all data to be re-routed to another centre.[33] Resilience, rather than total security, was the overarching strategy for Barclays here.

Barclays: Security Snapshot

An internal Barclays document entitled *Data Processing Security* from May 1985 provides a detailed insight into the type of operations within the bank that utilised computer and network technology and how the bank understood the threats to the security of these operations at that time. The document serves as an example of how a major London clearing bank understood and dealt with computer security and allows for inference on how similar banks may also have done so.

Conceptualising the threats to these telecommunications systems, Barclays identified the problems of data confidentiality and data integrity as particularly pertinent. These 'major' threats formed the core of the banks' concerns.[34] 'Unauthorised observation of data' could occur on leased lines and public networks, using 'sophisticated equipment', with neither the sender or receiver being aware of the eavesdropping and breach of data confidentiality.[35] Barclays summarised the motivations of a potential intruder in this scenario as such: 'the intruder is solely interested in reading the information for use in some other connection and does not intend to interfere with the messages or the system in any other way.'[36] This threat scenario concerned sensitive information being seen by those without permission.

However, data manipulation was the second threat cited by Barclays. In this case, the bank noted that 'sophisticated equipment would be necessary' to enable changes to be made 'without any delays to the flow of data being apparent at either end point'.[37] Barclays saw three potential goals of intruders attempting to breach data integrity: 'to change data (e.g. amounts or account details), add data (e.g. complete transactions) or delete data (e.g. prevent a transaction being transmitted).'[38] This

---

[33] Ibid., p. 3.

[34] Barclays File 0036-0078, 'Data Processing Security', May 1985, p. 4.

[35] Ibid. p. 4

[36] Ibid. p. 4

[37] Ibid., p. 4.

[38] Barclays File 0036-0078, 'Data Processing Security', May 1985, p. 4.

definition would be recognisable to cyber security professionals in modern day financial institutions, and other sectors, as a threat to data integrity.

The bank was markedly aware of the potential damage that could be done if unpermitted individuals could intercept or even alter communication traffic, even attempting to understand the specific methods and motivations of the criminals involved. Having been able to more easily manage the confidentiality and integrity of communications and transactions historically, given the manual nature of their undertaking, banks had to offer a comparable or greater level of security in these electronic equivalents in order to maintain their prized attribute: the trust of their customers.

The bank saw wiretapping as the primary attack its telecommunications systems were vulnerable to. Barclays' telecommunications environment consisted of four key technologies at the time: leased lines, 'rented for exclusive use linking specific end points', generally from terminals such as computer terminals in a branch to a large computer centre; the Public Switch Network, the 'ordinary telephone system using dial-up enabling any two end points to be linked'; the Packet Switched System, the 'modern British Telecom data communication system available for general use' which used a dial-up facility similar to the Public Switch Network; and Prestel, the 'public viewdata system enabling television receivers to display frames of information received via the public telephone system either into "private" files accessible by a closed group of subscribers or into publicly available files.'[39] Barclays saw the main threat to the leased lines as wiretapping, as they were not connected to the public telephone system, and wiretapping was also a concern in the Public Switch Network, in addition to 'unauthorised dialling into a system', described by the bank as 'hacking'.[40] Both the Packet Switched System and the Prestel system faced 'similar' threats.[41] The physical infrastructure involved in these communications, spread geographically across London, was potentially vulnerable to unauthorised parties intercepting the transmissions that it carried. Keeping data sent across them confidential was a key concern for Barclays given the potentially sensitive nature of their content.

Barclays also described two further threats whose validity they felt was slightly more questionable. The first of these 'other threats' was 'electronic eavesdropping by receiving the signals emanating from computer equipment', such as Visual Display Units (VDUs), which the bank said was receiving 'some attention in the media.'[42] Preliminary assessments by the bank concluded that there was only a 'small risk … of sensitive information being read by this means' although a detailed study had yet to take place. 'Protection may be achieved by encasing terminals and computers in a protective "Faraday cage" to prevent electro-magnetic radiation, but the cost may be prohibitive. In the Bank's main computer

---

[39] Ibid., p. 3.

[40] Ibid., p. 3.

[41] Ibid., p. 3.

[42] Barclays File 0036-0078, 'Data Processing Security', May 1985, p. 6.

centres the number of devices emitting signals is sufficiently large to create a noise background from which any individual signal would be indiscernible.'[43] Rather than attempting to defend against this threat, Barclays was taking a chance in thinking that the sheer quantity of emissions from its computer centres would make the take of interception and interpretation prohibitively difficult for would-be attackers.

Barclays' scepticism over the credibility of this threat is clear. However, as outlined in Chap. 2, there was some reality to this threat as early as ten years previously when the Bank of England discussed this issue with the Communications Electronic Security Group within the Ministry of Defence. Reference to cost also highlights how the bank was still in the mindset of proportionality, recognising that total and complete security may not be achievable, but that sufficient disincentive could be created by requisite investment, resulting in an acceptable equilibrium between the level of investment and the level of security.

Alongside this form of electronic eavesdropping Barclays specifically referred to hacking. Defined as 'the practice of using personal computer equipment and the public telephone network to attempt to gain unauthorised access to computer files', the bank noted that those partaking in this endeavour relied upon the fact that many computer terminal users within the bank were protected by passwords which were 'simple to determine' and which could be 'guessed relatively easily.'[44] A real-life example of such a potential vulnerability was explored, the 'well publicised' case of the 'penetration of Prestel's private user group files.' The bank noted that, according ti published reports, Prestel's development system was left connected to the main computer system and was protected only by 'easily discovered passwords' which, in turn, led to the 'master files containing other user passwords.'[45] Barclays stated that no system could be regarded as 'proof', or impenetrable, against hackers if it used the public telephone network whilst also noting how protection of system would depend on 'the adequacy and control of password systems', with effective passwords being those which were changed frequently.[46] While these two threats were not considered to be of the same magnitude as the two major threats of unauthorised data observation or manipulation, they are evidence that more widespread use of computers and telecommunications network broadened the potential dangers for banks. They had to adopt an agile and continuously evolving approach to how they defined security and how they perceived the threats to it.

---

[43] Ibid., p. 6.
[44] Barclays File 0036-0078, 'Data Processing Security', May 1985, p. 7.
[45] Ibid., p. 7.
[46] Ibid., p. 7.

Barclays: Protective Measures

Barclays outlined three protective measures available to them against the threats they had described earlier on in their *Data Processing Security* from 1985. There was significant continuity with the types of measures included in the major cross-sector infrastructure created in the previous decades and in the methods implemented within individual institutions.

The first of these was encryption which Barclays said could 'prevent the intelligence' of messages from being understood through a wiretap and prevent messages being altered, whether on leased lines, the telephone network or the packet switched system.[47] There were two options for employing encryption in the bank's opinion: either proprietary methods, or those defined in public standards which, Barclays said, had been 'promulgated only after exhaustive validation as being secure for commercial use', offering a high degree of reassurance.[48] The bank also described their pre-existing practice: although encryption was 'not normally applied' to data passing through their telecommunication networks, certain sensitive systems, such as Barclaycard, did have this protection. For so-called 'viewdata systems' such as Prestel, encryption was not practical, as user's would have required a computer at their end for encoding and decoding. Barclays speculated that cheaper microcomputers in the future could make such systems more attractive due to the improved security that was possible. Only particularly sensitive data files, including passwords, were stored in encrypted format. A project group was responsible for reviewing the efficacy of applying encrypting through different methods, and the bank also employed a dedicated team evaluating new systems during their development to to assess whether they would require encryption, as well as to periodically review the security requirements of existing systems.[49] With the commitment to build security in from the outset of new systems, Barclays was again foreshadowing later developments in cyber security practice.

Standard practice at Barclays, for both data at rest and in transit, was not to encrypt unless the communications were deemed particularly sensitive. They were aware of the danger of leaving passwords unencrypted on computers but had decided that insufficient benefit would be gained from investing in encryption, which created 'an unacceptable processing overhead'.[50] The cost of implementing encryption for Barclays, in most cases, was not justified by the importance of what it would protect.

Recognised here, and referred to more explicitly later in the document, was the sense that computer network security was an evolving endeavour, adapting as technology continued to develop apace. 'The future business of the Bank is likely to involve more direct connection of its networks to the outside world and therefore

---

[47] Barclays File 0036-0078, 'Data Processing Security', May 1985, p. 4.

[48] Ibid., p. 5.

[49] Ibid., p. 5.

[50] Barclays File 0036-0078, 'Data Processing Security', May 1985, p. 10.

the review of network security will be a continuing and important task' was the particularly accurate view included in one report from the mid-1980s.[51] Aware that encryption techniques were still developing, the topic was to be kept under review, 'particularly in the light of' the increasing number of smaller computers being used throughout the bank, where data was recorded on small diskettes and cassettes and could be removed more easily.[52] Barclays, and its peer banks, had to think deeply about new technology, understand both its benefits and flaws and then evaluate its usefulness to the business and its customers, with security a crucial informing factor in this process.

The second measure to protect against these threats was an application of cryptographic techniques and again highlights continuity from projects of preceding decades. Authentication applied a unique code word to a message, authenticating the main components, such as amount, beneficiary, payee bank and sender, enabling the recipient to be satisfied that the sender was legitimate and that the message had not been tampered with during the course of transmission.[53] Although this measure was not protection against a message being read, it could be used in conjunction with encryption of messages and was utilised in 'all the Bank's money transfer systems' including SWIFT and CHAPS.[54]

The third measure, underscoring this continuity, were sequence numbering and time stamping, and these data items could be contained within a message to guard against any delay caused by interception such as wiretapping.[55]

Despite these technical measures comprising a significant part of Barclays' security functions, the bank also relied upon physical access control measures and procedures for managing the security of their applications, their software programs and the data upon which they operated and generated.

For example, access control measures were used primarily for systems that comprised of several terminals linked via a network. These included each terminal in the bank which was deemed 'sensitive' requiring User Identification and password security and procedures emphasised that passwords used should be 'difficult to determine by guess or chance' and should be changed frequently.[56] Differing levels of authority were also applied by computers to limit operators to carrying out only specified tasks on a computer terminal, and these periods of duty at computer terminals had to be authorised by both management within the bank and the controlling computer, a process of authorisation that was used for the majority of the bank's systems, with individual authorisations regularly reviewed.[57] Physical control of

[51] Ibid., p. 5.

[52] Ibid., p. 10.

[53] Barclays File 0036-0078, 'Data Processing Security', May 1985, p. 6.

[54] Ibid., p. 6.

[55] Ibid., p. 6.

[56] Ibid., p. 8.

[57] Ibid., p. 8.

terminals was also practiced, by having keylock systems fitted to each of them, in addition to control of the rooms in which the terminals were situated.[58]

Clerical procedures were also in place to oversee input and output to computer systems and ensure that inputs were properly authorised.[59] Most systems provided reports that could be used to check the inputs against.[60] Barclays' major accounting systems were considered to be 'well controlled in this way' and such practices, in their view, had stood the test of time given that no frauds had so far been detected 'due to manipulation by computer means.'[61] Again, the bank's awareness of the need to be agile and adaptive in face of the evolving security threat was explicit. 'There is no complacency and systems are periodically reviewed,' the Bank stated. 'As more complex on-line real time systems are introduced which process items immediately upon input, the above control principles are enhanced, where appropriate, by the use of automated controls such as encryption, authentication and multi-level passwords.'[62] Barclays also stated that all their applications and programs contained controls to ensure the completeness and accuracy of data files during their processing, either through printed reports or built-in data integrity checks.[63]

Further, the bank described data file protection as 'another vital element of security' and described RACF, their own proprietary security system installed in its computer centres, which used passwords to control who had access to individual data and program files and for what purposes, for example to read, write or modify.[64] All files were protected in this way against unauthorised access or manipulation, and the provision of RACF at the bank's computer centres holding its mainframes was deemed to give the Bank 'adequate file protection'.[65] Barclays also described how data files 'should always' be provided with back-up copies for continuity in the event of a disaster, and noted that this had been given a 'high level' of importance within the bank.[66]

Barclays knew, however, that a strong record on computer security also depended on individuals. Despite the protective measures described, the bank said, the people working on computers still had to be trusted: 'the Bank still has to rely on the integrity of those who install and amend software protection facilities.'[67] People, in these privileged, sensitive positions, and likely possessing technical knowledge shared by very few others, represented a crucial vulnerability even given the thoroughness of thought around security by Barclays.

---

[58] Ibid., p. 8.

[59] Barclays File 0036-0078, 'Data Processing Security', May 1985, p. 9.

[60] Ibid., p. 9.

[61] Ibid., p. 9.

[62] Ibid., p. 9.

[63] Ibid., p. 9.

[64] Ibid., p. 10.

[65] Ibid., p. 10.

[66] Barclays File 0036-0078, 'Data Processing Security', May 1985, p. 10.

[67] Ibid., p. 10.

Barclays: Software

A combination of technical and physical measures helped manage Barclays' computer network security at a broader level, but the bank also had to consider security in minute detail when it came to the programs it ran on its computers. They described how, despite the matter being 'of great concern' to the bank over 'many years', the issue had 'not been resolved to any degree of satisfaction.'[68]

According to Barclays, the problem could be viewed in two parts, the first concerning the initial authoring of these programs: 'Ensuring that when programs are written, they contain only the code which is required for the functions they are designed to carry out and that there is no illegal or unauthorised coding within them ('Trojan horses').' Prior to this, the bank had been dependent largely upon 'trust that code is only what it purports to be', supplemented by a technical overview of the program code during development. 'We do not subject code to independent scrutiny and certification prior to it being incorporated into a live computer system; this applies to major enhancements as well as to new systems,' read one Barclays memo, in stark contrast to the thorough review processes routinely followed today. Such scrutiny was not possible due to 'lack of resources of sufficient calibre'. Though this approach was already under review by Barclays by 1985. Checking only covered the functionality of systems, and deeper code review constituted a trade off of productivity against security, a price which Barclays had not yet been prepared to pay. The bank was particularly sensitive to what it described as 'sudden resignations', which did cause them to take some steps towards protecting themselves and their software against the possibility the the employee concerned had 'perpetrated an unwelcome act', through no detail on these steps was offered.[69]

Depending upon trust that coders were acting wholly in accordance with their instructions opened Barclays up to a vulnerability, especially because the code that was written was not subject to any third-party scrutiny. Lack of resources was cited as a reason for, by their own admission, unsatisfactory procedures in place here, the trade-off between security and costs again being apparent.

Second, related to the first issue, there was the problem of overseeing edits to the code of programs already running on Barclays' computers, to ensure that no extraneous code had been subsequently introduced by unauthorised means. A facility existed at Barclays' mainframe computer centres to compare the operational programs used with 'secured (management) copies but which have limited use to ensure computer program integrity.' To be effective, the bank knew, this monitoring had to be combined with 'strong controls in the programming area.'[70] In this case there *was* some level of control given the facility to compare operations programs with stored copies, but the difficulty still existed, as by the time the check had taken place the operational program could well have been amended. Price Waterhouse

---

[68] Ibid., p. 11.

[69] Barclays File 0036-0078, 'Data Processing Security', May 1985, p. 11.

[70] Ibid., p. 12.

Associates had been commissioned by May 1985 to conduct a review of program and data security, part of which would be proposals for enhanced methods of controlling program amendments alongside applying stronger controls over original programming.[71]

Barclays were less concerned with the security of their four computer centres which contained their mainframe installations, as, in particular their two primary centres at Gloucester and Wythenshawe, were 'purpose built' and practiced 'strict access control and emergency procedures which were regularly tested.[72]

Contingency planning was also a core constituent of Barclays' effort for managing the risk inherent in their growing utilisation of technology. They viewed the purpose of such planning as minimising the effect on users of failures of all or part of automated services in the bank's computer centres.[73] An annual policy statement set out the objectives of the bank's contingency plans, including explanations of any constraints which applied, and as of 1985 the policy stated that there must be 'sufficient processing capacity' to cover intra- and inter-centre contingency.[74] For its telecommunications networks used for data processing, the bank's plan was to fall back on the Public Switched Telephone Network.[75] Despite realising the importance of contingency plans, staff shortages and increased workloads at computer centres meant that contingency testing had lapsed by early 1985, although the bank hoped to restart this process by June.[76] Investigations were also underway to find a more efficient way of managing the difficulties when transferring databases from one computer centre to another, for example in the event of a complete failure at one computer centre.[77]

Discussions within Barclays further highlight just how seriously the issue of tampering with data within new telecommunications systems was taken. Consideration was given to the creation of a real-time dealing system in 1985 for Barclays de Zoete Wedd (BZW), the original name for the investment banking arm of the bank. In March of that year, while the business was deciding whether to build or buy a dealing support system, major areas of consideration were highlighted, including the performance of any system, its resilience and its functionality, with the biggest priority being data integrity.[78] An assessment of the risks involved in real-time systems included the description that given the direct user input to any system, there was 'less discipline' verification did not occur and data could not be suspended, but had to be dealt with immediately.[79] File and transaction security, the

[71] Barclays File 0036-0078, 'Data Processing Security', May 1985, p. 12.

[72] Ibid., p. 11.

[73] Ibid., p. 14.

[74] Ibid., p. 14.

[75] Ibid., p. 114.

[76] Ibid., p. 14.

[77] Ibid., p. 14.

[78] Barclays File 0222-0049, 'Real-time Dealing System for BZW', 27 March 1985, p. 2.

[79] Barclays File 0222-0049, 'Real-time Systems Development', 22 March 1985, p. 2.

bank said, 'had to occur in flight'.[80] While a batch system might have afforded the bank slightly more control and therefore reassurance over its running, a real-time system offered greater performance benefits. Such a trade-off, between functionality and security, was not taken lightly.

Taking Stock

In January 1987 the Committee on the Review of Banking Services Law was appointed, reporting jointly to the Chancellor of the Exchequer and the Governor of the Bank of England.[81] Over a two-year period the enquiry's terms of reference were to 'examine the law and its practical implications from the points of view of banker, customer and the general public interest in the availability, reliability, security and effective operation of payment, remittance and other banking services'.[82] The report offers a detailed exploration of the legal status of banking services alongside extremely useful and detailed outline of the broader themes that were challenging the sector, with particular focus on new technological development.

Explicit in the report was an awareness of the importance of a belief that the banking system was secure. Four objectives seen as priorities when considering new solutions to problems of law and practice were listed, one of which was 'to maintain confidence in the security of the banking system.'[83] The report continued: 'We have seen how the opportunities for banking fraud, already enhanced by new technology and by the international spread of banking ... It is important to see banking fraud as something more than an item in banks' profit and loss accounts: on that view, anti-fraud measures could be left wholly to their commercial judgement.'[84] Rather than being considered in the context of its purely financial impact, the report encouraged the banks to consider computer security in its more abstract context in instilling confidence in the banking system as a whole.

This sentiment was a key theme throughout the Review. The Committee recognised that their investigations required caution, and that the banks would be nervous about discussing security in the open: 'Banks are naturally and properly concerned to ensure that confidence in the banking system is maintained. For this reason, it is quite understandable that they should wish to discourage any public discussion of

---

[80] Ibid., p. 2.

[81] The National Archives, 'Committee on the Review of Banking Services Law (Jack Committee): Report and Government Response', http://discovery.nationalarchives.gov.uk/details/r/C14027 [Accessed 21 December 2015].

[82] Professor R B Jack, *Banking Services: Law and Practice: Report by the Review Committee*, CM 622, 30 December 1988, p. 2.

[83] Ibid., p. 24.

[84] Ibid., p. 24.

systems security which might cast doubt on how efficacious that security is.'[85] The Review Committee stressed that it fully shared the banks' wish not to upset confidence, which it agreed was integral to the whole activity and business of banking.

The Review Committee reinforced the view of the banks that trust and consumer confidence was vital for their modern operations' success. They also alluded to the recurring trade-off for banks between implementing security measures and the justification for doing so in terms of cost. 'Expedients of a more technical kind are available to banks to improve levels of security on existing systems', the Committee noted. 'We are advised that encryption is the best available means of preventing internal interception of electronically transmitted information within the banking system ... that "end-to-end encryption" eliminates 90 per cent of such fraud.' Though recognising the utility of this capability, which was being progressively introduced for both ATM networks and other systems such as SWIFT, it noted that end-to-end encryption was not yet universal and that problems existed that limited its application, such as operational performance and facility of maintenance. 'There is also some question how far the cost is justified by the nature of the threat it is aimed against, given that fraud within the banks, as one might well expect, is said to be a relatively minor element in the overall scene,' the report concluded.[86] The Committee showed an awareness of the various issues that banks had to evaluate before deciding how to secure their assets. Specifically, they recognised the importance of confidentiality in communications that was fundamental to the trust between customers and banks.

It seems that by the late-1980s awareness was spreading further outside of the banks and into the realms of the public sector. It was reported that City firms' defences were tested on their computer security by the City of London Police. In an operation codenamed Comcheck, City firms were required to track the number of authorised log-ons over Easter bank holiday weekend in 1989, with the results reportedly proving slightly worrying.[87] Some companies were unable to ascertain whether hackers had penetrated their networks and others 'lacked any security defences and had to produce special software merely to take part in the exercise.'[88] A spokesman for the City of London Fraud Squad was quoted as saying that the exercise revealed 'significant weaknesses' in the procedures of some firms.[89] Detective Inspector Norman Russell of the City of London Police at the time said that his organisation had seen 'some incredible things in banks and finance houses'

---

[85] Professor R B Jack, *Banking Services: Law and Practice: Report by the Review Committee*, CM 622, 30 December 1988, p. 82.

[86] Ibid., p. 87.

[87] See Richard Caseby, 'City "pays off" hackers to keep silent on crime", *The Sunday Times*, 4 June 1989; Richard Caseby, 'Worried Firms Pay Hush Money To "Hackers"', *The Sunday Times*, 12 June 1989; "The Comcheck Initiative', *Computer Fraud & Security Bulletin*, November 1989, p. 4.

[88] Richard Caseby, 'City "pays off" hackers to keep silent on crime", *The Sunday Times*, 4 June 1989.

[89] 'Computer crime- how to avoid a hack attack', *Management Today*, 30 January 1990.

in terms of these businesses' lack of awareness on computer security, and was reported as saying that some firms had security systems in name only.[90]

Computer security was also raised at the highest level of politics in the late 1980s. Baroness Nicholson of Winterbourne described how she had had 'a very long interview with the prime minister about this' and that Mrs Thatcher 'understood the real concerns I was putting out in front of her'.[91] Nicholson was also confident that the cabinet ministers she had briefed on the issue also understood the magnitude of the situation.[92]

In October 1989, the Law Commission published a report on Computer Misuse that included many observations on businesses and their use of computer technology. Their report referred to just how computers had become much more active in business operations rather than simply static means of holding large amounts of information: 'Although computers are sometimes thought of principally as a sophisticated means of collating and holding information, many computers are now used in 'operational' as opposed to purely information-storing roles. Such systems administered not only financial transactions (for instance, world-wide inter-bank fund transfer systems) but also a wide variety of complex operations.' The report listed other uses of computers such as in air traffic control systems and hospital systems for calculating drug doses, as well as stock control and automatic reordering in retail businesses, robot control of machines in manufacturing and the programming of computers to trade on Stock Exchanges in response to economic data and price movements inputted by other systems.[93] In fact, the report went as far as to state that the extent to which and the complexity with which such operations were being computerised appeared to be increasing day-by-day. The variety of operations underpinned by computer usage emphasised the extent of dependence being placed on these machines.

The Commission also reflected in detail on how unauthorised access to a banking computer system might be dealt with by the law, and the various problems associated with proving an offence. The first of those concerned hackers who gained unauthorised access to a system. Further security checks stood in the way of that individual transfers funds between banks accounts, including potentially secret passwords, meaning the hacker had to try a large number of alternatives in order to find one that worked. Should they have been successful, they would have committed theft, but the question raised by the Commission was exactly when was that theft committed? Attempting various passwords, in their view, probably did not amount to an act that was more than merely preparatory to theft, particularly if further steps were actually require to complete the funds transfer. However the Commission felt it was 'undesirable' that such a person could only be prosecuted for a serious offence

[90] Lindsay Nicolle and Tony Collins, 'The computer fraud conspiracy of silence', *The Independent*, 19 June 1989, pp. 18–19.

[91] Channel 4 Dispatches, 11 October 1989.

[92] Ibid.

[93] The Law Commission, 'Criminal Law: Computer Misuse', No. 186, *October 1989*, p. 3.

if they actually succeeded in stealing the money. 'The speed with which such a theft may be carried out using a computer and the consequent difficulty of detecting the perpetrator require in our view a special extension of the criminal law in order to discourage such conduct, by exposing the hacker to prosecution at an early stage', the Commission felt. 'Under our proposed ulterior intent offence such a person, if he were detected trying to find the password, would at that stage have committed the offence of obtaining unauthorised access to a computer with intent to steal.'[94] New means through which crime could be perpetrated, at unprecedented speeds, created difficulty not just for the banks but also the way in which crime and fraud was handled by the United Kingdom's legal system. By the early 1990s, with most banks operating technology with greater functionality than ever before, great thought had to be placed on what exactly amounted to crime and wrongdoing in these new systems.

Computer Viruses

By the late 1980s, awareness of the threat from malicious attempts to undermine financial sector operations became prevalent. Barclays Bank provides an insightful case study here.

Firstly, they recognised the need for expertise. Trevor Nicholson, Chief Information Officer at Barclays at the time said: 'We house not only specialist teams who are responsible for security in our computer centres, our mainframe computer centres. We have also specialist teams who deal with hacking. We have a specialist who has written programmes to detect computer viruses. We personally have a pro-gramme mounted in our personal computers that will spot some 200 different known viruses.'[95]

Barclays also clearly appreciated the rapid pace of change in security practices. 'Every time you produce a programme to spot 200 new viruses', Nicholson said, 'someone invents a few more for you which you haven't built in a defence for.'[96] Clearly there was a need to stay on top of emerging threats to maintain stability for their customers and shareholders.

Barclays therefore invested heavily to mitigate their risk to malware and the malicious actors targeting them. In 1989 Barclays said it spent 'in excess of £20m a year ... on merely making our systems secure.' Nicholson added: 'I don't think it matters how big you are, how knowledgeable you are, how prepared you are. You can still be hit by a virus.' Driven by the fear of being caught unprepared for this emerging type of threat, Barclays was taking a proactive approach secure their networks.

---

[94] The Law Commission, 'Criminal Law: Computer Misuse', No. 186, *October 1989,* p. 25.
[95] Channel 4 Dispatches, 11 October 1989.
[96] Ibid.

Nicholson said in 1989 that, 'We've had one virus since we started very actively looking for this over the last few years, which was the well-known 'Friday 13th virus'. This occurred in a small network of personal computers, 10 or 12 systems joined together in a Local Area Network where we were developing an expert system.'[97]

The worry for the next Friday 13th in October 1989 was the Datacrime virus. It was in response to this threat that County NatWest were said to have turned their clock forward by 24 hours in order to avoid Friday 13th entirely.[98]

The threat was evolving and banks had to learn along the way. First, in terms of motivations. Awareness was growing yet there was still minimal understanding of the motivations and abilities of those able to breach the banks' systems. In 1989 Barclays had suffered three "hacks" according to Channel 4's Dispatches. Trevor Nicholson said: 'In the first case we don't actually know why he was in the system, because it merely occurred that when the proper user logged into his system to use it he found that someone was already there. He had logged in, we had found earlier from the audit trail, some 40 minutes or so before the real user. And as far as we could tell, and this is always a problem of course, you're never quite sure if you've found everything, as far as we could tell, nothing had taken place from that particular hacking.'[99]

The actual occurrences ranged from small to large scale fraud. Trevor Nicholson said, 'There have been attempts to transfer funds from bank accounts out to other accounts in other parts of the world, but fortunately, so far, to best of our knowledge, they've been thwarted. The largest I can recall is something like £900,000 which is a fairly sizeable sum of money, particularly if you're on the losing side.'[100]

Doomsday Scenarios

Despite seemingly feeling in control of the computer security risks, potential worst-case scenarios were still in the minds of those working in this area within the banks in the early 1990s.

Asked about her bank's computers crashing and emergency backups not existing, Jill Van Looy, an Assistant Director in charge of treasury support operations at Schroders in 1992, typified this fear. Interviewed by Sue Fenton of Midland Bank's Press Office, Van Looy reportedly pulled a face of mock horror in response, and said: 'We could effectively lose track of all our money overnight. We would be exposed on all treasury positions, we wouldn't know whether we were long or short on our Nostro accounts [accounts held by UK banks with a foreign bank], we

---

[97] Channel 4 Dispatches, 11 October 1989.

[98] 'Hygiene sees off computer viruses', *Financial Times,* 14 October 1989.

[99] Channel 4 Dispatches, 11 October 1989.

[100] Ibid.

couldn't monitor what we had to pay or were due to receive, we couldn't deal and we couldn't produce the daily capital adequacy reports the Bank of England demands.'[101] The potential ramifications for Schroders were clearly serious, in both financial and repetitional terms.

A similarly bleak retort was recorded from Sheila Phillips-Byrne, Van Looy's counterpart at Allied Irish Bank: 'If a payment isn't where it should be on value day it can cost us a lot of money.'[102] Both interviewees insisted that their employers' contingency systems were too good to allow such dramatic emergencies to occur, but they did acknowledge that occasionally some noteworthy incidents did occur. For example, Schroders had to invoke its disaster recovery plan after a 'hardware fault in its banking system made it impossible to start the system at the beginning of the day'.[103] Jill Van Looy took her back office staff and the system software to Safetynet, a company specialising in IT backup to City institutions, and once the software had been installed a leased line was brought into action between Safetynet and the City.[104] Business continued as normal while technicians at Schroders in the City worked on the hardware, and a weekend of 24-hour shifts ensued, allowing for dealing to continue without disruption and, vitally, with the outside world unaware of what had occurred.

Van Looy saw the potential losses not only in terms of loss of income as a result of having to take the system 'down for two or three days' if a backup site had not existed but also in terms of consumer confidence.[105] 'The more serious problem would have been the unquantifiable damage which could have resulted from loss of client and market confidence,' Van Looy noted, whilst also describing how Schroders learned a significant amount from having to 'weigh up the situation' and the 'consequences of taking certain decisions' such as 'spending less time trying to mend the system before invoking the emergency procedures.'[106]

Both Schroders and Allied Irish Bank had clear plans for their contingency operations. Each of them had annual contingency tests that involved sending numerous messages via various routes.[107] The importance of such contingencies was underlined by Colin Tyne, Midland Bank's Head of Payments Product Management, who noted their importance in the products they offered customers. 'We spend a lot of time thinking about backup for the services we provide to customers,' Tyne acknowledged, including 'dual data centres in Bootle and Sheffield.'[108]

For Schroders, contingency meant utilising Safetynet's site in Chiswick, in case of a hardware fault at their primary site, from where it could use its software which

---

[101] HSBC File UNKNOWN, *Electronic Banking News*, Issue 11, September 1992, p. 4.

[102] HSBC File UNKNOWN, *Electronic Banking News*, Issue 11, September 1992, p. 4.

[103] Ibid., p. 4.

[104] Ibid., p. 5.

[105] Ibid., p. 5.

[106] Ibid., p. 5.

[107] Ibid., p. 6.

[108] HSBC File UNKNOWN, *Electronic Banking News*, Issue 11, September 1992, p. 6.

had been installed there on identical equipment; contingency reports containing 'all manner of information required to continue the business' were stored off-site in paper form in fireproof cabinets, and software backups were taken nightly an also kept off site.[109] For Jill Van Looy, these plans were required given the shift of focus in the business to computer power. 'Things used to be done manually, by people, rather than by machines. It was possible to operate without computers because business was based on what people could handle: now it's based on what computers can handle,' was Van Looy's rather philosophical assessment. 'Computerisation has increased volumes of business and we can do transactions today we could never have done before, but we are more reliant on computers so contingency is uppermost in our minds.'[110] This explicit reference to the new reliance on computers and the need for resilience should a disaster scenario occur. Should such an incident occur, institutions needed clear plans to minimise the impact and return to normal service as quickly and efficiently as possible.

A slightly different computer set up at Allied Irish Bank (AIB) meant a different contingency scenario albeit with the same focus and attention placed upon it as with Schroders. The bank did not keep off site files as they had two computer centres in Dublin, where all records were microfilmed or stored on disk so that Allied Irish could retrieve records up to the end of the preceding day.[111] Operations could be switched from London to Dublin without this becoming public knowledge, should total power failure or a similar issue occur, and should those links to Dublin be lost, it could use its retail banking network to access Dublin via Northampton, which utilised its own backup site in Uxbridge.[112] Despite this reliance on computers, Sheila Phillips-Byrne noted how in-house engineers made their contingency plans less likely to be invoked but stressed that despite computers largely replacing people, people were an indispensable part of AIB's contingency plans.

For Midland Bank, the contingency process involved calling together its Major Incident Control Panel. This body consisted of senior managers from the technical, operations and business management sectors of the bank which would help it resolve 'any problems as quickly as possible' and to 'fulfil its prime concern of continuing customer service'.[113] Midland also undertook work with some of its major customers to prepare comprehensive contingency plans for 'all types of system and logistical emergencies', copies of which would be held with the customer at their premises, and at two Midland premises.[114] Each plan dealt with the detail for making payments, and procedures for making paper payments, should telecommunications be disrupted or computers were rendered inoperable as well as 'very rare' events with the potential for longer term disruption and damage such as water

---

[109] Ibid., p. 5.

[110] Ibid., p. 5.

[111] HSBC File UNKNOWN, *Electronic Banking News*, Issue 11, September 1992, p. 5.

[112] Ibid., p. 5.

[113] Ibid., p. 6.

[114] Ibid., p. 6.

damage or loss of power supply.[115] Whilst these plans offered some level of reassurance, Colin Tyne from Midland Bank stressed the need for them to be undertaken 'without any effect on the customer', although he was aware that this was not a simple task: 'It is the reality of having to use the contingency that we all fear. It will really test the skills of both customer and Midland alike.'[116]

Entrenched Understanding

Banks had established a way of understanding computer security over the course of the 1960s to 1980s and this had become entrenched as the 1990s begun. For example, Midland Bank described Information Technology Security in 1995 as the need to protect the confidentiality, integrity and availability of information managed by their computer systems.[117] The bank had developed over time a broad strategic outline for its computer security.

An internal Midland booklet from 1995 entitled *Information Technology – Security Guidelines* set out a series of 'DO' and 'DO NOT' bullet points to staff including management and staff responsibility.[118] The positives were a combination of the more specific and more general: 'review System Administrator activity periodically' and 'be tough on sloppy security'.[119] Similar can be said of the 'DO NOT' points: 'use bank owned PCs for unauthorised personal or private purposes' and 'divulge confidential information, such as customer information'.[120]

Three priorities were outlined should staff become aware that a security breach had occurred. Primacy was given to 'contain[ing] the business impact quickly', to be followed by communicating the facts to management and keeping a complete record of events.[121]

Advice on passwords included specific suggestions such as using passwords of at least six characters, comprised of alphabetic and numeric characters, avoiding repeated characters and names, themes or common words.[122] Changing passwords once per month was recommended.[123]

Particularly harsh warning was given in relation to unpermitted software. 'The use of unauthorised software will be treated as Gross Misconduct', the bank said,

---

[115] Ibid., p. 6.

[116] Ibid., p. 6.

[117] HSBC File UK 1286, 'Information Technology – Security Guidelines', 1995, p. 7.

[118] Ibid., p. 7.

[119] Ibid., p. 8

[120] Ibid., pp. 9–10.

[121] Ibid., p. 11.

[122] Ibid., p. 12.

[123] Ibid., p. 12.

'and may result in dismissal.'[124] Staff were urged not to assume that all software was authorised and banned software included 'games of any sort', 'public domain software', 'software distributed with magazines' and 'software you have written yourself unless it has been specifically authorised.'[125]

The relatively recent phenomenon of computer viruses was worthy of detailed exploration. 'The effects are varied and range from the comical and humorous to total destruction of data and files', was the opening of the section on this malicious software written by Midland.[126] Following this was the assertion that at their most damaging, viruses could render systems and data 'useless', which could be 'disastrous' with 'serious disruption of business and of customer service.'[127] Employees were advised to follow the guidelines on unauthorised software and to report the receipt of unexpected or unsolicited diskettes or other media to their line managers, while in bold, one instruction stood out: 'Hold infected or suspicious diskettes in a secure place and do not use or release until you have authority from your PC Support team.'[128]

Alongside the advice on the more technical aspects of computer security was advice on physical security, still a prominent consideration for banks. Described as the 'first line of defence to protect computing and communications facilities' they were seen as protecting Midland from theft, physical damage and potential misuse by unauthorised persons.[129] Specific guidance included locking cabinets containing communications and processing equipment, changing access codes periodically and wearing identification passes visibly, challenging strangers as to their reason for being on the premises.[130] No equipment was to be left unattended in an insecure location and maintenance staff were not to be left alone with sensitive equipment, while Personal Computers (PCs) and Visual Display Units (VDUs) were not to be placed adjacent to windows through which they may be observed.[131]

Specific direction was also provided on the management of encryption keys, namely the 'protection of encryption keys and other secret values used to safeguard Midland's data.'[132] Secure handling of these was described as 'vital', for example the keys used to protect Automatic Teller Machine (ATM) systems.[133] Shortly after this Midland included a section on computer crime, explained as 'a criminal offence where the target of the crime is computer equipment, data or software' which could

---

[124] HSBC File UK 1286, 'Information Technology – Security Guidelines', 1995, p. 12.

[125] Ibid., p. 19.

[126] Ibid., p. 20.

[127] Ibid., p. 20.

[128] Ibid., p. 20.

[129] Ibid., p. 20.

[130] Ibid., p. 22.

[131] HSBC File UK 1286, 'Information Technology – Security Guidelines', 1995, p. 22.

[132] Ibid., p. 29.

[133] Ibid., p. 29.

mean equipment theft, a computer virus or unauthorised access to IT systems.[134] Measures to prevent such crime included monitoring sensitive systems for suspicious activity using activity logs or direct observation, recording and retaining evidence and evaluating any data loss, the data confidentiality and the business impact resulting from equipment theft or unauthorised access.[135] Staff were told not to destroy evidence unless it was 'unavoidable in tackling the breach' and not to 'publicise the incident unnecessarily' while investigations were ongoing.[136]

Computer Security as a Business Fundamental

Midland by the mid-1990s understood the fundamental importance of computer security to their overall prosperity as a business. 'IT Security is important because our success would be threatened if the security of our systems is seriously compromised', the bank warned.[137] Prefacing a booklet for staff on IT security guidelines, authored in 1995, were two paragraphs which left little room for uncertainty over the paramount importance of the issue:

> Midland depends critically on its computer and communications systems. Information technology lies at the heart of our business, storing and processing details of our customers and their business with us. A direct threat to the security of our systems means a direct threat to our business.

> Midland is focusing the full power of its systems to strengthen our position in the marketplace to deliver ever increasing value to our customers. These systems are under your control. IT Security therefore matters to you and it is important you recognise and understand your role in protecting Midland's assets and services.[138]

Responsibility had been placed firmly with the employees at the forefront of Midland's computer operations. Having stressed the critical importance of computer security to the company's success, the bank spoke directly to employees and explicitly placed the expectation upon them for helping maintain the security of their systems. Banks by the 1990s were highly dependent on strong computer security for their success.

---

[134] Ibid., p. 30.

[135] Ibid., p. 30.

[136] Ibid., p. 30.

[137] Ibid., p. 7.

[138] HSBC File UK 1286, 'Information Technology – Security Guidelines', 1995, p. 3.

Conclusion

In the opening scenes of the 1983 film *Superman III* an armed and masked robber slides down a ledge outside the Century Savings Bank, a large bag stuffed full of cash secured under his arm, pursued, and shot at, by three Metropolis Police officers. Shortly after, the audience meets the actor Richard Pryor who plays a newly-employed electronic data processor at Webscoe Industries called August Gorman. A new colleague of Pryor's soon informs him that any half cents in payroll calculations are rounded down instead of being paid to their recipients. Pryor proceeds to use his computer skills to funnel these half cent amounts into his own personal payroll account. His next weekly pay packet is then supplemented by a cheque for $85,789.90.

Having broken the news to Ross Webster, Chief of Webscoe, an assistant, Simpson, proclaims:

> In the old days it was simple. We kept books, we had ledgers, we knew what was going in and what was paid out. If somebody wanted to rob you, they'd come in with a gun and say, "Stick them up!" Now they get these blasted computers to do their dirty work.[1]

Webster, baring a wry smile, replies: 'My friend, you are yesterday. Whoever pulled this caper off, is tomorrow.'[2]

Although coming from a fictional (and not-very-well-regarded) movie, the conversation between Webster and Simpson is illustrative of the transformation that had begun and was ongoing when *Superman III* was released in the early 1980s. It gives an indication of how transitory the period was for industry, particularly those dealing directly with money, following the advent of commercially-viable computing power. It also alludes to the increasing level of dependence upon "blasted computers" as time progressed, with those used to old-fashioned methods of manual record-keeping scornful at the presence of these machines which they could not and did not wish to understand. Simpson almost nostalgically refers to the prospect of

---

[1] *Superman III*, (1983), approximately at 29:00 into the film.
[2] Ibid.

© Springer Nature Switzerland AG 2022
A. Sweetman, *Cyber and the City*, History of Computing,
https://doi.org/10.1007/978-3-031-07933-7

old-fashioned robbery, giving the sense that this more straightforward approach could at least be confronted by all, rather than only by a new brand of computer security experts.

This book has sought to provide previously unattainable detail on the transitionary period between 1960 and 1990 in which financial sector institutions in the United Kingdom, primarily the major London clearing banks, became steadily more reliant on computers for a growing proportion of their operations. Previously unexplored and newly released archival material has made this possible. As demonstrated in the introduction of this research, the existing literature is piecemeal and unfocused, small fragments of relevant detail appearing unpredictably in volumes which are somewhat related yet tangential. By focusing more specifically on computer security this research has been able to delve deeper, attempting to develop new depth of understanding. Presented here are its conclusions.

Three research questions were posed at the outset in order to drive this book' analysis. How exactly did the London clearing banks, and their counterparts in the Bank of England, *understand* and *define* computer security in this period? What did these institutions perceive to be the main threats to this security? What practical measures did they enact to mitigate the risk they faced? Resulting from these questions and the adopted approach of detailed case study examinations interspersed with broader overview chapters are specific, detailed answers together with broader thematic insights.

A key theme to acknowledge before an exploration of more specific answers is that of consensus and continuity. Across the three decades of this period and across the key institutions involved, there existed remarkable consensus in the areas probed by this book' three research questions. Little divergence existed between the major banks in either their understanding of what computer security meant to them, the primary dangers they believed they faced or the methods for combating the risk of these threats. Cutting across this work throughout each of its six core chapters, this theme is arguably *the* key overall message of this research. Computer security in this period was a burgeoning issue for the major banks from almost the same time in the early 1960s when they first purchased these machines, and their representative interest group, the Committee of London Clearing Bankers (CLCB), together with their only being a handful of institutions, facilitated collaboration rather than competition on this issue. Formative experiences such as those detailed in this book like the creation of Bankers' Automated Clearing Services (BACS), Clearing House Automated Payments System (CHAPS) and the Society for Worldwide Interbank Financial Telecommunication (SWIFT), each beginning at the beginning of the 1970s and in which the importance of security to their success was undisputed, facilitated the sharing of knowledge on computer security, seemingly helping to disseminate shared knowledge, expectations and standards into the decision-making of these individual institutions. By the time these services had launched in the early-mid 1980s the banks and institutions involved had intensively acquired a vast amount of practical experience. That no catastrophic computer security-related incident had occurred, to the best of our knowledge, in either these payment and telecommunication systems or individual institutions by the end of the period 1960–1990 suggests that consensus had not resulted in complacency. Regardless, it is noteworthy that such consensus existed and persisted over time. Continuity was perhaps possible because once the power of this new technology had been harnessed and embedded into banking operations, there was no fundamental change in its functionality between by the end of the 1980s. Over the next decade, and the widespread adoption of the Internet and the World Wide Web by consumers and financial institutions, there would likely be sufficient stimulus for banks to alter their understanding of computer security and certainly the risks they faced and measures of protection, though this falls slightly outside the purview of this research.

Explored below are the specific conclusions of this book, a discussion of their wider implications and identification of areas for further research, before an examination of the contemporary relevance of this work.

Defining Computer Security

The major London clearing banks, together with the Bank of England, took security to mean the maintenance of three distinct qualities: confidentiality, integrity and availability. Whether in relation to their internal computer networks or to external, sector-wide telecommunication and payment infrastructure, these factors comprised the very core of the definition of computer security held by these institutions.

Underpinning the banks' understanding and management was a crucial objective upon which they fixated: the need to maintain the trust of their individual and corporate customers. The banks felt it vital that new hardware and software could transmit sensitive customer information confidentially and privately. They also recognised it as paramount that customers could feel certain that messages or transactions relevant to them were received by the intended recipient in the exact way intended, unaltered during transmission and originating from an authorised and authentic source. These institutions also deemed it crucial that time-sensitive customer data and payments could be made in a timely and reliable manner, requiring high levels of system availability. Given the rapid uptake of computers by the banks in this period, as soon as these machines became truly commercially viable after World War II, the banks acutely felt the need to reassure customers of these machines' utility in general terms, given the mystique and lack of knowledge around them. They also felt they needed to specifically endorse the presence of computers in operations dealing with some of their customers' most delicate personal or business matters, those relating to finances. It was unlikely, even within their corporate customers' business, that many individuals had come into regular contact with or acquired detailed technical knowledge of computers. If such understanding or expertise was present, it was likely isolated to a very small number of individuals. Compounded by press coverage describing the potential unemployment that would accompany corporate computerisation, banks were both at the forefront of defending the security of computers and networks and at the forefront of the defence of the *idea* of computers, having to justify their usage for processing and storing sensitive and personal information and wealth.

Persisting alongside the three factors of confidentiality, integrity and availability was an overall view that security should be conceptualised in terms of resilience. The key institutions pursued a pragmatic approach: assuming it inevitable that some form of computer security-related incident would occur and planning for a timely recovery. Security, it was felt, was not just about preventing an unwanted incident but also about recovering from it in a specified time to resume operations with minimal disruption. Partly this was driven by the recognition that perfect security was unattainable. It was also framed by the same crucial requirement of banks to maintain customer trust in their services, or at least to attenuate the loss of customer confidence resulting from a major incident.

Banks' understanding of computer security through the lens of resilience arose out of the trade-off between cost and security which permeated the thinking and decision-making of the key institutions throughout this period. It is a key theme in this book. Often, sacrifices in the level of security were made if costs were too high. The banks adopted the approach of developing sufficiently high disincentives, so that the cost of attempting to, for example, transmit fraudulent payment messages or physically attack a computer centre, was too high to warrant perpetrating the required actions. Consensus emerged that when understanding security, the aim was to achieve a level of risk, particularly in the cross-sector infrastructure such as BACS and CHAPS in which numerous stakeholders were invested, that was acceptable to all. However, the banks did have to contend with the fact that the rewards involved in fraud or "bank robbery" via technical means, such as sending an illegitimate instruction for payment to a bank across a payment system, could be an inordinately higher for the perpetrators than crime via traditional means. Nevertheless, the banks were willing to deal with these higher stakes provided the risk involved – considering factors like the cost to the perpetrators, the technical skill required, the level of collusion and the understanding of the relevant system required – was tolerable for all parties involved.

Such consensus over security thinking occurred because of the small group of major London clearing banks, often in conjunction with the Bank of England, being heavily involved in the creation of cross-sector infrastructure such as BACS, CHAPS and SWIFT examined here. As stakeholders in these facilities, in some cases owner-operators, it was in the banks' interests to build security into these operations from the outset. This rested on the premise that they saw computer security as a worthwhile endeavour, but this judgement was unwavering in the banks throughout the period 1960 to 1990. Being so closely involved in these projects, and having an interest group in the Committee of London Clearing Bankers (CLCB) which provided the platform for their views to coalesce, recognition of computer security and its importance emerged and persisted throughout the three decades upon which this book focuses.

A further factor in creating this consistency of understanding was that computer security was inextricably linked to the motivation of the major clearing banks to sustain London's pre-eminence as a global financial centre. Such motivation played a role in justifying the creation of major payment platforms, and this overarching strategic purpose – which would ultimately benefit each of the banks as global businesses – likely superseded any disagreement over security. Securing new systems, both internal and sector-wide, would garner customer trust and confidence, help deliver growth and profitability through cost savings and new business.

Computer security existed as a concern on two key levels: for and within institutions, and across the financial sector in its entirety. Whilst being a management issue in the payment and telecommunication systems created for cross-sector use, the banks recognised that a reputation for strong computer security could be a marketable asset. It could be both a tangible and symbolic quality.

Throughout the period there was also no distinguishable priority given to either one of the qualities of confidentiality, integrity and availability. Often debate could focus on one of these values in isolation, referring to the likelihood of a breach of confidentiality, for example, how this risk could be mitigated by encryption and what the cost of this would be versus the potential impact of a breach. In the development of BACS, for example, the perennial issue of a contingency computer centre was provoked by concern over a physical attack at the Edgware computer centre that might have rendered the service unavailable. Yet none of these qualities assumed an importance that surpassed the others. It could be argued that because most threats were discussed as theoretical possibilities rather than tangible historical examples that the banks lacked evidence with which to prioritise certain issues. However, the banks' overall objective was to maintain customer trust, and so prioritisation was perhaps unnecessary when a breach of any of these qualities resulting in an impact on customer confidence was possible.

Perceived Threats

Perhaps unsurprisingly given the transitionary nature of this period for banking operations in the United Kingdom, from manual to computer-based, these institutions' perceptions of threat embraced both the physical and the technical. Often mentioned together in discussions were concerns over, for example, some form of destructive attack aimed at hardware held at computer centres alongside the potential for new payment and telecommunications systems to be misused rather than damaged. Neither the physical or technical was prioritised systematically. Both vectors could ultimately cause significant disruption, and so both were evaluated in terms of their potential impact upon customer trust through either a breach of confidentiality, integrity or availability. If it had the potential to impact upon one of these areas, the issue was deemed a threat regardless of how it could come to fruition. For example, as telecommunication lines linking various sites became increasingly used, their remote nature opened the risk to somebody "tapping" the line and eavesdropping. As this posed a threat to confidentiality, it was deemed a serious threat.

Again, the trend here is continuity throughout the period and across the institutions in the sector. It could be argued that physical security assumed a greater importance as computer operations grew and the number of sites and back-up sites holding critical computer equipment followed suit, therefore making the potential impact of systems being unavailable far greater. Concurrently, however, as increasing numbers of payment instructions and messages for growing sums of money were sent between institutions using computer software, hardware and telecommunication infrastructure, so the importance of confidentiality and integrity of this information warranted greater focus.

Resulting from the banks' method of identifying threats to computer security was a perception on the part of the major financial sector institutions that security dangers could arise which were both deliberate and non-deliberate. For example, it was thought that criminals could actively manipulate these new systems. With enough knowledge, they may be able to use the system for fraudulent gain, perhaps by impersonating legitimate users and sending payment instructions across networks. There was also significant concern that new technology could be taken advantage of by those trying to gain access to privileged information about financial markets, creating specific worries over the privacy of communications and transactions. Banks were concerned both about manipulation by outsiders but also the potential for employees with pernicious intentions manipulating their legitimate access for unauthorised purposes. The institutions in the sector were also concerned by the potential for new services to be deliberately damaged or made unavailable, specifically through destructive physical attacks or attempts to gain access to the networks without permission.

However, security for the financial sector, in relation to the availability of systems, also encompassed non-deliberate causes for the new services becoming unavailable. Accidents and faults were discussed under the heading of security alongside deliberate threats. The reason for this was because the systems becoming unavailable would have had largely the same practical and symbolic impact regardless of whether this was done intentionally or not. Embedding new technology into operations for banks meant that security also encompassed certainty and predictability that these new functions would work as expected. Reliability was therefore crucial, not just of individual banks' computer hardware and software but also the wider infrastructure underpinning it such as power supplies and telecommunication links.

It would be incorrect to say that the major London clearing banks and their public sector peers took greater care over threats to their computer security as the period progressed. If anything, the resources and effort involved in discussing, planning and implementing computer security persisted at a remarkably high level throughout. What is true, however, is that they recognised their growing exposure over time, as a greater proportion of their operations became dependent upon computers. Increased reliance upon these machines for a continually enlarging scale of operations magnified the possible impact of a major incident, whether the number of payment instructions either lost or delayed due to physical damage or the amount of transmitted traffic that could be read through a wiretap. By the end of the period, threats such as computer viruses had the potential to cause greater disruption than previously, but the banks were equally, if not slightly more, focused on computer security. Computers by this time had become critical to these banks' overall business functions, and so credible threats developed an enhanced importance and computer security continued to be seen a relatively mainstream business issue in these institutions, directly related to customer trust.

Worth noting here is that often the banks' discussions revolved around theoretical threats as opposed to concrete ones. Although as noted in the literature review, some early work had recorded crimes of fraud and embezzlement by the mid-late 1970s, the banks were new adapters of computer equipment and so were having to consider the threats in this specific context for the first time. There were occasions when they received specific warnings, yet often their assessments were a result of their own thinking or advice from consultant experts. Therefore, it is difficult to assess, generally, the validity or accuracy of the threats to the bank in this period. It is possible to conclude, however, that the potential existed for significant reputational and even financial damage, the prospect of which was the banks were broadly unwilling to contemplate, and so invested heavily in lowering the level of risk they faced.

Mitigation Measures

Measures to mitigate these threats were developed as specific and direct responses to the perceived dangers. Some of these methods were purely technical, with the aim of managing information in transit. Encryption of message traffic, for example, became relied upon by the banks for discouraging eavesdropping on communication lines. Maintaining confidentiality by scrambling transmissions became a significant aspect of the major banks' measures for minimising the risk they faced.

Also, authentication measures, applications of cryptographic technology, could ensure that messages were not tampered with in transit and were sent by a legitimate operator with permission to use a certain service. Ensuring message integrity through technical methods like this facilitated the building of customer trust in these systems.

Certain measures within systems also helped keep track of their usage. Password controls often acted as a first barrier to entry, and privileges to access certain functions on computer terminals were employed. Logs of computer usage also became a vital measure for checking whether either employees or anyone remotely able to access computer networks had, for example, inserted illegitimate payment messages. Numbering these messages and checking of daily print-outs did not necessarily prevent any such action happening, but meant that they could be spotted relatively easily and their impact managed.

Some of the measures were non-technical, with the primary aim of managing people and spaces. Access controls could regulate entry to computer rooms, physical locks could be placed upon certain computers and file stores. Perimeter security of sites containing computer equipment often involved patrolling security guards, choosing a location which was itself remote or benefitted from the surrounding security of other buildings, and using identification cards to monitor entry and movement of individuals. In their view of computer security throughout the period, the banks felt that strict access security would decrease the likelihood of somebody misrepresenting themselves as a legitimate employee and accessing the system by directly sitting at a terminal at their computer site.

The banks' view of computer security through resilience meant they paid great attention throughout the period to contingency planning. Emphasising the need to restart operations as soon as possible following an incident with the minimal possible level of disruption, investment was made in measures such as back-up premises and remote storage of information, as well as reserve computer processing power, in attempts to try and minimise the impact, particularly of a destructive incident. As explored in the sections prior to this, there persisted a trade-off between cost and protection afforded by certain measures. Computer security measures were not meant to eliminate all risk or vulnerability, but to bring them to acceptable levels for the institution or institutions involved.

Wider Considerations

The specific conclusions arising from this book' exploration of archival evidence provide a new level of detail that can be added to existing understanding of computer security in the UK financial sector in the second half of the twentieth century. Alongside this direct impact on knowledge, the findings of this book also prompt wider considerations.

For example, it is interesting to consider the extent to which the banks' thinking and action over computer security in this period was different to their longer-term consideration of security more generally. Whilst not examining in detail security in the banks in the centuries and decades before and after 1960 to 1990, this book' findings suggest significant levels of continuity. Motivating the banks to pursue robust computer security in this period was their objective of instilling and maintaining customer trust and confidence in their new methods of working. While the specific services and technologies were new and therefore different, the broad aim was likely a continuation of longer-term thinking. Confidentiality, integrity and availability can be applied specifically to computer-based operations, but all remain a concern for banks in other contexts. Confidentiality gets to the heart of the banker-customer relationship which has existed for centuries, such discretion and privacy arguably being a priority in this relationship long before and after this book' period of focus. Integrity of communications would also have been an issue in paper-based systems, albeit with a more recognisable means of managing this issue via the individuals transporting, for example, the paper on which a signature and payment instructions would have been placed. Availability is arguably more specifically relevant to computer-based systems, but, for example, widespread industrial action in this period and before could likely have resulted in a similar effect, and was cited by the banks as a security concern. Though this continuity exists, computer security thinking likely differed in that the banks recognised the potential speed and scale of criminal actions and their impacts could be far greater. The very benefits that these new systems offered – speed and ease of communication, linkages to other institutions and substantial processing power – were the very qualities that made them potentially dangerous to the banks should they be misused. Computer security became a component of overall security management for the banks rather than a separate matter.

A second wider issue to consider is the extent to which the thoroughness of the banks' approach to security in this period facilitated the success of the City of London as a financial centre. Their role in embedding security in sector-wide financial infrastructure from the outset arguably contributed to a level of stability and a perception of openness to technological innovation in London. A detailed assessment would be required to evaluate the relative weight and influence of various factors, including deregulation of the financial sector under the Thatcher government in the mid-1980s, resulting in "Big Bang" in 1986. The robust and thorough planning and building-in of computer security from the very creation, particularly of the sector-wide payment and telecommunication systems such as BACS, SWIFT and CHAPS, but also in internal bank networks, certainly laid a foundation for reliable and trustworthy computer-based operations, dependence on which would only grow throughout this period and thereafter.

Thirdly, though this research has not sought to develop a direct comparison to current day cyber security thinking in those same institutions, a wider issue to consider is the extent to which banks' understanding and management of computer security in the period of focus of this book forms the origins of contemporary cyber security in those organisations. Particularly in relation to their definition of security, this book' findings suggest there is continuity in this area. Specific threats may have changed resulting from new technological developments and broader developments in banking and financial sector business, as may mitigation measures, particularly given how consumers now expect internet-enabled banking services on a variety of smart devices. However, banks ultimately continue to require the trust and confidence of their customers to operate profitably. A consequence of the banks' consistent and shared understanding of computer security during this period has resulted in such thinking becoming entrenched. The trio of confidentiality, integrity and availability are still the way major banks frame and manage computer security risk. It could be argued that such deeply embedded ideas have led to a lack of innovation in computer security or risk management thinking in recent decades, though it is equally true that as expertise has evolved, there has seemingly been no strong argument to support a different model. Regardless, such consistency of understanding ultimately led to banks producing foundational financial sector infrastructure from the 1960s onwards, embedding computers into their operations so deeply – having felt able to sufficiently secure themselves and their customers – that began a general trend for those institutions of embracing technological change that continues today.

Further Research

A natural area for further research is to consider the continuities and changes in computer security thinking and actions in the UK financial sector up to the current day. This book considers the period 1960–1990 in relative isolation, but fruitful research could be conducted which extends that period or explicitly compares that period to today. Beginning research in an earlier time period to assess the continuities and changes in security thinking within the financial sector more broadly, taking into consideration but not focusing specifically on computer security, could also significantly bolster the existing literature. A second potential research path would be to widen this book' geographical focus, perhaps in the initial instance to evoke direct comparison with the banks in the United States. This book refers to some aspects of similar developments in America, including representations from British banks travelling to America to seek expert advice, but archival research in that nation was not within the scope of this research. A third area of potentially relevant research would be to look at the thinking and actions of other areas of non-military infrastructure, often categorised now as critical national infrastructure, to evaluate the similarities and differences in understanding and approach to the financial sector.

Contemporary Relevance

This book provides in-depth context to a pivotal area of concern for banks in the United Kingdom and across the globe today. Broader cyber security matters are now regularly covered in the mainstream quality press. Governments devote increasing resources to cyber security, both for offensive and defensive purposes, and strategic thinking around issues such as cyber deterrence occupy the minds of policymakers and academics. Within the financial sector, this book is relevant to an increasingly troublesome issue faced by the banks, the shift from criminals targeting customers to the banks and even global payment infrastructure. The case studies explored in this book are therefore directly relevant to contemporary threats faced in the UK financial sector. These case studies' relevance may even enhance in the short-term. For example, Barclays estimates that payments systems such as BACS, with SWIFT having been the particular focus in the year to 2017, 'have already' or 'will in the near future come increasingly under attack by sophisticated threat actors.'[3] Though not necessarily offering guidance to such institutions on how to manage the contemporary threat, this book provides focused and relevant historical context which could to some extent inform contemporary decision-making by understanding part of the story of how banks' computer security thinking and action has evolved to its current state.

---

[3] Ibid., p. 11.

Cyber security persists as a vital issue for the vast global financial sector. Private sector institutions are tasked with defending some of the most critical parts of countries' national infrastructure, the breakdown of which could have a catastrophic impact on the functioning of everyday life. A deeper understanding of cyber security's history, its origins and development, will serve to enhance the management of cyber security today. This book hopes to contribute, in some way, to such understanding.

Bibliography

Archival Material

Barclays Files:

0156-0017, 0156-0019, 0178-0001, 0178-0003, 0178-0004, 0036-0067, 0036-0078, 0080-2165, 0080-2827, 0080-4134, 0080-6198, 1683-0023, 1683-0024, 1683-0003, 1023-1053, 1023-1146, 0235-0020, 1682-0023, 0300-0957, 0328-0026, 0717-0161, 0222-0049.

Bank of England Files:

1A18/1, 1A18/3, 1A18/4, 1A18/5, 2A183/1, 2A89/1, 2A89/2, 2A89/3, 2A89/4, 3A34/1, 3A34/2, 3A34/4, 3A34/5, 3A34/6, 3A34/8, 3A34/9, 3A34/10, 3A34/11, 3A34/12, 3A34/13, 3A34/14, 5A199/4, 5A199/6, 7A371/5, 7A383/1, 7A383/2, 7A383/3, 7A383/4, 7A386/1, 7A386/2, 7A386/3, 7A386/4, 71383/3, 8A464/1, 11A70/1, 11A70/2, 11A70/4, 11A270/1, 11A270/2, 13A75/1, 13A75/2, 13A75/3, 13A75/4, 13A75/5, 13A75/6, 13A75/7, 13A75/8, 13A75/9, 13A75/10, 13A75/11, 13A75/12, 13A75/14, 13A75/15, 13A75/16, 14A017/2, 14A107/1, 14A107/2, 14A64/2, G1/13, G13/5.

HSBC Files:

UK1793-0013, UK0009-0017, UK0200-1014A, UK 0200-1024A, UK1286, UK0649.

Lloyds Files:

9595, 10131, 10133, 10599, 11521/2, *Banknotes.*

© Springer Nature Switzerland AG 2022
A. Sweetman, *Cyber and the City*, History of Computing,
https://doi.org/10.1007/978-3-031-07933-7

London Metropolitan Archive Files:

MS32157X/1, M32145X/1, M32145X/2, M32145X/3, M32145X/4, M32145X/5, M32145X/6, MS32456/2, MS32041/6, MS32452X/2.

Royal Bank of Scotland Files:

NWB/1372, RB/1453/1.

The National Archives Files:

T390/698, T471/45.

Published Sources

Margaret Ackrill and Leslie Hannah, *Barclays: The Business of Banking 1690–1996* (Cambridge: Cambridge University Press, 2001).

Jon Agar, *The Government Machine: A Revolutionary History of the Computer* (Cambridge: M.I.T. Press, 2003).

R. E. Anderson, *Bank Security* (Massachusetts: Butterworth, 1981).

Christopher Andrew, *The Secret World: A History of Intelligence* (London: Allen Lane, 2018).

Paul Armer, 'Computer Aspects of Technological Change, Automation, and Economic Progress', *The RAND Corporation,* February 1966.

Jamie Bartlett, *The Dark Net* (London: Windmill, 2014).

Bernardo Batiz-Lazo, *Cash and Dash: How ATMs and Computers Changed Banking* (Oxford: Oxford University Press, 2018).

Peter Bird, *LEO: The First Business Computer* (Wokingham: Hasler Publishing, 1994).

Mark Bowden, *Worm: The First Digital World War* (London: Grove Press, 2011).

Joel Brenner, *America The Vulnerable: Inside the New Threat Matrix of Digital Espionage, Crime, and Warfare* (New York: Penguin Press, 2011).

British Bankers' Association and PricewaterhouseCoopers, *The cyber threat to banking: A global industry challenge,* May 2014.

BT Global Services, 'Cyber Threats and the Financial Sector: Is anybody safe?', 2011.

Martin Campbell-Kelly, *ICL: A Business and Technical History* (Oxford: Clarendon Press, 1989).

Martin Campbell-Kelly and Daniel Garcia-Swartz, *From Mainframes to Smartphones: A History of the International Computer Industry* (Cambridge: Harvard University Press, 2015).

Paul Ceruzzi, *A History of Modern Computing: Second Edition* (Cambridge: MIT Press, 2003).

Martin Campbell-Kelly, *From Airline Reservations to Sonic the Hedgehog: A History of the Software Industry* (London: MIT Press), 2003.

Martin Campbell-Kelly, William Aspray, Nathan Esmenger and Jeffrey Yost, *Computer: A History of the Information Machine* (Boulder: Westview Press, 2014).

John Cooper, *The Management and Regulation of Banks* (Basingstoke: Macmillan, 1984).

Gordon Corera, *Intercept: The Secret History of Computers and Spies* (London: Weidenfeld & Nicolson, 2015).

James Cortada, *The Digital Hand: How Computers Changed the Work of American Financial, Telecommunications, Media, and Entertainment Industries, Volume II* (Oxford: Oxford University Press, 2006).

Adam Cummings, Todd Lewellen, David McIntire, Andrew P. Moore and Randall Trzeciak, 'Insider Threat Study: Illicit Cyber Activity Involving Fraud in the U.S. Financial Services Sector', *Carnegie Mellon Software Engineering Institute*, July 2012.

Depository Trust & Clearing Corporation (DTCC), *Cyber Risk – A Global Systemic Threat*, October 2014.

Charles Eames and Ray Eames, *A Computer Perspective: Background to the Computer Age* (Cambridge: Harvard University Press, 1990)

James Essinger, *Computers in Financial Trading* (Oxford: Elsevier, 1988).

James Essinger, *Computer Security in Financial Organizations* (Oxford: Elsevier Advanced Technology, 1990).

James Essinger, *Controlling Computer Security: A Guide For Financial Institutions* (London: Financial Times Business Information, 1992).

Kenneth Flamm, *Creating the Computer: Government, Industry and High Technology* (Washington, DC: Brookings Institution, 2007).

Thomas Glaessner, Tom Kellerman and Valerie McNevin, 'Electronic Security: Risk Mitigation in Financial Transactions – Public Policy Issues', *The World Bank: Policy Research Working Paper*, 2870, (2002).

Thomas Gleassner, Tom Kellermann & Valerie McNevin, *Electronic Soundness: Securing Finance in a New Age* (Washington: The World Bank, 2004), World Bank Working Paper No.26.

Misha Glenny, *DarkMarket: How Hackers Became The New Mafia* (Oxford: The Bodley Head, 2011).

Herman Goldstine, *The Computer from Pascal to von Neumann* (Princeton: Princeton University Press, 1972).

John Grady and Martin Weale, *British Banking: 1960–85* (Basingstoke: Macmillan, 1986).

James Graham et al., 'Cyber Fraud: Tactics, Techniques, and Procedures', *iDefense,* (Florida: Auerbach Publications, 2009).

Her Majesty's Government and Institute of Chartered Accountants in England and Wales, 'Cyber-Security in Corporate Finance', 2014.

Professor R B Jack, *Banking Services: Law and Practice: Report by the Review Committee,* CM 622, 30 December 1988.

Peter Jenner and Michael Rentell, *Breakdowns in Computer Security: Commentary and Analysis* (Surrey: Computer Weekly, 1991).

John Kemeny, *Man and the Computer* (New York: Charles Scribner's Sons, 1972).

Kenneth Kraemer and Kent Colton (eds), *Computers and Banking: Electronic Funds Transfer Systems and Public Policy* (New York: Plenum Press, 1980).

Simon Lavington, *History of Manchester Computers* (Manchester: NCC Publications, 1975).

Simon Lavington, *Early British Computers* (Bedford: Digital Press, 1980).

Steven Levy, *Crypto: How the Code Rebels Beat the Government – Saving Privacy in the Digital Age* (London: Penguin, 2001).

Lloyds Banking Group, *250: 1765-2015* (London: Lloyds Banking Group, 2015).

Gerald M Lowrie, 'ACM '70 Proceedings of the 1970 25th annual conference on Computer and crisis: how computers are shaping our future', *American Bankers Association,* (1970).

Gerald McKnight, *Computer Crime* (London: Michael Joseph, 1973).

Nick Metropolis, J. Howlett and Gian-Carlo Rota (eds), *A History of Computing in the Twentieth Century* (New York: Academic Press, 1980); James Beniger, *The Control Revolution: Technological and Economic Origins of the Information Society* (Cambridge: Harvard University Press, 1986).

William Mitford, *The History of Greece: Volume I* (London: T.Cadell, 1829).

Kevin Mitnick, *Ghost in the Wires: My Adventures as the World's Most Wanted Hacker* (New York: Back Bay Books, 2011).

Philip Molyneux, *Banking: an introductory text* (Basingstoke: Macmillan, 1990).

New York State Department of Financial Services, *Report on Cyber Security in the Banking Sector* (May 2014).

New York State Department of Financial Services, *Update on Report on Cyber Security in the Banking Sector* (April 2015).

David Omand, *Securing the State:* (London: Hurst & Company, 2010).

Donn Parker, *Crime By Computer: Startling New Kinds of Million-Dollar Fraud, Theft, Larceny and Embezzlement* (New York: Charles Scribner's Sons, 1976a).

Alan Peachey, *Great Financial Disasters of Our Time* (Berlin: BWV, 2006).

Ben Pimlott, *Harold Wilson* (London: HarperCollins, 1992).

Kevin Poulsen, *Kingpin: How One Hacker Took Over the Billion-Dollar Cybercrime Underground* (New York: Broadway Paperbacks, 2011).

Marisa Randazzo, Michelle Keeney, Eileen Kowalski, Dawn Cappelli and Andrew Moore, 'Insider Threat Study: Illicit Cyber Activity in the Banking and Finance Sector', *Carnegie Mellon Software Engineering Institute,* June 2005.

Brian Randell, *The Origins of Digital Computers: Selected Papers* (Berlin: Springer-Verlag, 1975).

Thomas Rid, *Rise of the Machines: A Cybernetic History* (London: W.W. Norton & Company, 2016).

Richard Roberts and David Kynaston, *The Lion Wakes: A Modern History of HSBC* (London: Profile Books, 2015).

Henry Roseveare, *The Evolution of a British Institution: The Treasury* (London: Allen Lane, 1969).

Brian Ruder and J.D. Madden, *Computer Science and Technology: an Analysis of Computer Security Safeguards for Detecting and Preventing Intentional Computer Misuse,* (Washington: US Department of Commerce, 1978).

Ken Slater, *Information Security in Financial Services* (Basingstoke: Macmillan, 1991).

Peter Salus, *A Quarter Century of UNIX* (Reading: Addison-Wesley, 1994).

Peter Salus, *Casting the Net: From ARPANET to INTERNET and Beyond...*(Reading: Addison-Wesley, 1995).

Wayne Sandholtz, *High-Tech Europe: The Politics of International Cooperation* (Berkeley, University of California Press, 1992).

Simon Singh, *The Code Book: The Secret History of Codes and Code-Breaking* (London: Fourth Estate, 2000).

Ruth Taplin (ed.), *Managing Cyber Risk in the Financial Sector: Lessons from Asia, Europe and the USA* (London: Routledge, 2016).

Paul A Taylor, *Hackers: Crime in the digital sublime* (London: Routledge, 1999).

Rein Turn and H.E. Petersen, 'Security of Computerized Information Systems', *The RAND Corporation,* July 1970.

Thomas Whiteside, *Computer Capers: tales of electronic thievery, embezzlement, and fraud* (New York: Crowell, 1978).

Harold Wilson, *The Labour Government, 1964–70* (London: Weidenfeld & Nicolson, 1971)

The Law Commission, 'Criminal Law: Computer Misuse', No. 186, *October 1989.*

Jeffery Yost, *The Computer Industry* (London: Greenwood Press, 2005).

Journal Articles

Jon Agar, 'Putting the spooks back in? The UK secret state and the history of computing', *Information & Culture,* 51/1 (2016), pp.102–124.

David Ambrosia, 'New SWIFT Rules on the Liability of Financial Institutions for Interest Losses Caused by Delay in International Fund Transfers', *Cornell International Law Journal,* 13/2 (1980), pp.311–328.

James Baker and Ezra Byler, 'SWIFT: A Partial Answer to Worldwide Funds Transfer', *Foreign Trade Review*, 17/1 (1982), pp.15–30.

James Baker and Ezra Byler, 'S.W.I.F.T.: A Fast Method to Facilitate Financial Transaction', *Journal of World Trade*, 17/5 (1983), pp. 458–465.

Bernardo Batiz-Lazo and Douglas Wood, 'A Historical Appraisal of Information Technology in Commercial Banking', *Electronic Markets*, 12/3 (2002), pp. 192–205.

James Baxendale, 'Commercial Banking and the Checkless Society', *Rutgers Journal of Computers & Law*, 88 (1970), pp.88–98.

Jay Becker, 'The Trial of a Computer Crime', *Computer*, 441 (1980), pp. 441–456.

Jay Becker, 'International Computer Crime: Where Terrorism and Transborder Data Flow Meet', *Computers & Security*, 1/1 (1982), pp.41–53.

Jay Becker, 'Computer Crime Update: The View as we Exit 1984', *Western New England Law Review*, 7/3 (1985), pp.627–650.

August Bequai, 'The Problem of Crime in the Electronic Society', *Commercial Law Journal*, 83/3 (1978), pp.139–145.

Dennis Branstad, 'Security of Computer Communication', *IEEE Communications Society Magazine*, 16/6 (1978), pp.33–40.

Mark Budnitz, 'The Finicky Computer, the Paperless Telex and the Fallible Swiss: Bank Technology and the Law', *Boston College Law Review*, 25/2 (1984), pp.259–303.

Holger Burk and Andreas Pftizmann, 'Digital Payment Systems Enabling Security and Unobservability', *Computers & Security*, 8 (1989), pp.399–416.

Leslie Chalmers, 'An Analysis Of The Differences Between The Computer Security Practices In The Military And Private Sectors,' *1986 IEEE Symposium on Security and Privacy*, (1986), pp. 71–74.

Dean Champion and Edward Dager, 'Automation man in the counting house', *Trans-action*, 3/3 (1966), pp.34–36.

David Chaum, 'Security Without Identification: Transaction Systems to Make Big Brother Obsolete', *Communications of the ACM*, 28/10 (1985), pp. 1030–1044.

R.T. Clark, 'Electronic funds transfer: The creeping revolution', *Environment and Planning A: Economy and Space*, 16/4 (1984), pp. 437–450.

Joris Claessens, Valentin Dem, Danny De Cock, Bart Preneel, Joos Vandewalle, 'On the Security of Today's Online Electronic Banking Systems', *Computers & Security*, 21/3 (2002), pp. 253–265.

Davide Consoli, 'The dynamics of technological change in UK retail banking services: An evolutionary perspective', *Research Policy*, 34 (2005), pp. 461–480

Nick Cowan, 'The Technical Environment of Banks and Its Implications', *International Journal of Bank Marketing*, 5/4 (1987), pp. 15–31

Dorothy Denning and Peter Denning, 'Data Security', *ACM Computing Surveys*, 11/3 (1979), pp.227–249

Michael Dierks, 'Computer Network Abuse', *Harvard Journal of Law & Technology*, 6/2 (1993), pp. 307–342.

Kurt Engemann and Holmes Miller, 'Operations Risk Management at a Major Bank', *Interfaces*, 22/6 (1992), pp. 140–149.

Ivan Ekebrink, 'Data security in terminalized system', *Computers & Security*, 5/4 (1986), pp. 325–327.

Craig Ford, 'Electronic Funds Transfer: The State of the Art – Present and Project', *University of Pittsburgh Law Review*, 37/4 (1976), pp. 629–640.

Tom Forester and Perry Morrison, 'Computer unreliability and social vulnerability', *Futures*, 22/5 (1990), pp. 462–474.

Roy Freed, 'Computer fraud – a management trap: Risks are legal, economic, professional', *Business Horizons*, 12/3 (1969), pp.25–30.

Heather Fulford and Neil Doherty, 'The application of information security policies in large UK-based organisations: an exploratory investigation', *Information Management and Computer Security*, 11/3 (2003), pp.106–114

Gloria Gonzalez Fuster, Paul De Hert and Serge Gutwirth, 'SWIFT and the vulnerability of trans-atlantic data transfers', *International Review of Law, Computers & Technology*, 22/1–2 (2008), pp.191–202.

Richard Stockton Gaines, 'Some security principles and their application to computer security', *ACM SIGOPS Operating Systems Review*, 12/3 (1978), pp.19–28.

Giles Garon and Richard Outerbridge, 'DES Watch: An examination of the sufficiency of the Data Encryption Standard for financial institution information security', *Cryptologia*, 15/3 (1991), pp.177–193.

Michael Gemignani, 'What is Computer Crime, and Why Should we Care?', *University of Arkansas at Little Rock Law Journal*, 10/1 (1987–88), pp.55–68.

Elizabeth Glynn, 'Computer Abuse: The Emerging Crime and the Need for Legislation', *Fordham Urban Law Journal*, 12/1 (1983–1984), pp.73–102.

James Grant, 'Electronic banking and telecommunications', *Information & Management*, 11/1 (1986), pp.3–7.

Jason Haines and Peter Johnstone, 'Global Cybercrime: New Toys for the Money Launderers', *Journal of Money Laundering Control*, 2/3 (1999), pp.317–325.

Brahim Herbane, 'The evolution of business continuity management: A historical review of practices and drivers', *Business History*, 52/6 (2010), pp. 978–1002.

Arvid Hoffman and Cornelia Birnbrich, 'The impact of fraud prevention on bank-customer relationships: an empirical investigation in retail banking', *International Journal of Bank Marketing*, 30/5 (2012), pp. 390–407.

Henry Holloway, 'Information Technology and Company Policy: 4. Banking', *Journal of Information Technology*, 3/4 (1988), pp. 265–271.

J.B. Howcroft and John Lavis, 'Evolution of the Payment Systems of London Clearing Banks', *The Service Industries Journal*, 7/2 (2006), pp. 176–194.

Peter Johnstone and Jason Haines, 'Future Trends in Financial Crime', *Journal of Financial Crime*, 6/3 (1999), pp.269–275.

Peter Johnstone, 'Financial Crime: Prevention and Regulation in the Intangible Environment', *Journal of Money Laundering Control*, 2/3 (1999), pp.253–263.

Brian Kearvell-White, 'KPMG's UK Computer Security Review 1994', *Information Management & Computer Security*, 4/2 (1996a), pp. 42–51.

Brian Kearvell-White, 'National (UK) Computer Security Survey 1996', *Information Management & Computer Security*, 4/3 (1996b), pp.3–17

Andrew Kinnon and Robert Davis, 'Audit and Security Implications of Electronic Funds Transfer', *Computers & Security*, 5/1 (1986), pp. 17–23.

Gina Bari Kolata, 'Computer Encryption and the National Security Agency Connection', *Science*, 197/4302 (1977), pp.438–440.

Monica Lagazio, Nazneen Sherif and Mike Cushman, 'A multi-level approach to understanding the impact of cyber crime on the financial sector', *Computers & Security*, 45 (2014), pp. 58–74.

John Langdale, 'Electronic funds transfer and the internationalisation of the banking and finance industry', *Geoforum*, 16/1 (1985), pp. 1–13.

Colin Lewis, 'Information management: the industrial need', *ASLIB Proceedings*, 37/3 (1985), pp. 137–145.

J.C.R. Licklider and Robert Taylor, 'The Computer as a Communication Device', *Science and Technology*, April 1968, pp. 21–41.

Herbert Lingl, 'Risk Allocation in International Interbank Electronic Fund Transfers: CHIPS & SWIFT', *Harvard International Law Journal*, 22/3 (1981), pp. 621–660.

Jerome Lobel, 'The State-of-the-Art in Computer Security', *Computers & Security*, 2/3 (1983), pp. 218–222.

Wayne Madsen, 'The World Meganetwork and Terrorism', *Computers & Security*, 7/4 (1988), pp. 347–352.

J.N. Marshall and J.F. Bachtler, 'Spatial Perspectives on Technological Changes in the Banking Sector of the United Kingdom', *Environment and Planning A: Economy and Space,* 16/4 (1984), pp. 437–450.

Ian Martin, 'Too Far Ahead of Its Time: Barclays, Burroughs, and Real-Time Banking', *IEEE Annals of the History of Computing,* 34/2 (2012), pp.5–19.

John Meng, 'The Computer Game', *American Scientist,* 56/4 (1968), pp. 414–419.

Ruth Mitchell, Rita Marcella and Graeme Baxter, 'Corporate Information Security Management', *New Library World,* 100/5 (1999), pp.213–227.

Glenis Moore, 'An end to the paper chase?', *Electronics and Power,* 33/9 (1987), pp.554–556.

Susan Hubbell Nycum, 'Security for Electronic Funds Transfer System', *University of Pittsburgh Law Review,* 709 (1976), pp.709–724.

Ronald Paans and Israel Herschberg, 'Computer Security: The Long Road Ahead', *Computers & Security,* 6 (1987), pp.403–416.

Donn Parker, 'Computer abuse perpetrators and vulnerabilities of computer systems', *AFIPS '76: Proceedings of the June 7–10, 1976, national computer conference and exposition,* (1976b), pp. 65–73.

Donn Parker and Susan Nycum, 'Computer Crime', *Communications of the ACM,* 27/4 (1984), pp.313–315.

Donn Parker, 'The Strategic Values of Information Security in Business', *Computers & Security,* 16/7 (1992), pp/ 572–582.

Malcolm Pattinson, Marcus Batavicius, Kathryn Parsons, Agata McCormac, Dragana Calic, 'Managing information security awareness at an Australian bank: a comparative study', *Information & Computer Security,* 25/2 (2017), pp. 181–189.

Gerald Popek and Charles Kline, 'Encryption and Secure Computer Networks', *ACM Computing Surveys,* 11/4 (1979), pp. 331–356.

A.R. Raghavan and Latha Parthiban, 'The effect of cybercrime on a Bank's finances', *International Journal of Current Research and Academic Review,* 2/2 (2014), pp.173–178.

Jerome Roache, 'Computer Crime Deterrence', *American Journal of Criminal Law,* (1986), pp.391–416.

Juhani Saari, 'Computer Crime – Numbers Lie', *Computers & Security,* 6/2 (1987), pp.111–117.

Jerome Saltzer and Michael Schroeder, 'The Protection of Information in Computer Systems', *Proceedings of the IEEE,* 63/9 (1975), pp. 1278-1308.

Ali Sanayei and Ali Noroozi, 'Security of Internet Banking Services and its linkage with Users' Trust: A Case Study of Parsian Bank of Iran and CIMB Bank of Malaysia', *2009 International Conference on Information Management and Engineering,* (2009), pp. 3–7.

Harry Scarbrough and Ronnie Lannon, 'The Successful Exploitation of New Technology in Banking', *Journal of General Management,* 13/3 (1988), pp.38–51

Andreas Schaad, Jonathan Moffett, Jeremy Jacob, 'The role-based access control system of a European Bank: a case study and discussion', *SACMAT '01 Proceedings of the sixth ACM symposium on Access control models and technologies,* pp.3–9

Susan Scott, 'Origins and development of SWIFT, 1973–2009', *Business History,* 54/3 (2012), pp. 462–482.

K.S Shankar, 'Special Feature: The Total Computer Security Problem: an Overview', *Computer,* 10/6 (1977), pp. 50–73.

Daniel Sin, Matthew Sag & Ronald Laurie, 'Source Code versus Object Code: Patent Implications for the Open Source Community', *Santa Clara High Technology Law Journal,* 18/2 (2002), p.238.

Diana Smith, 'Who is Calling Your Computer Next? Hacker!', *Criminal Justice Journal,* 89 (1985), pp.89–114.

Stanley Sokolik, 'Computer Crime – The Need for Different Legislation', *Computer Law Journal,* 353 (1980), pp.353–383.

Artur Solarz, 'Computer-Related Embezzlement', *Computers & Security,* 6/1 (1987), pp. 49–53.

Roussow von Solms, 'Information security management: The second generation', *Computers & Security,* 15/4 (1996), pp.281–288.

Detmar Straub and William Nance, 'Discovering and Disciplining Computer Abuse in Organizations: A Field Study', *MIS Quarterly,* 14/1 (1990), pp.45–60.

Bruce Summers, 'Electronic Payments in Retrospect', *FRB Richmond Economic Review,* 74/2 (1988), pp. 16–19.

Ashley Sweetman, 'TEMPEST and the Bank of England', *Intelligence & National Security,* 33/7 (2018), pp.1084–1091.

Lewis Taffer, 'The Making of the Electronic Fund Transfer Act: A Look at Consumer Liability and Error Resolution', *University of San Francisco Law Review,* 13/2 (1979), pp.231–244

Dennie van Tassel, 'Proceedings of the May 14–16, 1969, spring joint computer conference', *American Federation of Information Processing Societies,* (1969), pp.367–372.

Theodosios Tsiakis and George Sthephanides, 'The concept of security and trust in electronic payments', *Computers & Security,* 24/1 (2005), pp. 10–15

The Law Commission, 'Criminal Law: Computer Misuse', No. 186, *October 1989*

Rein Turn, 'Protection and Security in Transnational Data Processing Systems', *Stanford Journal of International Law,* 16 (1980), pp.67–86.

Mary Volgyes, 'The Investigation, Prosecution, and Prevention of Computer Crime: A State-of-the-Art Review', *Computer Law Journal,* 385 (1980), pp.385–402.

Michael Warner, 'Cybersecurity: A Pre-history', *Intelligence and National Security,* 27/5 (2012), pp.781–799.

Steve Weingart, Steve White and William Arnold, 'An Evaluation System for the Physical Security of Computing Systems', *Proceedings of the Sixth Annual Computer Security Applications Conference 1990,* pp.232–243.

Fred Weingarten, 'Communications Technology: New Challenges to Privacy', *John Marshall Law Review,* 21/4 (1988), pp. 735–754.

Barney Wharf, 'Telecommunications and the Globalization of Financial Services', *Professional Geographer,* 41/3 (1989), pp.257–271.

Stanley Winkler and Lee Danner, 'Data security in the computer communication environment', *Computer,* 7/2 (1974), pp.23–31.

John Winthrop, 'Layman's View of Computer Power', *Financial Analysts Journal,* (1969), pp.101–103.

Charles Wood, 'Future Applications of Cryptography', *Computers & Security,* 1/1 (1982), pp. 65–71.

Charles Wood, 'Policies for Deterring Computer Abuse', *Computers & Security,* 1/2 (1982), pp.139–145.

Charles Wood, 'Effective information security with password controls', *Computers & Security,* 2/1 (1983), pp.5–10.

Paul Young et al, 'Robbing the bank with a theorem prover', *University of Cambridge Computer Laboratory: Technical Report,* 644 (2005).

Bernard Zajac, 'Computer viruses: Can they be prevented?', *Computers & Security,* 9/1 (1990), pp. 25–31.

Chapters in Edited Collections

Wayne Harrop and Ashley Matteson, 'Cyber Resilience: A Review of Critical National Infrastructure and Cyber-Security Protection Measures Applied in the UK and USA' in Frederic Lemieux (ed.), *Current and Emerging Trends in Cyber Operations* (Basingstoke: Macmillan, 2015), pp.149–166.

Dianne Martin and Fred Weingarten, 'The Less-Cash/Less-Check Society: Banking in the Information Age', in Elinor Harris Solomon (ed.), *Electronic Money Flows: The Moulding of a new Financial Order* (Boston: Kluwer Academic Publishers, 1991), pp. 187–217.

Ian Martin, 'Britain's First Computer Centre for Banking: What Did This Building Do?', in Batiz-Lazo et al (eds), *Technological Innovation in Retail Finance: International Historical Perspectives* (London: Routledge, 2011), pp. 37–71.

M. Williamson, 'Electronic Funds Transfer in Perspective', in Elton, Lucas and Conrath (eds), *Evaluating New Telecommunications Services: NATO Conference Series, 6,* 1978, pp. 643–660.

Newspapers & Magazines

Computer Fraud & Security Bulletin
Daily Express
Financial Times
Management Today
Motherboard
The Economist
The Independent
The New Scientist
The Sunday Times
The Telegraph & Sunday Telegraph
Wired

Online Sources

Archived webpage of HM Treasury, 'History of the Treasury', 13/03/2013, http://webarchive. nationalarchives.gov.uk/20130319161430/http:/hm-treasury.gov.uk/about_history.htm

Bacs, 'Bacs corporate information', http://www.bacs.co.uk/Bacs/Corporate/CorporateOverview/ Pages/Overview.aspx [24 February 2016].

BAE Systems, 'Two bytes to $951m', http://bit.ly/2i5Z7V7 [Accessed 20 February 2018a].

BAE Systems, 'Cyber Heist Attribution', http://bit.ly/2spm7Hk [Accessed 20 February 2018b].

Bank of England, 'Quarterly Bulletin: 1968, Q3', http://www.bankofengland.co.uk/archive/ Documents/historicpubs/qb/1968/qb68q3262270.pdf

CESG, 'About Us', https://www.cesg.gov.uk/articles/cesg-information-security-arm-gchq [Accessed 19 February 2016].

CHAPS Co, 'About CHAPS', http://www.chapsco.co.uk/about-chaps [Accessed 8 February 2017].

CHAPS Co, 'History of CHAPS', http://www.chapsco.co.uk/about_chaps/timeline/ [Accessed 14 December 2015].

CHAPS Co, 'Who uses the CHAPS system' http://www.chapsco.co.uk/about-chaps/who-uses-chaps-system [Accessed 8 February 2017].

Cheque Credit & Clearing Company, 'Emergence of Technology', https://www.chequeandcredit. co.uk/information-hub/history-cheque/emergence-technology [Accessed 16 February 2016].

Joseph Cox, *Motherboard,* 'Cunning Malware Covered Hackers' Tracks in $81m Bangladesh Bank Heist', http://bit.ly/2s9wCKs [Accessed 7 February 2018].

EMIDEC, 'EMIDEC Computer News 1', http://www.emidec.org.uk/emipicbr.pdf [Accessed 16 November 2017].

European Commission, 'APACS Response to the European Commission Interim Report on Payment Cards', http://ec.europa.eu/competition/sectors/financial_services/inquiries/replies_report_1/05.pdf [Accessed 20 February 2017].

Hansard, HC Deb 27 April 1965 vol 711 cc196-7, http://hansard.millbanksystems.com/commons/1965/apr/27/computer-advisory-unit [Accessed 1 February 2016].

London Stock Exchange, 'Gilts', http://www.londonstockexchange.com/traders-and-brokers/security-types/gilts/gilts.htm [Accessed 9 May 2017].

National Physical Laboratory, 'History', http://www.npl.co.uk/about/history/ [Accessed 10 November 2017].

National Physical Laboratory, 'NPL's History Highlights', http://www.npl.co.uk/upload/pdf/npl-history.pdf [Accessed 10 November 2017].

National Physical Laboratory, 'What is NPL?', http://www.npl.co.uk/about/what-is-npl/ [Accessed 20 February 2017].

Science Museum, 'The Pegasus Computer', https://blog.sciencemuseum.org.uk/the-pegasus-computer/ [Accessed 15 November 2017].

Sigma 6/9 Sales Guide', 20 February 1972, http://www.mirrorservice.org/sites/www.bitsavers.org/pdf/sds/sigma/Sigma_6_9_Sales_Guide_Feb72.pdf [Accessed 10 May 2017].

SRI International, 'About Us', https://www.sri.com/about [Accessed 21 December 2015].

SWIFT, 'SWIFT History', https://www.swift.com/about_swift/company_information/swift_history# [Accessed 10 December 2015].

The National Archives, 'Committee on the Review of Banking Services Law (Jack Committee): Report and Government Response', http://discovery.nationalarchives.gov.uk/details/r/C14027 [Accessed 21 December 2015].

UK Debt Management Office, 'Gilt Market', http://www.dmo.gov.uk/index.aspx?page=gilts/about_gilts [Accessed 25 February 2016].

United States Federal Reserve, 'International Finance Discussion Papers, *An Appraisal of the CHAPS Payments Mechanism*, Number 217, February 1983', https://www.federalreserve.gov/pubs/ifdp/1983/217/ifdp217.pdf [Accessed 8 February 2017].

Kim Zetter, *Wired*, 'That Insane, '$81m Bangladesh Bank Heist? Here's What We Know', http://bit.ly/1TXMSHl [Accessed 18 February 2018].

Other

Bank of England Archive Display, 'Technology and the Bank of England: Early developments in automation and technology', viewed 26 January 2015.

Channel 4 Dispatches, 11 October 1989.

Hansard, House of Lords Debate, 30 June 1982, Vol. 432, cc. 23.

Printed in the United States
by Baker & Taylor Publisher Services